KT-512-075

Mike Rossiter is an independent documentary film-maker, whose work has been nominated for BAFTA and Emmy awards. In 2001 he filmed the search for and recovery of the body of Donald Campbell and his record-breaking boat *Bluebird* from Coniston Water. He produced the series *War at Sea* for the BBC and discovered and filmed the wreck of the aircraft carrier *Ark Royal*. He is also the author of *Ark Royal* and *Sink the Belgrano*.

Also by Mike Rossiter

**ARK ROYAL
SINK THE BELGRANO**

and published by Corgi Books

TARGET BASRA

MIKE ROSSITER

CORGI BOOKS

TRANSWORLD PUBLISHERS
61–63 Uxbridge Road, London W5 5SA
A Random House Group Company
www.rbooks.co.uk

TARGET BASRA
A CORGI BOOK: 9780552157001

First published in Great Britain
in 2008 by Bantam Press
a division of Transworld Publishers
Corgi edition published 2009

A CIP catalogue record for this book
is available from the British Library.

Addresses for Random House Group Ltd companies outside the UK
can be found at: www.randomhouse.co.uk
The Random House Group Ltd Reg. No. 954009

The Random House Group Limited supports The Forest Stewardship Council
(FSC), the leading international forest certification organisation. All our
titles that are printed on Greenpeace approved FSC certified paper carry
the FSC logo. Our paper procurement policy can be found at
www.rbooks.co.uk/environment

Typeset in 12/15.5pt Times New Roman by
Falcon Oast Graphic Art Ltd.
Printed in the UK by CPI Cox & Wyman, Reading, RG1 8EX.

2 4 6 8 10 9 7 5 3

CONTENTS

AUTHOR'S NOTE

Target Basra is set during the invasion of Iraq by US and British forces in 2003. It is not meant to be a definitive description of that war, or a complete description of the capture of Basra by the British Army. I have tried to tell the story of two units of Royal Marine Commandos who landed on the al-Faw peninsula and arrived a few days later on the outskirts of Basra, and describe the planning and negotiation that went on in the months leading up to their assault on Iraq.

One of the first documentaries I made was about chemical warfare, when I interviewed UN observers of the Iran–Iraq war, and Kurdish refugees from Halabja. Subsequently I made *Hellfighters of Kuwait*, a documentary about the efforts to extinguish the oil-well fires after Saddam Hussein's invasion. Despite this contingent interest in Iraq, the subject of *Target Basra* was suggested to me by Rear Admiral Tim

McClement, who thought that the story might throw into sharp relief some of the advantages of an alliance with the US in military operations, but also some of the compromises and problems that might come in its wake.

Whether it does or not must be the reader's judgement, but I think it reveals an untold story about the first days of the war that says much about the training and mentality of some of Britain's armed forces, and the way they approached a military operation that was probably the most politically contentious in British history. For the Royal Marines, particularly Operation Telic, as Britain called the invasion of Iraq, it was a uniquely challenging and hazardous mission.

I was given an enormous amount of help by Captain Mike Davis Marks, and Lieutenant Commander Harvey Burwin in the Ministry of Defence. Beyond that, the book makes clear who else I talked to. Everyone gave me assistance, although they had only a vague idea of the particular story I was pursuing. Most of those to whom I spoke are still serving in the forces, and were concerned about security and the considerable pressure on their time, but I could not have finished this book without the courtesy and consideration they were prepared to show me. Similarly, with limited material being published, I was dependent on notes and diaries kept at the time. I have chosen to tell the story largely from the viewpoint of company commanders: they have a unique perspective that encompasses fighting on the ground as well as the overall plan of the operation. All stressed that they were never in as much danger or in the thick of the fighting as the rank-and-file marines.

There will inevitably be incidents and actions that I have not covered, or have not described adequately. Some marines were impossible to contact, and I have restricted myself to information I have obtained from a reliable written record or first-hand interview. If there are any errors or mistakes they are mine.

I must thank my agent Luigi Bonomi, for his cheerfulness and optimism, and my editor at Transworld, Simon Thorogood, for his calm and judicious advice. Vivien Garrett, Transworld's Production Editor, and Hazel Orme polished my text as much as was possible, and Sheila Lee put some striking images together. Moira Hall transcribed the interviews quickly and efficiently, and I would have been lost without her. Finally, I have to thank my wife, Anne, and my sons, Max and Alex, for their patience.

Mike Rossiter, March 2008

INTRODUCTION:
THE POINT OF THE SPEAR

The few hundred men of 40 Commando who were waiting tensely to board their helicopters on the night of 20 March 2003 were in a uniquely hazardous position. They knew that they were going to be the first troops on the ground in Iraq as part of Operation Iraqi Freedom. Some knew they were going to be the first British troops to make a helicopter-borne assault in more than fifty years. One or two of their commanding officers were aware that, with members of 42 Commando, who would be airborne an hour later, this would be the largest helicopter-borne operation carried out since the Vietnam war. None of this made the operation more of a gamble than it should have been. What did was that, in defiance of well-established military convention, the attack they were about to launch would be against well-defended targets that were surrounded by concentrations of enemy troops.

They were embarking on a mission of high strategic importance, and would take severe risks to ensure success.

The Marines were waiting on that desert evening in Kuwait because negotiations about their deployment had been taking place long before the controversy about invading Iraq had surfaced. That controversy centred in Britain on the legal justification to intervene militarily in a foreign country, and on the extent to which Saddam Hussein's government was in breach of United Nations resolutions ordering him to destroy his stocks of chemical and nuclear weapons. He had used chemical weapons against Iran, and against his own population in Kurdistan. During the war in 1991 to remove Saddam Hussein's forces from Kuwait, ground troops had behaved as though chemical warfare was possible, and in 2003 the marines in Kuwait were fully trained to take precautions against the danger of chemical weapons and nerve agents. In the first few days of the war they did so frequently, and were conscious that the ground they walked on was contaminated by bombardment from chemical weapons used in the Iran–Iraq war.

However, the political debate about the existence of chemical weapons in Iraq was a sideshow. The invasion of Iraq was, for the United States government, a necessary conclusion to the war in 1991 when Saddam's forces had been driven out of Kuwait. That conflict had ended inconclusively, a reminder of US impotence in the region. The destruction of the World Trade Center in New York, with the resulting war on terror, proved the catalyst. The question for the British government was how far to support the US in its invasion of Iraq while pursuing the fundamental policy of remaining America's closest ally: the public's distaste for war was well known.

Despite statements to the contrary in the 1970s, no British government has found it possible to lose military interest in the world outside Europe. The war between Iraq and Iran, and then the invasion of Kuwait, had meant that, once more, British forces were dragged east of Suez. By 1998 the government planned to create a military unit called a Joint Rapid Reaction Force, with the ability to mount and sustain a medium-scale war-fighting operation. It would be more or less permanently established, so that it could be sent quickly into action, and would be composed of special forces, an attack submarine, surface warships and a task force drawn from the Royal Marines of 3 Commando Brigade, the Parachute Regiment, tanks and artillery, with helicopter and combat-aircraft support. In a complete reversal of the previous thirty years of military planning Britain was preparing to intervene anywhere around the world.

In Iraq 40 Commando was the point of a very long spear, whose shaft was the ships and helicopters of the Navy Task Group that had carried them through the Mediterranean, with the sailors that supported them. Without that back-up, they could never have been the effective fighting force that they were. The Royal Marines of 3 Commando Brigade were the first to land in Iraq, and kicked down the door to Basra, but they were never originally intended to be there. Their presence as part of a coalition with US forces was the product of a much wider tail of alliances and collaborations, within which the senior officers of the Royal Navy were working to maximize the involvement of British forces, despite the political debates that were taking place. These relationships occur and continue outside the public gaze, but the senior liaison officers, joint exercises and exchanges, without which much of the planning for 40 Commando's assault would not have taken place, are part of a long-standing strategic British policy that culminated in the assault on the al-Faw peninsula. Behind it lie the self-confidence and desire to put into practice the war-fighting skills honed over many years. As one officer remarked, 'It's like training to drive a bus and never being given the opportunity.'

3 Commando Brigade is far more deadly than a bus but they were sent to the deserts of Kuwait when the British fleet was in an extremely weak state. Two landing ships, HMS *Fearless* and HMS *Intrepid*, had been recently scrapped, and the one new replacement in service, HMS *Ocean*, was in refit. The Task Group

was centred on HMS *Ark Royal*, an aircraft-carrier that was rapidly converted to carry helicopters, and HMS *Ocean*, rushed out of dry dock to sea. Despite the government's intention behind the Joint Rapid Reaction Force, the Commandos would be heavily dependent on their US allies for air support and helicopter transport.

On the first day of the operation US support vanished, creating the potential for the failure of the whole operation. This was avoided by quick, flexible planning, which became a hallmark of the Commandos' operations on the al-Faw peninsula and in the key actions prior to the assault on Basra. This city, the second largest in Iraq, had never been an element of the US military campaign, which was focused entirely on Baghdad and the expected rapid collapse of Saddam's regime. As the campaign encountered difficulties, Basra became increasingly important politically as well as militarily. It was the first major city in Iraq to fall to Allied forces, and did so without the enormous casualties that would normally result from fierce urban fighting. As CNN headlined the day after the city had fallen, 'Basra offers a lesson on taking Baghdad.'

Whether it did or not, the Commandos of 40 Commando, who had spent weeks meticulously planning an assault on the very first day of the war, found themselves ten days later fighting a battle on the outskirts of Basra based on a plan that barely covered the back of an envelope. In both battles, and in the intervening days of rapid deployments and fire-fights, aggression, flexibility, determination and belief in themselves brought them out on top.

On 20 March, gathered round their small individual portable stoves for a last brew before the bullets started flying, the Royal Marines had no illusions as to the strategic importance of their preliminary objectives that night and how vital it was that they succeeded. They had no idea however that just over a week later they would be in the midst of an operation that would break the back of the resistance in Basra and claim the first major victory for the Alliance. Neither would their commanding officers have put money on them all being alive to see it.

The Royal Marines of 3 Commando Brigade were probably the first soldiers in Iraq to understand that the military planning was based on poor intelligence. The substantial Iraqi armed forces that had been employed in the Iran–Iraq war and in the invasion of Kuwait no longer existed. Instead, the enemy was politically motivated, and had become embedded in the civilian population. The dream of an early collapse of resistance was precisely that: a dream.

When the fighting was over, many company commanders took responsibility for the day-to-day tasks of running a country that the overthrown regime was no longer there to carry out. In the vacuum of any contingency planning for post-war operations, the young officers of 3 Commando Brigade found themselves in charge of towns and villages on which, days previously, they had unleashed violent assaults. It was absurd, but the commanders of A and B companies, in charge of towns in which some of the hardest fighting had taken place, tried to discharge their responsibilities conscientiously and sympathetically. One officer commented that overnight the lads had had to make the transition from fighting to peacekeeping, and had done it as well as they had fought on the al-Faw peninsula.

The war in Iraq was unpopular, motivated solely by politics, and badly planned. The company commanders, acting as quasi-mayors, were not only in the forefront of the fighting but also had advance notice of the conflicts and problems that had been waiting to erupt with the collapse of Saddam's regime.

1

AS MIDNIGHT APPROACHES

On the morning of 20 March 2003 two bulldozers ripped out a huge square pit in the Kuwaiti desert and three companies of 40 Commando Royal Marines assembled at one end and began to fire their Heckler & Koch SA80 assault rifles into roughly erected targets. They were at their tactical assembly area (TAA) in northern Kuwait, just a few miles from the Iraqi border, known to everyone as TAA Viking. It was a noisy location, with the perpetual sound of helicopters beating through the air overhead and military vehicles grinding their way along the desert road. And the heat was intense.

The firing range had been dug out so that the marines could zero their weapons, set their sights for a predetermined range and align them accurately. The sharp crack of gunfire was heard all morning. Major Matt Jackson, the commanding officer of B Company, was glad that his men had this last chance to test their weapons. The day before, all the activity in the camp had come to a complete halt when a suffocating sandstorm had filled his ears and nose with dust and particles of grit, and cut visibility to a few metres. The sand infiltrated everywhere, and Jackson had wrapped his assault rifle in a blanket and plastic bin liners in an attempt to stop it becoming clogged. All the marines were now thinking longingly of the ships from which they had recently disembarked, with their clean bunks, air-conditioning and hot showers. They were now poised, in their tarpaulin-covered dug-outs in the desert, just a few hours from the start of a US-led invasion of Iraq.

40 Commando was a force of around eight hundred men, which, with two other Commandos, 42 and 45, made up 3 Commando Brigade, Royal Marines. The Royal Marines were formed in 1664 to maintain authority and discipline on Royal Navy warships, but also to serve as sharpshooters in boarding parties and to be an amphibious infantry. They captured Gibraltar in 1703, and served on board Nelson's fleet at the battle of Trafalgar. They were also trained as gunners, and normally formed the crew of a gun or gun turret on major ships, a tradition that survived until the 1960s.

The name 'Commando' was coined in 1942 when Winston Churchill, desperate to sustain the war against Hitler, called for groups of specially trained, unconventional forces to be set up to raid the coastline of Europe and harass the occupying Nazi forces. The Commandos were recruited from the Royal Marines and the regular army. At the end of the war they became a purely Royal Marines force and now, with the post-war decline of the Royal Navy, they are the principal element of the Royal Marines. They are an elite force, highly trained in a variety of fighting environments – jungle, mountain and the Arctic – as well as amphibious landings. With the Paras and the Joint Helicopter Force, the Commandos are among the UK's Joint Rapid Reaction Force. Each Commando is made up of six company-sized units. The Command Company supports the headquarters of a Commando and has a long-range heavy-mortar troop as part of its complement. The Logistics Company is responsible for supplies, transport and casualties. The rest are either designated as close-combat companies, in which the majority of the troops are armed with assault rifles, or stand-off companies, armed with heavy machine-guns and anti-tank missiles mounted on vehicles. Major Jackson's B, or Bravo, Company was a stand-off company, although one troop was a close-combat troop. Jackson was new to B Company, and young to be a company commander. So far he had had no problems, but he knew that his youth and relative inexperience would raise doubt in his men. 'You always have a slight credibility problem when you take over. It's either, "We've got somebody wet behind the ears", or "What wizard idea might the thrusting young CO have in store for us?"'

There were other reasons for the men of B Company, and indeed the whole of 40 Commando, to be apprehensive. They were about to invade another country, Iraq, and although they had known this for some time, the onset of battle was fast approaching. Few had experienced warfare. They were volunteers to a man, and to become Royal Marines they had had to show a high level of commitment and ability, mentally and physically. They were well trained, but they knew that no amount of training could prepare them for their first moment of action. Firing guns on the makeshift range was easy. What would it be like when the targets were firing back?

Some kilometres to the west of 40 Commando's TAA, there was another, much larger, encampment and helicopter landing zone, TAA Swallow. This was the desert home of their sister organization, 42 Commando. Along with Brigade Headquarters and support staff, 40 and 42 Commando had been sent to Kuwait to take part in President Bush's Operation Iraqi Freedom. The invasion would be dominated, of course, by the United States, with its massive build-up of troops, warplanes and the presence at sea of the US Fifth Fleet, with five aircraft-carrier task groups in the area. In all there were 150,000 US servicemen in the Gulf. The UK's presence of 45,000 men, with a fleet of twenty-two ships, *Ark Royal* and the helicopter assault ship *Ocean*, struggling to find sea room in the crowded waters of the northern Arabian Gulf, seemed far more significant than a mere 3000 men of 3 Commando Brigade. But their mission was of the utmost importance, the key to success for the entire enterprise. They had to secure the oil infrastructure in the al-Faw peninsula, the small area of land that jutted into the sea between Kuwait and Iran, and through which 90 per cent of Iraq's oil was exported. In addition, they had to occupy the bank of the Khawr 'Abd Allah waterway so that ships could reach Umm Qasr port to unload humanitarian supplies for the relief of the Iraqi civilian population.

This was the main immediate task facing the two Commandos now waiting in Kuwait for the war to start. The final limit of the British zone of military exploitation was the city of Basra, on the banks of the Shatt al-Arab to the north of the al-Faw peninsula. Basra was the second largest city in Iraq, the leading metropolis and port of the south, through which all roads and ship canals passed, the political and cultural centre of the southern Iraqi oilfields.

In 1916 Basra had been occupied by the British in the war against the Ottoman Empire; in 1919 some consideration had been given to carving a separate country out of Mesopotamia, as it was then called, with Basra as its capital. In 1941, the British Army had again occupied Basra and the southern provinces it dominated to secure the vital Iraqi oilfields for the benefit of the Royal Navy, and deny them to Hitler. The marines were aware of the importance of Basra, and its historic connection with the British Empire, but now their role in its capture was uncertain, low down on a lengthy list of things they should be prepared to do. Foremost in their minds was their immediate mission, that was about to be launched in just a few hours' time.

The first landings were to be made by 40 Commando. An hour later, while they fought the Iraqi forces guarding the oil installations, 42 Commando, under the command of Colonel Buster Howes, would follow and set up positions to defend 40 Commando against Iraqi forces to the north.

42 Commando had arrived in Kuwait by air several weeks before, and had been living in tents ever since. They had had to build their camp from scratch, and although they had showers and mess tents, there wasn't enough cooking equipment or food, and the men were losing weight.

Colonel Howes and 42 Commando's operations officer had spent days planning the assault. Speed was of the essence: it was vital to assemble the maximum concentration of forces as quickly as possible, but in TAA Swallow where they were assembled, an area of six square kilometres, enormous dustclouds formed by the passage of troop convoys and the rotors of huge transport helicopters took some time to clear, especially between landings and take-offs, which might cause serious delays to the build-up of 42 Commando's forces. The mechanics of making sure that each man was in the right place at the right time were daunting. Moreover, everyone had to be self-sufficient in water, rations and ammunition, so was carrying at least sixty-nine kilos in his back-pack. They couldn't fight with that on their backs so when they landed they would ditch their loads and take up defensive positions. It was a high-risk mission.

As they waited, the tension mounted. They knew that the war they were about to start was unpopular: they had seen on television the large demonstrations against it in London and around the world, while the debate in the UN, in Parliament and among heads of state had been going on for months. But they remained focused on their forthcoming task.

In fact, 40 Commando had only been in Kuwait for three days, just recently landed from HMS *Ocean* and other transports. They were living in shell scrapes, holes dug in the ground covered by a tarpaulin, and already they were tired of waiting. Their view was that if it was going to be war, then bring it on quickly. President Bush had issued an ultimatum to Saddam, that he should flee Iraq with his sons, and the dead-line had expired on 18 March. Even though the BBC

World Service had announced that missiles had landed in Baghdad, there had still been no order to move to their helicopter landing zone.

By 20 March the sandstorm had ended and they were on four hours' notice to board their helicopters and invade Iraq. This was their last chance to test their rifles, and to set their sights for a range of 100 metres. The firing was interrupted by several warnings of incoming Iraqi Scud missiles, and gas masks were pulled over faces, straps tightened, in anticipation of a gas attack. It never came.

The company commanders had a briefing at 1000 and were told that H-hour, the time that the helicopters were scheduled to lift off, was set for 2200, local time. At noon the commanding officer of 40 Commando, Colonel Gordon Messenger, assembled his troops in the firing range for a final address. He is a charismatic figure, and his men had enormous respect for him. They would, as one said, 'follow him over a cliff'. He is quietly spoken and matter-of-fact; he knows war is a nasty business, and that no commander, or soldier, can afford to dwell on its bloody outcome. Save for the clatter of a helicopter in the distance there was silence as his men gathered around him. It was a scene that contained echoes of another war, more than six hundred years ago, when a small group of Englishmen prepared to take on the French Army at Agincourt, a moment immortalized by Shakespeare in *Henry V*. Standing bare headed, his helmet in his hand, Gordon Messenger made three points. It was natural, he said to his men, to be scared at the prospect of battle, but they should have courage. They were marines, and they should be confident that their training and weapons were far better than those of the enemy they would face. And they should consider themselves privileged to be there because this action would go down in the annals of the Royal Marines, and be part of the history of 3 Commando Brigade.

There was a moment of thought and introspection before 40 Commando disbanded, back to their Company areas. Then the Company commanders took the opportunity to address their own group of men. Major Matt Jackson, the young, fair-haired Commander of B Company, reiterated his Commanding Officer's remarks, and added the thought that their strongest weapon was trust, trust in themselves, in each other and in their unit.

Then Gordon Messenger wandered around TAA Viking, talking to the men gathered round their fires, making a last brew, the flames casting shadows as dusk fell. He was relaxed: 'I had done as much as I could, and the pressure, for the moment, was off. I had no idea how it would unfold. I knew there was the possibility that people would be killed, but I was comfortable that if people were going to die then it would not be through a fault of mine.'

* * *

At TAA Swallow, some people were very unhappy. Captain Chris Haw was in 3 Commando Brigade Reconnaissance Force (BRF), an elite group trained to deploy far forward and act as an early warning of enemy attack. He had been taken off the planning effort for a special operation that had been abandoned. Now he was with a standby formation, ready to deal with accidents or mechanical failures. He was gutted: here was a big operation, and he was just a bystander.

Walking around the landing zone, he passed his mates quietly waiting to board their helicopters. 'People were talking in little groups. There were intelligence updates, the possibility of tanks in the area of operations, and so on.' He shook hands with his friends in the BRF, who were going to take off first, doing the job he should have been doing. Some had written letters to their loved ones, which they handed to him. He thought nothing of the goodbyes: 'It was just like saying goodbye to your missus when she leaves for work. You know you'll see her again in the evening.'

A group of marines, D Company, was still on board HMS *Ark Royal*, sailing close to the Iraqi coast in the Gulf and preparing to embark on helicopters. They had been led through the ship by seamen to the hangar decks, each section assigned their own member of *Ark Royal's* crew, and then they waited for the helicopters to take them off. There were ninety men, faces blackened, their bulky packs, radios, small arms and portable anti-tank missiles surrounding them. The captain of *Ark Royal*, Alan Massey, was walking around the ship. The commandos' faces were tense but there was quiet activity as each man made last-minute adjustments to his kit.

Alan Massey had his own concerns about the approaching H-hour. First, his crew were young men and women, most of whom had never experienced the stress and nervous anticipation of war. They looked to him for assurance and leadership. Then he had to consider, 'Was there sufficient sea room between the shallow coast and the fleet of ships behind us? Did we have enough headway into the wind? Had our minesweeping been adequate? All the things where a slight lack of focus might jeopardize the mission.'

Out at sea on HMS *Ocean*, the helicopter assault ship, preparations were being made for the second stream of helicopters that would ferry out supplies and vehicles, and potentially bring back casualties. Her captain, Adrian Johns, had already seen Tomahawk cruise missiles fly low over his ship on the way to Baghdad, and he had to make sure that their flight lines and his outbound helicopters were kept properly separated.

His mind returned to 40 Commando's last days on board *Ocean*. Colonel Messenger had been organizing a group photo. He had stressed to Adrian Johns that it was important to capture this moment, and to make sure that everyone was in the picture. 'Because', he remarked, 'they won't all come back, you know.' The words had sent a cold shiver down Captain Johns's spine. He knew that it had been estimated that two helicopters would crash, with possibly sixty deaths. After that, who knew? Most of the planning had been carried out for the first day of the landing, but everything was subject to the vagaries of battle, the enemy, and the fortunes of the wider war. This operation, with *Ocean*, *Ark Royal* and the fleet of helicopters taking their cargo of commandos into enemy territory, had grown over eight months from almost nothing.

Major Matt Jackson and his fellow commandos knew that what they were about to do was extremely dangerous. They would be the first to set foot in Iraq, jumping out of helicopters, invading against entrenched enemy soldiers, forewarned of their arrival. Most modern forces, including Britain's, would choose any option but this. But the nature of the mission demanded it. Their only advantage would be their mobility, the hoped-for rapid concentration of forces and the determination to be as aggressive as possible.

As H-hour approached, the men of 40 and 42 Commandos were taken by lorry to board their helicopters. Then they walked up the ramps, the rotor blades started to turn and the roar of the engines drowned conversation. The sand and dust were whipped up in an impenetrable cloud, the pilots shifted their hands on the collective pitch levers and the aircraft lifted into the night. As the minutes and seconds, no longer hours or days, ticked away, each man looked inside himself and considered the imminent prospect of violent action.

2

THE CLOCK STARTS TICKING

On 14 August 2002, just eight months before that tense night in the Kuwait desert, Commodore David Snelson's Gulf Air flight from London Heathrow landed at Manama airport in Bahrain. Temperatures in the city were around 50°C and, even towards the end of the day, leaving the air-conditioned chill of the terminal building was like walking into a furnace.

Snelson is a slim man in his fifties, quietly spoken and engaging. He has a persuasive manner, and successfully led people with a mixture of charm and encouragement. A senior officer in the Royal Navy, he had once been in command of the aircraft-carrier HMS *Ark Royal*, and could reasonably expect eventual promotion to rear admiral. All of his talents would be exercised to the full in the coming months. Snelson was arriving to take up a post as deputy commander of an extraordinarily complex structure of naval forces in the Gulf region, and he knew that highly secret plans were being developed for the invasion of Iraq, several hundred miles to the north.

Bahrain is a small island off the east coast of Saudi Arabia, and was once a British protectorate, becoming independent in 1971. But the most important reason for Snelson to take residence there was that Bahrain was now the headquarters of the US Navy's Fifth Fleet, which had been wound up at the end of the Second World War, then re-created in 1997. It was now the permanently based presence in the region of the United States Central Command, or CentCom, which had its headquarters in Tampa, Florida. The permanent stationing of a US Navy fleet in the Arabian Gulf and Commodore Snelson's presence in Bahrain were the end result of a slow process of US military intervention in the area that had started in 1980.

On 22 September 1980 Saddam Hussein's Iraq declared war on its eastern neighbour, Iran. Both countries were vast, occupying strategic areas in the Middle East. Iraq shared a border with Turkey, Syria and Jordan: Iran dominated the eastern shore of the Arabian Gulf and bordered Afghanistan and Pakistan. Both countries benefited from substantial oil revenues. There had been minor disputes between them in the past, principally over control of the Shatt al-Arab, a wide waterway between the two countries that gave Iraq, and its ancient southern city of Basra, access to the Gulf. A dispute over this border was the ostensible reason for the 1980 conflict, but there were other underlying issues.

In the previous year, a revolution had overthrown the Shah of Iran, an autocratic ruler who had been installed by the US and Britain after a coup by Iranian armed forces in the 1950s. The mass revolt against his government was waged by both religious and secular political organizations, but when the leading Iranian Shia leader, Ayatollah Khomeini, returned to Iran from Paris, where he had been exiled by the Shah, it was a signal for the radical Shia organizations to seize political power. Their militia, the Revolutionary Guards, stormed the US embassy in Teheran and held many staff and diplomats hostage. Over the next few months, most secular Iranian politicians were killed or driven into exile, and their organizations destroyed. Iran became an Islamic state.

Saddam Hussein had seized absolute power in Iraq through the Ba'ath Party, a political organization that had its origins in Arab nationalism. Its founders had taken their ideas from European Fascist organizations, espousing a form of socialist nationalism that was avowedly non-religious. The Ba'ath Party in Iraq was mainly a vehicle for Sunni ascendancy over the population's Shia majority, but its secular rhetoric provided a useful smokescreen under which Saddam could constantly play off tribal and religious antagonisms against each other. His regime was threatened by the rise of a fundamentalist Shia theocracy in Iran, particularly when Ayatollah Khomeini proclaimed a policy of exporting the Iranian revolution, and called on oppressed Shias around the world to rise up against their governments. Saddam believed that Iran was politically weakened, and that a military assault against his neighbouring country would be successful, bringing him and Iraq greater influence in the region.

The war between Iran and Iraq was one of the longest and bloodiest since the end of the Second World War. Initially the Iraqis gained the upper hand, seizing Iranian territory and attacking Iranian air bases. Under the Shah, the Iranian military had been supplied with arms by the US, but with the embassy staff held hostage in Teheran this source of equipment was, officially at least, no longer available. Stalemate followed the first Iraqi advances, but Iran's Revolutionary Guards had gained control of the large sums of money the Shah had accumulated during his reign, and used them to seek alternative sources of weapons. They also started to raise their own military units. These forces were often composed of young boys, semi-literate, who could be persuaded to seek martyrdom on the battlefield. A year after the initial Iraqi invasion, Iranian forces counter-attacked. By May 1982 they had driven the Iraqis out of Iran, and were beginning to penetrate Iraq. During the next three years they threatened to take the city of Basra and occupied the al-Faw peninsula.

It was this period of fighting that saw the worst excesses of both regimes. By 1983 the Iraqi forces now numbered half a million men, and had established a highly developed network of defensive bunkers and artillery fire points. The Iranians launched human-wave assaults against the Iraqis' defences, losing tens of thousands of men. Often young, religious volunteers were used to clear minefields and over-whelm Iraqi trenches and frontline positions. In the offensive against Basra, five such human-wave attacks were repulsed by artillery and machine-guns – many observers likened this stage of the war to the battlefields of France between 1914 and 1918, and the slaughter of thousands of combatants brought almost no advantage to either side. Another simil-arity to the First World War was that Iraq adopted chemical weapons against the massed ranks of the Iranians – mustard gas and cyanide, but also modern chemicals that attacked the central nervous system in the same way that pesticides killed insects. It was the first time the latter had ever been used by military forces. The nerve agents were particularly potent against unprepared troops. Most of the chemicals used to make these weapons came from factories in Europe and the United States, and they became an important part of Saddam Hussein's arsenal.

Around a quarter of a million artillery shells were produced to discharge chemical weapons, as were bombs and missile warheads. UN inspectors, who made several visits to the battlefields during the course of the war, found enough evidence of their use to suggest that it had become routine on the part of Iraqi forces.

Despite high numbers of fatalities on both sides, the war ground on, neither country achieving a breakthrough. This led them to seek alternative ways to outflank their opponents. Iraq started what became known as the War of the Cities, launching air raids against Teheran and other Iranian towns. In retaliation, the Iranians fired Scud missiles against Baghdad. Schools, apartment blocks, passenger trains and airports were hit, causing large numbers of civilian deaths.

The Arab states were as threatened as Saddam was by the rise of militant Shiism, and in any event were motivated to support Iraq out of a sense of Arab solidarity. In particular, Saudi Arabia and Kuwait provided Saddam Hussein with money and loans. Because Iranian control of the al-Faw peninsula had cut off Iraq from the Gulf, Iraq's Arab neighbours also provided access to their ports and facilities for Iraq to raise money by exporting its crude oil. It was this last assistance that prompted the Iranians to attempt to cut off Iraq's oil trade through the Arabian Gulf. They mined several areas of the waters, and placed Silkworm anti-ship missiles along their coast. Ships sailing through the Strait of Hormuz became especially vulnerable. In May 1984, Iran attacked a Kuwaiti tanker near Bahrain, and a Saudi tanker was hit in Saudi Arabian waters. In all, around 546 ships were damaged during the war, and more than four hundred sailors lost their lives.

The threat to the oil trade acted as a spur to intervention by the US and Britain. At the start of the war Britain had established a presence in the Gulf, sending three warships to patrol the area. The US had declared its support for Iraq in 1982, saying, in a directive from President Reagan, that the US 'would do whatever was necessary to prevent Iraq from losing the war with Iran'.

This policy never wavered, despite Saddam Hussein's continued use of chemical weapons. The US supplied Iraq with intelligence about Iranian troop movements, and allowed some covert weapons transfers. Towards the end of the war its support escalated, when it allowed Kuwaiti and Saudi Arabian oil tankers to sail under the protection of the American flag, and its warships became increasingly aggressive against Iranian forces, even though in May 1987 an Iraqi jet attacked the USS *Stark*, killing thirty-seven crew.

In October 1987 the US Navy attacked Iranian oil platforms in retaliation for an Iranian attack on *Sea Isle City*, a US-flagged Kuwaiti tanker. In 1988, in response to damage caused to a US Navy frigate by a supposed Iranian mine, two Iranian oil platforms were attacked, then two Iranian ships and six gunboats were sunk. Four months later an Aegis guided-missile cruiser, the USS *Vincennes*, shot down an Iran Air passenger plane on its way to Dubai, killing 229 passengers and crew. The US claimed it was an accident and, after several investigations, paid almost $132 million in compensation to the Iranian government.

By now the war was taking its toll on Iran, and its ruling clerics were facing severe economic problems and political unrest. It may be that the tragedy of the Iran Air flight was the last straw: perhaps it brought home to the leadership that their war was no longer purely with Iraq and made them wonder how aggressive the US might become. In August 1988 Iran accepted a UN resolution calling for a ceasefire and a negotiated settlement of outstanding border disputes.

The eight-year war had been an unmitigated disaster for both countries, and a seemingly endless tragedy for the civilian populations, with more than a million deaths. Its callous brutality was underlined in March 1988 when chemical weapons were used against Kurdish rebels in the town of Halabja. Press photographers were close by, and the images they captured of poor villagers, women and children killed by Iraqi chemical weapons dropped from Mig-23s became an appalling symbol of the death that had spread over the region for so long, and helped to establish the belief that under Saddam Hussein Iraq was a rogue state.

Iraq suffered little diplomatic fallout from its egregious breaches of international law, and the US, Britain and other European nations were keen to seize any economic benefits from an oil-rich country that needed to rebuild its economy. But Saddam Hussein had run up huge debts to the tune of $80 billion, much of which was owed to Kuwait and other Arab states. Iraq had a huge standing army, and Saddam believed he could solve his economic problems by force. He asked Kuwait for a gift of $27 billion and suggested that Kuwait and Saudi Arabia should reduce their output of oil so that the price of crude would rise, thus increasing Iraq's revenues from its own production. Kuwait demurred, and in August 1990, Iraqi forces invaded. The royal family and most government ministers were out of the country, as usual in August, the hottest month of the year, and quickly set up a government in exile in London. Through its sovereign funds, the Kuwaiti government held massive assets in the stock exchanges of London and New York; Margaret Thatcher and George Bush Senior set about creating an international coalition to remove Saddam Hussein from Kuwait.

The previous US military intervention in a far-flung corner of the globe had been in Vietnam, and had resulted in a significant defeat. More recent interventions in the Middle East had been equally humiliating. A special-forces operation to rescue American hostages in Iran had ended in catastrophe, while in 1983 the US embassy and a marine barracks in Beirut had been obliterated by powerful car bombs in the Lebanese civil war.

US refusal to come to the aid of the royal family of Kuwait would mean severe loss of influence in the Middle East, yet another military embarrassment in the region would be equally damaging to US prestige and influence. It was this fear that governed the US actions to free Kuwait.

The military preparations to take on the Iraqi forces in Kuwait and drive them out of the country were based on the premise that overwhelming force was needed to ensure victory. The military build-up in the region took months, and the eventual battle was carefully orchestrated so that a massive bombardment of Iraqi forces in Kuwait and strategic targets in Iraq were destroyed before ground troops launched their assault. By the time US-led coalition forces attacked Iraq, and bombed Baghdad, on 16 January 1991, a massive army of almost 400,000 soldiers, with thousands of tanks and artillery pieces, had gathered in Saudi Arabia. There was a US fleet in the waters of the Gulf larger than any that had been assembled since the war against Japan. Six carrier-led battle groups, thirteen nuclear submarines and the battleship USS *Missouri* armed with 16-inch guns and

Tomahawk cruise missiles, were steaming into the waters of the northern Arabian Gulf. These ships normally were part of the US Sixth Fleet, stationed in the Mediterranean, and the Seventh Fleet operating in the western Pacific, with bases in Hawaii and Japan. Even with these forces, the US commander, General Norman Schwarzkopf, was expecting thousands of casualties. In fact, the battle showed the superiority of US weapons and technology against a large but poorly equipped and led Iraqi Army.

What was equally important to the initial success of Operation Desert Storm, as it was known, was a political decision to keep the aims of the war limited. In order to maintain international support for the US, and to prevent any possibility of US troops being trapped in a war of indeterminate length, the coalition would liberate Kuwait and go no further. There would be no occupation of Iraq, no foreign troops attempting to overthrow the leader of one of the most important states in the region.

Yet even this well-planned military operation had unexpected consequences. Saddam Hussein was determined to drive up the price of oil and set demolition charges on the heads of every oil-producing well in Kuwait. As his last convoy of troops drove through the Mutla Ridge – where they were strafed and killed by US fighter bombers – on their retreat to Iraq, almost eight hundred oil wells were on fire, sending a giant plume of oily smoke high into the atmosphere. The pumping stations on the coast were also destroyed, and at the start of the war Iraq had released an enormous oil slick into the Gulf to hamper any seaborne invasion. Kuwait had been looted – even the laboratories at the university had been gutted – and there was not a single working vehicle in the country. So determined was Saddam Hussein to wipe out Kuwait that even public buildings had been set with demolition charges.

However, Kuwait was a rich country, and several months later the oilfields had been repaired. Far more serious were post-war events in Iraq. President Bush's advisers had thought that in the wake of a decisive military defeat, Saddam Hussein would be removed in a coup staged by the Iraqi military, who had been led into two extremely damaging wars. This didn't happen. The opposition to Saddam and the regime came from below, with popular uprisings in the south of Iraq from the Shia population, and in the north from the Kurds, who had been struggling for their own national independence for a generation.

The US, Britain and their allies had withdrawn their troops from Iraq after the ceasefire in March, and made no attempt to prevent the massacres that followed.

The Shia revolt was brutally suppressed by the Iraqi Army and those brigades of the Republican Guard, specially equipped and loyal units, that had remained in Iraq to defend Saddam and Baghdad. In the north the civilian Kurdish population fled into the mountains, where they faced death from cold, lack of shelter and food. They threatened to spill over into Turkey and precipitate a political crisis, so US, French and British troops entered Iraq to create safe havens for the Kurds, with a 'no-fly zone' in which any Iraqi aircraft or helicopters would be shot down by Allied forces. The Iraqi Kurds had gained a measure of safety, but the Shia in the south continued to be subjected to brutal repression by Saddam's Republican Guards, so a few months later a 'no-fly zone' was established there too.

But Saddam Hussein remained in power. The no-fly zones continued to be patrolled by British and US warplanes, the military operations dubbed Southern Watch and Northern Watch respectively, and a US aircraft-carrier maintained a permanent presence in the Gulf. So, a war that had seemingly been marked by a large united coalition of countries, with limited aims and an initial military success, had become a stalemate.

The military victory had left what seemed to many a fudged and inconclusive situation in the Middle East. The UN sent in inspection teams to find and destroy Iraq's chemical and biological weapons, and economic sanctions were maintained. US and British fighters shot down any errant Iraqi helicopters, and mounted air attacks on Iraqi military installations and industrial buildings in retaliation for breaches of the UN inspection programme, or attempts to strengthen the Iraqi military.

President Clinton maintained this policy of containment, but right-wing Republicans saw Saddam Hussein's continued survival as a constant reminder of US impotence. They began increasingly to question the policy of no-fly zones, and the utility of the UN inspections. In 1998, Congress, now with a Republican majority, passed the Iraqi Liberation Act, which authorized $97 million to be spent on arming an insurgent force to overthrow Saddam.

Later that year, Saddam expelled the UN inspection team, and the US, with Britain, staged Operation Desert Fox, a blitz of 415 cruise missiles and 600 bombers that killed 1400 members of the Republican Guard, and allegedly set back Saddam's weapons programme by several years.

But if it was costly to Iraq, it showed again the limits of the strategy. Moreover, many were thinking of other, unforeseen, consequences of US policy. How would the Allies respond if one or, worse, several aircraft were shot down while enforcing the 'no-fly zones', and their crew held hostage? What could the US do to rescue them? Would it translate into another embarrassing hostage crisis similar to the Iranian one that had brought down President Carter?

When George W. Bush was sworn in as president in January 2001, the members of his conservative

Republican government immediately started to focus on policy towards Iraq, considering ways to bring the situation to a conclusion. One option examined by a group in the Pentagon was for a small invasion force to move into the south of Iraq and occupy the oilfields, thus obtaining a stranglehold on the country and the regime.

These plans were overshadowed by events later in the year.

In September 2001, the largest fleet of warships Britain had assembled since the war in the Falklands was preparing to travel through the Suez Canal. Three of the Navy's most important ships, the aircraft-carrier HMS *Illustrious*, the helicopter-carrier HMS *Ocean* and the amphibious-assault ship HMS *Fearless* were accompanied by three destroyers and two frigates, thirteen mine-sweepers, survey vessels and landing ships as they headed into the Arabian Gulf to take part, with Omani forces, in an exercise called Saif Sarrea 11. The fleet, the aircraft and the troops that accompanied them were testing the effectiveness of the new Joint Rapid Reaction Force.

On 11 September Captain Adrian Johns was in command of *Ocean*, capable of carrying 800 marines and eighteen helicopters. He was on the bridge overseeing the preparations to take on pilots and navigate the narrow waters of the canal. *Ocean* was newly built and Johns was her first commanding officer; he wanted everything to go well. The canal authorities could sometimes be overly bureaucratic. His principal warfare officer, who would normally be based in the operations room deep beneath the hangar decks, appeared on the bridge and seemed agitated. He said, with some urgency, 'Sir, I think you need to nip down to the bridge mess, switch on the television and see what's happening.'

Captain Johns was just in time to watch a United Airlines Boeing 767 smash into the south tower of New York's World Trade Center, in a giant fireball. He stood transfixed until the building collapsed. In his journal that night he recorded that life had been transformed, and would never be the same again. The world had entered into a different, darker era.

The ships of the Royal Navy's Task Group continued their transit of the Suez Canal and sailed down the Red Sea and into the Gulf to dock in Oman. They began their exercise, but were offered to the US government and CentCom as part of their military operation, Enduring Freedom, against the Taliban and al-Qaeda in Afghanistan. Some ships remained on station after the end of their scheduled visit to Oman. Special-forces units were launched from the flight deck of HMS *Illustrious*, and Tomahawk cruise missiles were fired from British nuclear submarines in the area.

Later, *Ocean* returned to the Gulf; some companies of 45 Commando flew from her directly into Afghanistan while the rest went via the ship's landing craft to Oman and were flown from there into action against the Taliban. It was a wholly unexpected baptism of fire for the Task Group and the new concept of far-reaching military intervention.

At the time that the Saif Sarrea exercise became transformed into a real war-fighting operation, the Royal Navy commanding officer, Rear Admiral James Burnell-Nugent, went ashore at Bahrain and set up an office in the building that housed the US Fifth Fleet headquarters. Burnell-Nugent is a forceful, dynamic character, having commanded the nuclear submarine HMS *Conqueror*, and all three of Britain's aircraft-carriers. It helped that he had a significant number of ships in the Gulf, and space was found for him and his team.

He quickly became commander of the United Kingdom Maritime Component, and put the case that he should also become deputy commander of the Coalition Force Maritime Component of Operation Enduring Freedom under Admiral Tim Keating, who commanded the US Fifth Fleet. This would place him close to the US centre of decision-making, and also make him, nominally at least, second in command of the warships from other coalition countries, much to their officers' irritation. The arrangement survived, and continued after the run down of the operation against the Taliban and al-Qaeda.

* * *

That was the history, and the command arrangements, into which Commodore Snelson was flying in August 2002. Admiral Tim Keating was still based in Bahrain, and the Fifth Fleet had a battle group created around the aircraft-carrier USS *Abraham Lincoln*, with two guided-missile cruisers, a group of destroyers and frigates, and a nuclear hunter-killer submarine, as well as a variety of support vessels. Ships carrying an amphibious ready group of US Marines had also recently become attached to the Fifth Fleet, and were due to begin a series of exercises in Kuwait. Keating was also head of Naval Forces Central Command, with an area of responsibility that encompassed the Middle East and stretched from the Suez Canal east to the Pakistan–India border, and south to the equator off the coast of Somalia. Also, he continued in command of the Coalition Force Maritime Component, which now included ships from around twenty-five countries that had offered to help the US to invade Afghanistan and destroy the bases of al-Qaeda. Commodore Snelson was in Bahrain to represent the interests of the Royal Navy and Britain against the overwhelming power and influence of the US. Delicate matters on the horizon might provide opportunities to cement Britain's relationship with the US, and what little influence Britain retained in the region, or might blow up in his face.

Before boarding his aircraft at Heathrow, David

Snelson had been thoroughly briefed by senior officers at Fleet Headquarters, located in a nuclear-bombproof bunker in Northwood, north London, the home of the Permanent Joint Headquarters, the nerve centre of Britain's armed forces. At this time, a plan to invade Iraq was being worked on by a small group of officers. It was kept extremely secret. Eighty-seven people were allowed to know about it, and their names were given to the secretary of state for defence, Geoff Hoon, for his approval. A year earlier, Brigadier Jim Dutton, the commanding officer of 3 Commando Brigade, had been privileged to see the start of the planning process at the Pentagon in Washington.

Shortly after the attack on the World Trade Center, Brigadier Dutton had been selected by the chief of the Defence Staff, Admiral Sir Mike Boyce, to take up a post as his liaison officer at the Pentagon. He had arrived in Washington on 10 October, the first foreign military officer to be allowed into the National Military Command Center. 'I used to go to their meetings at six thirty in the morning, and at four o'clock in the afternoon. I used to hang around the Pentagon during the day and talk to people. My role was meant to be assisting in a cross-flow of inform-ation, but it was ninety-five per cent one way: me reporting back to the UK.'

Dutton was in a sensitive position: at this time, the new US defence secretary, Donald Rumsfeld, was

attempting to streamline the US armed forces, intro-
duce new weapons and technology, cut manpower
and save money. The attacks on the World Trade
Center meant that the hawks in the administration
would feel able to move the question of what to
do about Saddam Hussein much higher on their
to-do list. The invasion of Iraq would be Rumsfeld's
primary objective, and his modernization of the
doctrines and structure of the armed forces would be
thoroughly road-tested.

The existing US operational plan, Op Plan 1003
98, to invade Iraq had last been modified, as its title
implies, in 1998; it was just one of the sixty-seven or
so op plans that the Pentagon maintains and regularly
updates as an insurance policy against the need to
mount sudden military action anywhere around the
world.

Op Plan 1003 called for the mobilization of around
380,000 troops, with an airborne corps occupying the
north of Iraq, another mechanized division taking
control of the area around Baghdad, and a Marine
Expeditionary Force occupying the south and Basra.
After the initial occupation it was assumed that total
troop figures would reach 400,000 and that the
occupation might continue for up to ten years.
Although last looked at in 1998, it was based on
the experience of Operation Desert Storm and the
assumptions that had been made, military and
political, at that time.

In November 2001 Rumsfeld met General Tommy Franks, the commander in chief of CentCom, at its headquarters in Tampa, Florida, and told him to start working on a different plan that would emphasize a much more rapid mobilization than the six months taken for the last war with Iraq. It would seek to maximize surprise and shock, and contribute to the momentum for regime change.

Within a month Franks had returned with a refined Op Plan 1003, in which troop numbers had been cut, but that was not enough for Rumsfeld. He wanted to change the plan fundamentally. It became clear to Franks that the reduction in numbers had to be drastic, and how and when the troops were mobilized must be radically rethought. There was no room in Rumsfeld's view of operations for a slow, deliberate build-up before the fighting started. If necessary, war would begin before all the forces required for victory were in place, as long as there was a properly worked-out timetable for their deployment.

Franks went away. The plans for invading Iraq would be built from the bottom up and would, Rumsfeld hoped, be testament to a new, revolutionary way of war fighting.

Brigadier Dutton, attending the two Joint Staff meetings every day, officially saw little of this arbitration between Franks and Rumsfeld. But in the meetings he attended he noticed that the Americans were talking less about Afghanistan and more about their own internal business and their war-fighting strategy. The most that General John Abizaid, Franks's deputy at the meetings, would say was that they were involved in a stock-take, an internal audit to discover whether or not it was possible to wage war in Afghanistan and Iraq at the same time. But they never asked Dutton to leave the meetings – he believes they were far too polite to exclude him – so he was free to form his own conclusions. The information he gathered was to prove invaluable to him. When he left Washington, in March 2002, Abizaid confessed that he would look down the table at him and sometimes wonder 'whether they really wanted this Brit in here'. But by then the cat was well and truly out of the bag.

In January 2002, President Bush had referred to an 'axis of evil' that included North Korea, Libya and Iraq. In the next months the military and diplomatic links that existed between Britain and the US meant that there was a fairly unobstructed flow of information. By 8 March, just before Dutton left the Pentagon, a document drafted for the Overseas and Defence Policy sub-committee of the cabinet stated confidently that 'The US administration has lost faith in containment and is now considering regime change.'

The British Prime Minister, Tony Blair, made a visit to President Bush in April 2002, and was entertained, with his wife, at President Bush's ranch at Crawford in Texas. By the time Blair had returned to London, his special military adviser, Lieutenant General Tony Piggott, deputy chief of the Defence Staff and responsible for operational planning, had called on Brigadier Dutton and asked him to work out what options were available for the UK to provide military assistance in an invasion of Iraq.

Dutton found this a thankless task because the proposition was anathema to other government departments. Working in a small, discreet team outside the hierarchy in the Ministry of Defence, he found it impossible to gain the attention of the rest of Whitehall – some departments would not return his telephone calls – but he was an experienced hand: he knew what resources were available, and what it would require to free them up. Ultimately he knew the decision was not military but political.

The options the team identified were recorded in a report to Tony Blair for a meeting in Downing Street on 23 July and were presented to him by the chief of the Defence Staff, Sir Michael Boyce. He said that there were just three possibilities: a limited offer of assistance, with access to base facilities in the islands of Diego Garcia and Cyprus and deploying three special-forces units; adding naval and air-force units to the special-forces contribution for longer-term operations; and, finally, an army contribution of 40,000 troops, to tie down two Iraqi divisions.

A week before this briefing, Dutton had left

Piggott's team to take command of 3 Commando Brigade, Royal Marines. There were other issues that he found equally pressing. The Royal Marines were changing their commando and company structure to make them more mobile and provide them with more centralized fire power. New weapons were to be introduced, which entailed more training, and reworking tactical doctrine. The fighting in Afghanistan, where 45 Commando was heavily committed, also called for a lot of his attention. But the Royal Marine Commandos were a major part of the Joint Rapid Reaction Force, so Dutton kept his eye on the developing plans for Iraq and maintained contact with Commodore Snelson. If there was going to be a war, he wanted to know about it and he wanted to be a part of it.

Snelson had been fully briefed about the current planning effort in Whitehall, but had not been told about the work that had been done by General Franks and Donald Rumsfeld. Neither had most of the US Navy officers in Bahrain. For them the old Plan 1003 was still the document they were working to, as was Snelson. The 600-page document that detailed the invasion of Iraq was still heavily influenced by the last Gulf War against Saddam Hussein, and its unfortunate aftermath. If there was another Shia uprising in the south, the US wanted to be in a better position to support it than they had been last time, which meant that the Iraqi port of

Umm Qasr, connected to the Arabian Gulf by the Khawr 'Abd Allah waterway, had to be occupied quickly so that it was open to relief vessels delivering emergency aid and equipment.

This waterway, and indeed the waters of the northern Gulf, had been mined by Saddam Hussein in the previous conflict, and it was expected that he would do so again in another war. The Admiralty had already sent a small flotilla of mine-sweepers to the Gulf, knowing they would take some weeks to get there. The Royal Navy has a reputation for its mine-sweeping skills, and Admiral Tim Keating, commander of the US Fifth Fleet in Bahrain, was happy to let the British plan an operation that would incorporate US and Australian mine-sweepers.

But Snelson, like Brigadier Dutton, wasn't the sort to watch a war take place around him without wanting to be actively involved. A few weeks after his arrival in Bahrain, the question of how to protect the mine-sweeping force arose. One bank of the Khawr 'Abd Allah was in Kuwait and would be secure; the other, on the eastern side, was part of the al-Faw peninsula and was Iraqi territory. The mine-sweepers would be vulnerable to attack from that shore. They were small vessels, not heavily armed, easily damaged by rocket and small-arms fire. The waterway was shallow and the dredged channels were narrow, not suitable for any larger warships that might provide a defensive screen. Moreover, during the last Gulf War, and also during the war with Iran, Iraqi forces had deployed Chinese-manufactured Silkworm anti-ship missiles, on the al-Faw peninsula, and intelligence suggested that the launchers were still in place.

It seemed to David Snelson that it was necessary to secure the east bank of the waterway, and the entire al-Faw peninsula. US plans did not make any provision for their troops to do this, so a UK force would have to take on that role. Current thinking in the Ministry of Defence was that any land forces involved in the US invasion of Iraq would take action in the north of Iraq, and make their way via Turkish roads and railways to their base camps on the Turkish–Iraqi border. At this stage, and the plans were still largely contained within the small secret group set up in April, the problems of Turkish agreement or, indeed, the suitability of transport routes in Turkey had not been properly addressed, but the army preferred to avoid a lengthy voyage to the ports in Kuwait.

If the docks of Umm Qasr could only be secured and used if the al-Faw peninsula was occupied, it made sense to mount an amphibious landing with a Royal Marines Commando. Snelson informed the Commander-in-Chief, Fleet, in Portsmouth, and the Joint Staff Headquarters in Northwood, of the new resources he would require. It was not an easy request to make. The number of ships that were available was limited: HMS *Ocean*, the purpose-built amphibious assault ship, was in dry dock, and the navy had only one operational aircraft-carrier, HMS *Ark Royal*. Deploying this to the Gulf, configured as a troop-carrier and transporting helicopters, would cause disruption to the navy's planned ship deployments. Clearing the waterway to Umm Qasr was now beginning to look like a significant operation, which caused tension with other service chiefs. There had still been no political decision to invade Iraq, but the heads of Britain's armed forces were keenly scouting opportunities to get involved.

In October Brigadier Dutton flew to San Diego: 40 Commando were taking part in exercises with the US Marine Corps at their 29 Palms training area in the Californian desert. At Camp Pendleton, the marines' headquarters on the Pacific coast, he met their new commander, Lieutenant General Jim Conway. It was a friendly visit and gave Dutton the opportunity to point out that 3 Commando Brigade was keen to take part in any action and that he would appreciate anything Conway could do to include them in the plans for Iraq. He returned to the UK, but other decisions in the planning mechanism were conspiring to bring the Royal Marine Commandos into the invasion of Iraq.

An American team had been put together at CentCom Headquarters in Tampa to consider whether Saddam Hussein would breach dams on the Tigris and Euphrates rivers to block the advance of the US military. Would he set fire to their oilfields to create a smokescreen, or release oil into the Gulf? He had invaded Kuwait to wipe out the large debts he had incurred with the country during his eight-year war with Iran. He had also wanted the Arab states in the region to cut their oil output to raise the price of crude oil and benefit the Iraqi economy, which was in crisis. It made perfect economic sense for him to destroy the oil infrastructure of Kuwait, but that didn't necessarily apply to Iraq's own oil industry. The planners in Tampa understood this, but were aware that, with the expected forthcoming invasion, Saddam would be desperate. The central aim of the US was to remove him from Iraq, and in their view it was sensible to assume that he would take any measures necessary to survive.

An analysis of the major southern oilfields, the routes of the pipelines and the locations of the pumping stations revealed that they all culminated in the al-Faw peninsula, where a staggering 90 per cent of Iraq's oil output left the country via two gas and oil platforms in the shallow waters of the Gulf, just a few miles from the coast.

It didn't take David Snelson long to realize that his plan to occupy the al-Faw peninsula and make it safe for mine clearance could potentially accommodate a much more strategic mission, which would be crucial for the success of the invasion and key to the future for Iraq, post Saddam Hussein.

The wrangling between General Franks and Donald Rumsfeld over the number of troops and the amount of time it would take to position them in the area was still absorbing the attention of David Snelson's American senior officers at CentCom in Bahrain. 'That's what the big discussions General McKiernan, the Land Component commander, was having were about, and that was where Admiral Keating's focus was. There was not a lot of attention on the detail of what actually needed to happen in the south.'

As far as the planners in Tampa were concerned, the seizure of strategic assets was a task for special forces, in this case the US Navy SEALS. Such troops are trained for sudden, violent action in a hostile area, but are poorly equipped to maintain a defensive position, and need a protective blanket of mobile forces to rapidly take over from them. David Snelson thought that 40 Commando, who were to mount an amphibious operation to secure the east bank of the Khawr 'Abd Allah waterway, would also be able to install a small occupying force on the oil infra-structure and relieve the SEALs. They could remain in place for seventy-two hours, then hand over to a larger US marines force.

On 5 November Snelson became a rear admiral. He was still in frequent communication with Brigadier Dutton, and a small team of Royal Marines had arrived in Bahrain to plan and arrange 40 Commando's deployment. They came rapidly to the conclusion that 40 Commando didn't have the manpower to do the job. The latest intelligence suggested that an Iraqi division was positioned south of Basra, and it seemed reasonable that they would counter-attack and threaten any forces that had landed in the al-Faw peninsula. The 800 troops of 40 Commando would be overwhelmed in a matter of hours.

Then it became clear that the commander of the US 1st Marine Expeditionary Force, which would replace 40 Commando after three days, would be expected to move his forces rapidly towards Baghdad. General Franks's campaign, under pressure from Donald Rumsfeld, was to mount a lightning strike on the Iraqi capital and bring about a collapse in the regime. It would be unnecessary to secure the whole of Iraq and, in any event, there would not be enough US forces to do so. CentCom's plan was largely to ignore the south of the country, apart from those areas between Kuwait and Baghdad.

The logical solution for David Snelson was to increase the size of the British Expeditionary Force, so 42 Commando was included in the plans for the amphibious landing. Snelson was now in charge of an operation significantly bigger than the mine-clearance task he had taken on just a few months before. It looked to many that an exercise in empire building was under way, and in London senior officers' hackles rose.

It was now that Snelson's talent for diplomacy and bureaucratic manoeuvring came to the fore. He had to influence US planning so that any British contribution would be properly considered, even though it would never be large enough to impact fundamentally on the success of US plans. Snelson knew that if the US wanted to do something they had enough resources to do it with or without the British. Part of his strategy from the beginning was to ensure that British elements of the task group would be placed under American tactical command: 'By doing that it forced the Americans to include us in the planning. It forced them to communicate with us, and then we would know exactly what was going on. It would also help reduce the risk of blue on blue,' the term used to describe friendly forces firing on each other.

Yet this handing over of control was viewed with suspicion in the Ministry of Defence. Now the growth of the navy's contribution to an amphibious landing set alarm bells ringing in Whitehall and at Northwood. 'That aspect of it was seen by the chief of Joint Operations, John Reith, as military adventurism on my part, largely a land campaign designed by a sailor who, he felt, probably didn't have much understanding of these things. So it was a question of balancing, influencing the American plan, and trying to win over my British bosses that it was the right thing to do.'

With 40 and 42 Commandos committed, in Snelson's

plan, both *Ark Royal* and *Ocean* would have to be sent to the Gulf, and they in turn would need escort vessels and Royal Fleet Auxiliaries to refuel and supply them. The Commander-in-Chief, Fleet, Admiral Jonathan Band, was happy to underwrite the mobilization of the warships, but with the main thrust of British land forces still planned for the north of Iraq via Turkey, the al-Faw peninsula landings seemed a dangerous and unnecessary sideshow. Snelson knew that he needed Brigadier Dutton, and 3 Commando Brigade Headquarters to be in theatre and involved in the detailed planning of the landings, alongside their US counterparts. He had approached several of the more senior US officers in CentCom, asking them to endorse his plans when they attended various component commanders' meetings, hoping that such support would quieten the criticism from London. The ploy was not successful, the US officers feeling, perhaps, that it was not their job to interfere in the British decision-making process.

On 14 December 2003 matters came to a head and General John Reith, chief of Joint Operations, made one of his fairly frequent visits to Bahrain. He wanted Admiral Snelson to abandon his plans and they argued about it quite forcefully. Snelson refused to give way, but had to call an end to the argument as both men were due to meet Admiral Keating, of the US Fifth Fleet, Snelson's commanding officer.

Protocol and good manners required that Snelson

and Reith present a united front to Keating, but Snelson couldn't restrain himself: he interrupted Reith in full flow and the argument between the two British officers started again, with some bitterness. It was an appalling breach of etiquette, but it produced results. For the first time Keating realized the pressure Snelson was under, and moved to back him. He told Reith that he had endorsed Snelson's plans, and that as far as CentCom and the Fifth Fleet were concerned, they were essential to the operation. This backing from the US was a significant victory for Snelson, and General Reith made a formal request to the chief of Defence Staff for 3 Commando Brigade Headquarters to be deployed to the Gulf.

A day after the bust-up in Admiral Tim Keating's office Brigadier Dutton was given permission to fly to Kuwait. In the six days he spent there, he met with the staffs of the US 1st Marine Expeditionary Force, who were based in a camp to the north-west of Kuwait City in their headquarters, which became known as Camp Commando. 'We spent a few days with them finding out if the whole brigade was involved, what could they do, what could we do, what tasks they wanted to hand to us in terms of screening and supporting while they moved up country.'

A problem remained. Dutton's Brigade Headquarters was normally in charge of the three Commandos, 40, 42 and 45, but only two were currently planned to be deployed in the invasion of Iraq. It was hard to justify the presence of the full brigade staff. Snelson and Lieutenant General Jim Conway, commander of the US 1st Marine Expeditionary Force, conferred and, over breakfast at Ricks Country Kitchen in Bahrain, worked out a solution.

It was a master stroke, Brigadier Dutton remembered: 'David Snelson managed to persuade the US and, indeed, John Reith and Northwood, the Permanent Joint Headquarters, to agree that if 3 Commando Brigade could stump up two commando units, the gunners, the engineers, the logisticians and all the rest of the stuff, the helicopters and things that went with the brigade, the Americans would provide a marine expeditionary unit, the equivalent of a commando to balance the brigade as the third unit. They would place it under my command, but they would only do that if we provided a substantial force for them to blister on to. But we could do that.'

Brigadier Dutton returned to the UK, then flew with his staff to San Diego to discuss with Conway how the US Marines and the Royal Marine Commandos would work together.

The ballooning plans of the UK maritime force commander in the Gulf had been kept under scrutiny by Admiral Band, the Permanent Joint Head Quarters (PJHQ), and the chiefs of the Defence Staff. Now, as the time approached for the Amphibious Task Group to sail for the Gulf, Snelson had to make a presentation of his plans to the naval officers who would be called upon to make them work.

On a cold January morning he addressed a packed conference room on Whale Island in Portsmouth naval base. He outlined the tasks and the planned deployment of ships and marines. What the assembled officers heard were the details of a challenging and audacious operation.

Ever since the Second World War, it had been a basic principle that forces should never make a landing where the enemy could oppose it. In the war to recover the Falklands, the landings had been on beaches some distance away from any significant Argentine forces. The al-Faw peninsula was, according to all the intelligence, well defended with an armoured division just a few hours away from the focus of the assault. The sea was shallow, and troops could only reach their objective by helicopter. The targets were time-urgent. In other words, any prior indication to the Iraqis that an attempt was being made to capture the oil facilities might trigger their demolition, and render the operation useless. For this reason the assault would be one of the very first actions of the war and would take place at night.

'When I revealed what we were going to be doing you could have heard a pin drop. I think probably the thing that hit people was the degree of risk we were going to be taking. They knew that we had an amphibious force that was not ideal. They knew that we hadn't been allowed to go out and buy the extra kit we needed until fairly late in November, so I think they were very much aware of the risks involved and there was a degree of surprise, astonishment, at the boldness of the plan. Somebody remarked to me that the Amphibious Task Group and 3 Commando Brigade in particular were the point of the spear. If you were the troop leader you were the tip of the spear. And there was that sort of realization – my goodness, we're the tip of the spear, I wonder how this is gonna go?'

As Snelson left the conference room, someone remarked that the meeting had reminded him of the film *A Bridge Too Far*, about the doomed airborne landings in Arnhem in 1944, which had proved a costly and bloody mistake. The film had opened with a scene similar to the briefing that Snelson had just given. Snelson hoped it was merely that scene which had crossed his companion's mind, not the mission's disastrous conclusion.

Six months after David Snelson had arrived in Bahrain a tentative plan for mine-clearance in Iraq had ballooned into a full-scale amphibious operation with a US Marine Corps unit under British command. The British government had yet to admit to the public that any plans existed to invade Iraq, and was still manoeuvring to get UN backing for any military action. But the navy had made its plans. It was time to start putting them into action.

3

THE FLEET SAILS

HMS *Ark Royal* moved majestically from her berth in Portsmouth, the masts of HMS *Victory*, Nelson's flagship at Trafalgar, sliding from view as she sailed past the round tower at the mouth of the harbour. The sightseers and well-wishers on the old sea walls could easily identify the ski-jump at the end of the flight deck that helped to propel heavily laden Harrier fighter-bombers into the air, but there were no fixed-wing aircraft on the flight deck, or in the hangar.

Ark Royal was not going to sea as an aircraft-carrier but as a helicopter landing platform, and as the flagship of Naval Task Group 03, which was heading, for public purposes at least, off on a series of exercises in the Far East. An enormous amount of work had been carried out inside *Ark Royal* while she had been tied up. She had been designed to play a variety of roles, but changing from one to another took time. All the bombs and missiles carried by Harriers had had to be removed from the magazine and unloaded, all the equipment packs and spares that lined the sides of the hangar had had to be taken out and replaced with the equipment needed for a variety of helicopters. The complement of marines needed more food and supplies than the normal crew of *Ark Royal* with its squadrons of aircraft. *Ark Royal* was also to be the command centre of an amphibious operation with all of its massive demand on communications: she needed more computers and communications suites, and her entire software had had to be changed. In the admiral's quarters, at the rear of the ship, the ceilings were ripped down to provide access to the internal wiring for computer connections, voice communications and fibreoptic cables so that the space could be transformed into an amphibious operations room. Similarly, the ward room became a large command and control centre that maintained a real-time electronic picture of everything happening in the battle space, whether on sea, land or in the air. It was a major transformation of the ship but the crew of 600 had done it before.

The day before *Ark Royal* left Portsmouth, Admiral Snelson, still in Portsmouth after his briefing to the assembled officers on Whale Island, held a press conference with the aircraft-carrier's captain, Alan Massey. To the assembled journalists, the story that the ship was sailing to the Far East seemed somewhat threadbare, but it had to be maintained because of political sensitivities. Snelson offered no hostages to fortune, but made the point that diplomacy was often more successful if the use of force was clearly an alternative option.

Ark Royal didn't head south-west, but set a course instead for the Irish Sea, then went north, docking at Glen Mallon on Loch Long, a Ministry of Defence armaments depot, to take on board the ammunition and stores that the commandos needed. Here, the story that the ship was heading for exercises in the Far East was more strictly adhered to. No orders had been given to place *Ark Royal* on a war footing, so loading anti-tank rockets, small-arms ammunition, claymore mines and hand grenades took several days because no overtime by the port workers had been sanctioned. The ship also found it hard to release from the stores more than a peacetime allocation of things like body bags, and other equipment. Gradually, though, she settled lower in the water under the weight of the enormous quantity of arms that were loaded on to her.

Ark Royal was finally ready. She was to join, and be the flagship of, a Royal Navy fleet, the size of which had not been seen since the Falklands war more than twenty years previously. There had been a lot of changes since then. This fleet sailing to the Gulf would have no independent air cover. There were women on board, as equal crew members, all the ratings had mobile phones, and twenty-four-hour streaming television to keep them in immediate touch with their friends, relations and the mood of the country about the war they were about to embark on in the Gulf. It was hoped the lack of aircraft would be more than made up for by the protection of US forces, but awareness of the controversy about the ultimate object of the mission would become a problem for Captain Massey and his crew as they sailed nearer to the Gulf.

Ark Royal and her crew of 460 men, and 140 women, some just boys and girls of eighteen, were sailing, perhaps, to war. For many, their only experience of war at sea was the training and exercises they had carried out when they worked up after a refit in port. As part of the Royal Navy's training programme, a series of exercises are held, culminating in what is known as a 'Thursday war' in the western approaches out of Plymouth. *Ark Royal* and her escort frigates, their gas turbine engines pushing them at close to thirty miles an hour, turn tightly as aircraft and submarines stage mock attacks. Crew members in anti-flash overalls, hoods and masks crouch by watertight doors at action stations ready to form stretcher parties or fire-fighting teams. In the operations room rows of young ratings, masks covering their faces, stare at computer screens, shouting closing speeds and ranges, the principal warfare officer and first officer on their feet, assessing in rapid succession how to evade the multiple threats. Then the cry goes up, 'Brace, brace, brace!' Around the ship, teams of inspectors assess how the ship's company, from junior rating to captain, bridge to engine room, deals with emergencies, asking, 'Is this crew ready to go to sea?' It's an exercise, a war game, but everyone on board knows that if the real thing ever happens this is what it will be like just seconds before a bomb, or shipwreck missile, blasts a fireball through the passageways and spaces of the vessel. Only the fear is missing. And everybody wonders secretly how they will behave when the fear and death are real.

So *Ark Royal* steamed on through the Bay of Biscay, prepared as far as a peacetime vessel could be for war.

In company with *Ark Royal* was HMS *Ocean*, larger than the aircraft-carrier, slower, and without the upward curve to the flight deck at the bow. She was newer than *Ark Royal*, just five years old, and specifically built as an LPH, or landing platform helicopter. Her job was to carry Royal Marine Commandos and get them ashore as quickly as possible using her four landing craft, Sea King or Chinook helicopters, and the ramp that could be extended from the stern to make a small floating jetty.

In June 2002 *Ocean* had returned from supporting the Royal Marines in Afghanistan and gone straight into a dry dock in Portsmouth for some serious maintenance work on the hull and propeller shafts. In December Captain Johns had received an instruction to ready her for sea as quickly as possible. They were afloat in record time, but then the ship was dogged by engine problems. *Ocean* doesn't launch fixed-wing aircraft, so she doesn't need to generate a huge wind speed over the flight deck. She is powered by diesel engines, driving one propeller, perfect for maintaining a steady cruising speed for thousands of miles, but not for rapid manoeuvres and sudden demands for a maximum speed of eighteen knots.

Ocean put to sea, and the port diesel engine blew its crank-case cover. She returned to dock, for extensive repairs to the engine. Once more she left Portsmouth for sea trials and again blew the port engine. With this second major breakdown, the ship continued on a single engine, with a great deal of anxiety being felt by Captain Johns, to her home port of Devonport.

There, despite the gloomy prognosis of the ship-yard, the engine was fixed and *Ocean* set off again, this time both engines running sweetly, to pick up ammunition at Southampton. On 15 January, with two companies of 40 Commando embarked, she headed west again to meet the helicopters that were flying from Yeovilton naval air station, nine Sea Kings Mark 4 from 845 Squadron, and six each of Lynx and Gazelle from 847 Squadron.

The task group headed south, and entered the Mediterranean, passing through the narrow Strait of

Gibraltar. It was now a significant fleet, with the two large ships, *Ark Royal* and *Ocean*, their escort of three destroyers, HMS *Edinburgh*, *York* and *Liverpool*, the frigate HMS *Marlborough*, three landing ships, carrying the rest of 40 Commando, HMS *Sir Tristram*, *Sir Galahad* and *Sir Percivale*, four other fleet auxiliaries, carrying fuel and supplies, and five chartered merchant ships. They sailed east for Cyprus where they would stage their first real exercises focused on the invasion of Iraq.

HMS *Ocean* and *Ark Royal* were heading a naval task group with an amphibious mission, to deliver more than 800 marines and their equipment to the al-Faw peninsula in Iraq. When D Company's commanding officer, Major Matt Pierson, had boarded *Ark Royal* Captain Massey had shaken his hand, and welcomed him aboard. Both men knew there were going to be many potential conflicts between the marines and the ship's crew, and that they would have to solve them. To put him at ease, Massey said to Pierson, 'You're the weapon, we're the delivery system.'

He need not have worried: the marines were quite capable of making themselves at home. Later in the voyage, when Matt Pierson saw that several gangways around the ship had been closed off with hazard-warning tape, he asked the quartermaster why. He was told that one of his marines had been taking pieces of metal from the gangways to make unofficial weapons mounts for the company's Pinzgauer 4×4 trucks. Soon all the trucks had been fitted with one of these mounts, and hazard warning tape was found in the most unusual places.

Colonel Messenger, the commanding officer of 40 Commando, had first become aware of the impending mission in November 2002, when he had met Brigadier Dutton, commanding 3 Commando Brigade, during his visit to the US to see members of 40 Commando training with the US Marines. He had lobbied with Brigadier Dutton for the US Marine Corps to write 40 Commando, with him as the CO, into the planning documents. Gordon Messenger knew nothing about any earlier plan to support a relief operation in Umm Qasr, or the discussions between Admiral Snelson and Brigadier Dutton. He thought 40 Commando had been plugged directly into an American plan for a US Marine Corps show with just one British Royal Marine Commando specifically directed towards the capture of the oil infrastructure on the al-Faw peninsula. He didn't need to know the background to the operation, just that it was strategic, key to the success of the overall war effort, and that he was entrusted with making it work.

Gordon Messenger had flown to Bahrain in December, where he had met up with the US Navy SEAL team, who were planning their assault on the oil facilities. He also went to a large meeting, called Exercise Internal Look, a tabletop exercise in which the movements of CentCom units taking part in Operation Iraqi Freedom were played out, so that the officers planning the operation could see where schedules needed to be adjusted and co-ordinated. It was a useful briefing, but not vitally important. As far as Gordon Messenger was concerned, the main focus was the Iraq oil-exporting facilities, and the al-Faw peninsula where they were located.

With Colonel Messenger on *Ocean* were his Company Headquarters, Captain Paul Lynch, the commanding officer of the Commandos Manoeuvre Support Group, the whole of B Company, under Major Matt Jackson, and C Company, under Major Duncan Dewar. A Company and the remainder of the Manoeuvre Support Group (MSG) were on board *Sir Galahad* and *Sir Percivale*.

Jackson thought it was a somewhat odd situation. The marines pride themselves on operating a system of 'mission command' in which commanding officers issue orders, and their subordinates are trusted to know how to carry them out without interference. Any commander who works 'with a long-handled screwdriver' is very unpopular, and considered a poor manager. Matt Jackson wondered whether there would be any difficulties sharing the space on HMS *Ocean* with his commanding officer and the command headquarters, but Gordon Messenger and his staff were ensconced behind secure doors, with strictly controlled access. To begin with, Jackson saw little of him, although this changed as the voyage progressed.

Major Pierson recalled that *Ark Royal* sank into the water by almost a metre under the weight of the ammunition and weapons loaded for his marines. A commando needs mobility, so *Ocean*, *Ark Royal* and the fleet auxiliaries were laden with vehicles, of which there was a fair variety. The two most important were the WMIK, and the Pinzgauer. The former is a stripped-down Land Rover with a weapons-mount installation kit fitted to it. It has a strengthened chassis and can carry two general-purpose machine-guns or a .5-calibre heavy machine-gun. It can also be fitted with a Milan anti-tank missile-launcher. It is used for reconnaissance and fire support. A Pinzgauer is a four-wheel-drive vehicle used to carry stores or up to ten passengers, and can also be modified to mount weapons. The marines also use a tracked vehicle, the BV10, which can carry stores or troops, and finally a complement of quad bikes for quick movement from one position to another. During the voyage the marines spent a lot of time working on these vehicles, stripping them down, modifying the cabs, adding Milan missile panniers and other pieces of equipment.

One person on *Ocean* who was quickly involved in the preparations for landing was Lieutenant

Commander Jon Pentreath, commanding officer of 845 Squadron, the Sea King helicopters that would, with the RAF Chinook helicopters on *Ark Royal*, transport the commandos into their landing zone. The Sea King pilots are known as Junglies because of their experience in inserting commandos or other special forces discreetly into areas of Borneo and Malaysia from ships at sea. They also have considerable expertise in the Arctic. They fly low over sea and land, making use of cover provided by contours, trees and buildings, navigating to small remote areas with limited room in which to land or hover. The Sea King helicopters are extremely reliable but have a limited payload.

The Chinooks of 18 Squadron are much bigger, with twin rotors. They are also noisier, but they can carry much larger loads, including vehicles, loading and unloading via the ramp at the rear, or carried slung beneath the fuselages.

Jon Pentreath had been told that an operation was possible back in December, and was ordered to start flying training with night-vision goggles over a gas mask but not to prepare overtly for Iraqi deployment, a set of instructions his aircrew found plainly absurd.

'The NBC [nuclear, biological and chemical] protective clothing was very hot and uncomfortable. Normally you want to get NVG [night-vision goggles] very close to your eyes to maximize the field of vision, but with the gas masks on, this was very much reduced. We were clearly directed by our joint helicopter command that we were not overtly to prepare for Iraqi deployment, so we couldn't add better equipment for the desert or anything. All we could do was prepare the paperwork for such time as we were able to request it.'

Just before Christmas, Pentreath decided to bring the squadron back from an exercise in Norway. He had not been formally told of their deployment to the Gulf, but he suspected it would happen. He calculated that his crews would at least have some Christmas leave before embarking on *Ocean*, and that the Sea King helicopters would be better maintained in preparation for Iraq. He was right.

The cover story for the departure of *Ark Royal* was that the ship was to take part in exercises in the eastern Mediterranean and Cyprus, and it is true that British sovereign bases on Cyprus traditionally provide facilities for Royal Navy amphibious exercises, known as Green Wader. However, the exercises would work up the ships and the marines for the landings in Iraq. Although everyone on the ships, and in the wider military effort supporting them, believed they were about to go to war, the government's official position was that they were embarked on a naval task group, heading for a goodwill visit to the Far East. Saddam Hussein's regime was still a matter for diplomacy and the United Nations.

This meant that the training on the ships had to be conducted at a relatively slow tempo. Damage control, missile hits, mines and fire-fighting measures were practised regularly, but had to be presented as a precaution rather than as a vital necessity. The senior officers were concerned at having to operate within an unpleasantly vague timescale, and hoped that there would be enough time to increase the pace of training, without allowing the crew to become too stressed and cynical about the constant exercises. The commandos and helicopter crews, however, had to take this opportunity to get their organization right. It was vitally important to rehearse the loading scheme of men and equipment on to the helicopters and ensure that the take-off sequence was timed and capable of delivering the force to the battlefield in the right order, in the right place.

The two helicopter platforms, *Ark Royal* and *Ocean*, took up position in a formation similar to the one they would adopt in the northern Gulf, off the coast of Iraq; there were five miles between them and they were on a parallel heading of 330 degrees, with the coast to the north. They would practise getting people off the ships, using stokers or stewards to lead a squad of marines along passageways and up ladders to the flight deck and their helicopters. They wanted to work out command and control procedures so that there would be no collisions between *Ocean*'s helicopters and *Ark Royal*'s.

Things didn't go well. The first problem, again, was that the task group was not going to war and had no priority. This hit home in Cyprus. Every winter the island is used by the RAF's display team the Red Arrows to rehearse for the forthcoming summer season of air shows and exhibitions. They had booked the air space well in advance and had priority. As Captain Johns recalled, 'We were trying to do amphibious and aviation rehearsals. At one time we had ten of my Sea King helicopters airborne, and air-traffic control in Cyprus held them up for an hour in the air while the Red Arrows went through their tricks and came back in again. I protested, but I couldn't say, "Don't you know there's a war on?" But it was very real for us.'

There were problems for the Commandos as well. There was a significant number of troops to get ashore, and *Ark Royal* had embarked five large twin-bladed Chinook helicopters, operated by 18 Squadron. The marines were not familiar with these machines, and found it difficult to work out how best to utilize their large lift capacity. To get the right capability in the right place at the right time by the right means takes considerable co-ordination, especially when flying into an inhabited and dangerous area at night. It's an extraordinarily complex operation. Everybody found the exercise in Cyprus difficult and unsatisfactory. Some necessary equipment was not on board the ships. Pentreath knew that a balance had to be struck between the planning and training schedules for the aircrews and flying time devoted to moving the marines. The Squadrons hadn't had enough time for training, but they had sorted out their crewing, coupling an experienced pilot with a less experienced one, then ensuring that they flew a lot together and developed a rapport in the cockpit. Familiarity with each other's habits and skills was important; the ability to second-guess each other's movements would be an enormous advantage in a fast-moving situation – it might make the difference between life and death to the marines who would be carried to their landing zone. But their training demanded time away from the exercises involving the marines, and there wasn't enough of that. The members of 40 Commando thought the failures were a serious wake-up call.

There was one small band of people on the task group, however, who were very happy, and they were the members of 849 Squadron, in particular their commanding officer, Warrant Officer Mack McKenzie. In 1982, in the Falklands, the Royal Navy had lacked an early-warning radar system carried by an aircraft that could be launched from the deck of an aircraft-carrier. Within a few years the Sea King had an ungainly looking piece of kit: the radar was housed in an inflatable dome on a tube that stuck out of the fuselage, which had to be folded back and deflated whenever the helicopter landed. It was cheap and cheerful, but it worked.

The radar was the key of course, and by December 2002 849 Squadron had been testing a Sea King Mark 7 fitted with a new Searchwater radar device. It was very advanced, and relied on interleaved pulse and pulse Doppler transmissions that could track moving targets over the sea. McKenzie had assembled four Searchwater-equipped Sea Kings on *Ark Royal*, with seven crews, enough to maintain operations twenty-four hours a day. On the test flight out of Culdrose in Scotland, the crews had been impressed with the power of the radar, and its ability to find very small targets against the back scatter of the waves.

On the way to Cyprus McKenzie had become frustrated by the problems caused by having five large Chinooks permanently parked on the flight deck. During exercise Green Wader, however, while the Chinooks had been grounded by the RAF's flight programme, McKenzie's Sea Kings had been doing their own exercises, using jet-skis to test how many and at what range they could track them from the air. The results were outstanding. The crews had also noticed something else. Although designed to discriminate between moving objects and the random reflections produced by waves, the Searchwater radar seemed to have an incredible range over land, and a similar ability to track small moving objects, such as cars or even motorcycles. This was something McKenzie wanted to explore.

The task group re-formed and sailed on for the

Suez Canal. There was clearly still a lot to do, but the question now was when and where they could improve on their experience in Cyprus. In Bahrain, Admiral Snelson knew that the task group had been almost thrown together, without the urgency that a clear threat to national survival would have engendered. Now the Americans were talking about fighting starting in the middle of February, which was barely a fortnight away. Time was pressing, and it was vital that the ships, the marines and the helicopter force were working well together. They could not afford mistakes.

Snelson was in constant touch with Commodore Jamie Miller, on *Ark Royal*, Captain Massey, and Captain Johns on *Ocean*. He was concerned about their lack of readiness. They needed one more rehearsal at least. With the assistance of the military attaché in Bahrain they looked for alternative places to mount some training exercises. Who in the Middle East would welcome a British military exercise in the current political climate?

After several days of telephone calls from *Ark Royal* to Bahrain, the British military attaché came up with a piece of desert in the United Arab Emirates that could be made available. Snelson flew down to visit and met the British ambassador with the military attaché. The logistic support for the exercise would not be ideal, but the government of the UAE was willing to assist, as long as discretion was maintained. He seized the opportunity. But time was now pressing, and the task group still had to negotiate the Suez Canal. Experienced sailors knew that this busy waterway, more than 160 kilometres long, could mean severe delays: pilots had to be taken on board, and southbound vessels had to moor in the Bitter Lakes to allow northbound vessels to pass. Transit through the canal could be achieved in eighteen hours, but might take much longer.

4

THE MOTHER OF ALL
REHEARSALS

Operation Green Wader in Cyprus had made everyone aware of the mission that lay ahead in Iraq and just how much work was needed if it wasn't going to end in failure. Everything had to be tightened up, and the details of the mission closely worked through. Entry to the Suez Canal added a real sense of danger. The huge convoy of ships passing through the narrow waterway was a tempting target for anybody close to the canal with a shoulder-launched missile. The crew were ordered to stay below as much as possible, and armed watchkeepers were posted on lookout around the ships. Force protection, defending yourself and your ship against attack, was as important a part of training as anything else.

This was the sixth time that Captain Johns had

travelled through the canal on HMS *Ocean*, but this
time he noticed a subtle difference in mood: the
operation was much quieter and faster than usual,
the Canal Authority's pilots coming aboard quickly.
Along the banks and in the villages fewer people were
hanging around to watch the ships go by, there
were fewer people on the big bridge that crosses the
canal, and the ferries had stopped working. The
journey was the most efficient and speedy he had ever
experienced.

He became aware that a US nuclear submarine had
joined the convoy, and its low black rounded hull
made a sinister contrast to the pale grey surface ships
of the Royal Navy. The Americans had impressed on
the Canal Authority that speed and an incident-free
passage would be greatly appreciated, and the
Egyptians had obviously taken this to heart. Captain
Johns understood that they had charged higher fees.
Nothing was allowed to interrupt the journey
through the canal, not even a patch of fog, and they
pressed on with Captain Johns on the bridge.

'The Egyptian pilot and I stood behind this radar
screen and we just kept ourselves in the middle of
these two little railway lines which were the banks
and, of course, that's not something they train you to
do in navigation school, but it worked and it was just
tremendous. That was one of the fastest transits we
ever did. It was a complete straight-through job.
We were through, and down the other side.'

Once in the Red Sea, however, engine problems recurred in *Ocean*. She and *Ark Royal* were attempting flying exercises with their helicopters, going to their maximum speed to get wind over the decks and provide some extra lift for the helicopters. They then turned round to repeat the procedure for landing, then made speed again to re-form with the rest of the fleet. The water in the Red Sea is among the saltiest and hottest in the world, reaching 30°C, and the water-cooled diesels on *Ocean* started to overheat, causing power reduction and other problems. Moreover, the Red Sea is shallow and narrow in places, giving the two big ships little room to manoeuvre. But it was excellent training for the waters, equally hot and shallow, that they would encounter in the north Arabian Gulf.

From the Mediterranean to the northern Gulf any maritime force has to pass through three choke points. The Suez Canal is the first, and the second is at the end of the Red Sea where the waters narrow even more between Yemen and Djibouti. Here, force protection became vital. On 12 October 2000 a US Navy guided-missile destroyer, USS *Cole*, had docked at Aden in the Yemen to take on fuel. Around eleven in the morning, a small boat with two people in it approached the port side, where it exploded against the hull, level with the waterline. The blast was enormous, punching a thirty-foot hole in the hull, killing seventeen sailors queuing for food in the galley and injuring thirty-nine others. It took almost twelve hours to control the flooding. The two occupants of the boat were killed, and it was generally assumed that this had been organized by al-Qaeda. The first vessel to reach the stricken *Cole* was, ironically, HMS *Marlborough*, now an escort for *Ark Royal* and *Ocean*.

More alarmingly, just four months earlier, in October 2002, a tanker, *The Limburg*, had been hit by another suicide vessel in the Gulf of Aden, killing a crew member and spilling thousands of gallons of oil into the sea. The ships in the fleet went past Aden at action stations, with *Ocean*'s armed landing craft in the water, and fully armed helicopters in the air. It was an extremely tense period, not helped by a great deal of small-boat activity – rigid inflatable boats with three or four armed people in them crossing the strait, perhaps Yemeni coastguard, smugglers or pirates on the hunt for a small cargo vessel. It was impossible to tell what their intentions were or if one was on a potential suicide mission. At night they were practically invisible, with the only warning of their presence a flitting radar contact. The watchkeepers were permanently at the ready, armed with machine-guns and flares, prepared to open fire if there was any sign that the motorboats were about to close on the ship.

Two days later they were in the Gulf, passing through the third choke point, the Strait of Hormuz, heading for a station off the coast of the United Arab Emirates. They were due to start another exercise, Sea Hawk, which would be more detailed, looking at the mistakes and problems encountered in Cyprus and putting them right. The process had begun immediately the ships had left Cyprus. They had a US Navy SEAL planning team on board, and Colonel Gordon Messenger started the in-depth planning that involved not just the SEAL officers but Lieutenant Commander Pentreath, for the Air Component, and the other company commanders in 40 Commando, particularly those of C Company who would be in the first wave of the assault with Gordon Messenger, Major Matt Jackson of B Company, and Paul Lynch of the Manoeuvre Support Group (MSG).

Matt Jackson had realized in Cyprus that 40 Commando's mission would be extremely hazardous, so after they had passed through the Suez Canal, Gordon Messenger had made him an offer. He would tell Jackson what their mission was and keep him abreast of the development of plans, but in return he must ask his company to give up their mobile phones and other forms of communication with the outside world. B Company wanted to know what they were going to do, and were happy to give up their phones in return for privileged information. The greater insight this allowed Matt Jackson didn't ease his concerns.

The main effort for 40 Commando, as part of the

brigade's objectives, was to capture the buildings and machinery that allowed Iraq to export its oil from the southern oilfields via the Gulf. It flowed through pipelines to a monitoring and metering station (MMS), an area roughly two kilometres square containing office buildings, several storage tanks and other large pieces of machinery that controlled the pressure and separated the residual gas from the oil. Then it was directed into two four-foot-diameter pipes, which went underground to emerge a few kilometres away at two buildings called Pipeline M and Pipeline K. These structures controlled the flow through another pipeline that took the oil and gas out to sea to two platforms, at which oil tankers could dock to load up with gas or crude oil.

The plan was that US Navy SEALs would make an initial assault on the sites of the Metering Station and the pipelines, and take control of specific valves and equipment. After thirty minutes the marines would take over. The SEALs would depart while the marines would set up a defensive perimeter against counter-attack, then move out to capture and control the surrounding al-Faw peninsula and the nearby town of al-Faw.

C Company, with Gordon Messenger's Head-quarters Company group and the Manoeuvre Support Group, would land on the metering station, closely followed by A Company. B Company, under Matt Jackson, would have the more difficult task of relieving the SEALs on the two pipeline buildings and holding them until D Company could land and clear and secure the area between the metering station and the pipelines, which were separated by about fifteen kilometres.

B Company's task was made harder because the pipeline outlets on the coast were almost two kilometres apart so the company would have to divide its limited forces and defend the two sites separately while D Company fought its way to them. The available intelligence, supplied mainly by satellite and spy-plane photographs, suggested there was an army barracks to the north of the metering station, which might hold a company of Iraqi soldiers, a trench complex between the metering station and al-Faw town to the east, and a large bunker complex two kilometres to the north of the buildings that Matt Jackson and his men would occupy. It seemed wise to expect strong resistance from Iraqi forces. Moreover, to make the situation even more hazardous, there was the reported presence, some seventy kilometres up the road in Basra, of an Iraqi armoured division, which could well overwhelm the 800 men of 40 Commando.

At the time Matt Jackson was told of the plans for the invasion of the al-Faw peninsula, an option was being discussed to take a squadron of Scimitar light tanks from the Queen's Dragoon Guards on to the beach beside the pipelines, using US Navy hovercraft to transport them over the mile-wide expanse of mudflats that was the Iraqi coastline. It was unclear whether or not the hovercraft would be available. Gordon Messenger thought the idea was mad and would never work but others at Brigade Headquarters in Kuwait believed the tanks might shift the balance of forces slightly more in 40 Commando's favour. On the other hand, B Company would have to clear the beach of mines, and mark out safe areas before the hovercraft would approach and the Scimitars drive on to land.

In any event, 42 Commando would be landed on the peninsula to the north of 40 Commando's positions, to create a blocking force against any incursion by Iraqi tanks or other forces from the north. No one knew how long these forces would need to resist attack, although the plan now was that the main British thrust by 1st Division land forces would overwhelm Basra, and Baghdad would be taken by the main US effort. If General Franks' and Donald Rumsfeld's plan worked, the Iraqi regime would not survive for long.

But it was easy to plan for a campaign that might take two or three weeks from the comfort of a high-tech and air-conditioned command centre in Bahrain or Tampa. For Matt Jackson and the other company commanders of 40 Commando, the prospect of holding on to a tenuous position for even two or three days was alarming. There was a relentless logic of war fighting for a lightly armed and mobile force that

Matt Jackson was struggling to reconcile with the limited lifting capability available to him.

Shortly after the exercises in Cyprus he was asked by 40 Commando planning group on *Ocean* to produce all-up weights for B Company and its equipment and supplies, and also to analyse the best way to deploy it in a hostile landing site to form a defensive perimeter. His Milan missile posts and heavy machine-guns could defend a maximum perimeter of three and a half kilometres. With his forces split into two, defending separate positions, he would not be able to clear forward from his original landing sites around the pipelines.

As a front-line unit prepared immediately on landing to engage the enemy, it was prudent to take ammunition to last for twenty-four hours. For the six heavy machine-guns in the company alone, that meant almost 10,000 pounds in weight. Heavy machine-guns' barrels have to be replaced every 300 rounds because they overheat, so spares would be required. B Company had an anti-tank troop and carried six firing posts for the Milan anti-tank missile. This missile needs compressed air to cool its heat-seeking infrared warhead, lithium batteries to power the launcher, other equipment and launch tubes so that the total weight of the full six anti-tank missile launchers and missiles came to 8826 pounds. The normal rate of fire for a Milan launcher is three missiles per minute, so the standard front-line supply of twelve missiles would provide only four minutes of continuous firing. Yet B Company might need to repel attacks for up to twenty-four hours without significant reinforcement, and its forces would be split to defend two perimeters.

With its forces divided, and the company fifteen kilometres from Commando Headquarters, a full set of forward fire control officers and communications were needed, as were the WMIK Land Rovers and Pinzgauers to provide mobile mountings for the machine-guns and missile-launchers. The conclusion was that for B Company to arrive at its two target destinations, the pipelines, in sufficient numbers to relieve the special forces and defend themselves against Iraqi attack, eight Sea King helicopters and four Chinooks would be required in seven separate combinations of passengers and underslung loads. That was almost the entire UK amphibious helicopter complement, with no provision for the other companies in 40 Commando, who were producing similar outline plans and conclusions.

A helicopter-transported assault was far more risky than a straight amphibious landing. As Matt Jackson pointed out, the availability of helicopters was determining the arrival sequence of men and equipment, not the tactical requirements of the mission. When he reached the end of one memo he asked the adjutant, 'Has your head exploded yet?'

Perhaps the exercises in the United Arab Emirates,

tailored to specific missions, might come up with some practical solutions to the problems.

Lieutenant Commander Pentreath, commanding 845 Squadron of Sea Kings on board *Ocean*, was also heavily involved in working out how the marines would be deployed from the Sea Kings on *Ocean* and the Chinooks on *Ark Royal*. He and Gordon Messenger's headquarters team spent hours looking at aerial and satellite reconnaissance of the oil installations on the al-Faw peninsula, trying to work out what types of troops needed to be landed where, and where and when equipment like anti-tank missiles, mortars and their supporting transport needed to be, and in what helicopters they could be delivered. The metering station was a large area, and there was some choice about where to land to secure the buildings or, alternatively, to prevent attacks from the bunkers and trench systems.

In the desert behind Jazirat al-Hamra, a small town on the coast of the United Arab Emirates, a full-scale outline of the buildings that 40 Commando would occupy had been constructed in the sand. Now it was easier to organize the marines into the right groups for the right aircraft. It was also apparent that there would be real problems with the sand- and duststorms whipped up by the rotor blades, cutting visibility, slowing transit times and causing mechanical failure. The heat was intense, water was vital, but the marines and the pilots were becoming acclimatized, and had

President George Bush and Prime Minister Tony Blair met in April 2002 at the President's ranch in Texas. Bush declared publicly that 'Saddam needs to go.' Blair urged the US President to seek the backing of the United Nations, and in September President Bush and the Secretary of State, Colin Powell (*bottom*), asked for a new UN resolution threatening severe consequences if Iraq did not account for all of its weapons of mass destruction.

Clockwise from above:
The Royal Marines of
40 Commando sailed
to the Gulf on HMS
Ocean, the purpose-
built amphibious
helicopter carrier,
and on HMS *Ark
Royal*, whose hangar
deck was stuffed with
vehicles and stores.
Also on board was 849
Squadron with Sea
King Mk VIIs fitted
with new search radar
in an inflatable dome
projecting from the
fuselage. They refined
its use while flying off
Kuwait City.

A few days before
the war started,
B Company set up
a temporary home
in the desert.

The Brigade Reconnaissance Force of 42 Commando zero the weapons on their WMIK Land Rovers on a desert range (*above left*). Colonel Gordon Messenger (*above right*) addresses 40 Commando, and Major Matt Jackson (*left*), the Commanding Officer of B Company, tries out his reflective identification patches. (*Below*) A Challenger II tank fires its main gun.

As H-hour approached, the HQ of 3 Commando Brigade waited for final confirmation (*left*), and D Company on *Ark Royal* (*below left*) made its final preparations.

(*Below*) The first wave of 40 Commando formed up with their US Marine CH53s behind them.

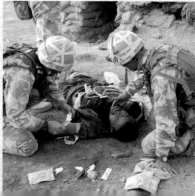

Major Justin Holt, Commanding
Officer of A Company (*above*), took
his company into al-Faw town. His
night attack on the Ba'ath Party HQ
(*right*) showed everyone that the
Royal Marines meant business.

Above right: Marines of 42
Commando fire a Milan missile at an
Iraqi hard point. (*Right*) B Company
survey the pipeline terminal the next
day. The quad bike was the only
transport to arrive with them.

Left: On the al-Faw peninsula Iraqi
conscripts were taken prisoner, and
some had their wounds treated.

A US marine raises a flag (*above right*) at Umm Qasr, the key Iraqi port (*far right*). Iraqi resistance continued, and Brigadier Jim Dutton (*centre right*) sent in 42 Commando, who were given just a few hours' notice of their deployment. They eventually secured the port area.

The occupation of the town was rapid and audacious (*above centre*). Within a day, they were patrolling the town (*far left*) and mingling with the civilian population, without their helmets (*right*).

Trained dolphins from the US Navy's Mammal Unit were used to locate mines in the waterway leading to Umm Qasr. It took several days before the Shatt al-Arab was declared safe for shipping and *Sir Galahad*, the Royal Fleet Auxiliary, could make its politically symbolic delivery of humanitarian supplies. The first phase of the Royal Marines' operation was over.

a much clearer idea of what they were getting into. Pentreath's Sea Kings were flying constantly, testing new anti-missile flares, and chaff dispensers, as well as carrying marines from the ships. The marines were engaged in other training, organizing mixed-weapon combat teams, and rehearsing anti-ambush procedures.

On *Ocean*, Captain Johns felt for the first time that everything was tightening up, that if they went to war they would be prepared. 'I went up to the flight operations room on the bridge one day and looked down at the flight deck. On the back end, the back third, they were firing live bullets at targets over the end of the ship. In the middle they were doing combat training, and at the front we were flying. Here we were, doing three very different things safely to work up the Commando so that they were at a peak when we pushed them off into Iraq. I realized that while I would have welcomed more time to do mission rehearsal, we were pretty much ready to go.'

Warrant Officer McKenzie, of 849 Squadron, was also pleased with progress. Throughout the exercise his radar observers had been flying out at sea, focusing on the coast road along the United Arab Emirates and further inland. It was clear that with the Searchwater radars they could build up a remarkable picture of daily movements along the roads and tracks of the country by vehicles and carts, and distinguish between the different types of target. All that was needed now was a way to route the pictures into the overall Link 16 communication network, and the tactical picture on the ground could be transmitted through the task group in real time, and forwarded to Brigade and Divisional Headquarters in Kuwait. This real-time battlefield surveillance was an unexpected and welcome asset.

With the exercise concluded, the task group continued up the Gulf. As it approached Bahrain, Admiral Snelson flew out to *Ark Royal* in a Merlin helicopter, which had just come into service. There he talked to Commodore Miller and Captain Massey about the readiness of the amphibious task group, and the latest developments in the US plans for the invasion of Iraq. Later they had a candle-lit dinner on the quarterdeck, with white tablecloths spread out, and a pipe band to play them in. Seated round the table, on a British warship making slow headway through the warm waters of the Gulf, served by smartly turned-out stewards, the candle flames reflecting in the silver serving dishes, it was possible to believe that the Empire had never ended.

The next day, Snelson flew to *Ocean*, meeting up once more with Captain Johns and Colonel Messenger. They had arrived in the area of operations on schedule, but it looked now that the start of fighting would not be in February. Snelson was concerned that the wait in the Gulf would sap the energy of the task group, and wanted them to pace themselves, allowing days for rest and relaxation during the on-board training regime.

A major rehearsal still lay ahead, 'The Mother of All Rehearsals' or MOAR. This was of particular importance for the Commandos on the ships, and Brigade Headquarters, that had been based in Kuwait since 20 January, particularly as their plans were still in a state of flux. Securing the oil facilities and the al-Faw peninsula required co-ordination not only with the helicopter carriers of the task group, but also with the US CentCom commanders of the Air, Land and Sea Components.

British forces, which had originally been going to invade Iraq in the north, through Turkey, had been refused permission for this by the Turkish government, and as a consequence the 1st (UK) Armoured Division would now be attached to the 1st (US) Marine Expeditionary Force to supplement the US Marines' push into Iraq. Then they would separate and advance on Basra while the US Marines continued to Baghdad. The Royal Marines were now under the UK divisional command, although 3 Commando Brigade, under Brigadier Dutton, was in command of the US 15th Marine Expeditionary Unit, as well as 40 and 42 Commando. In addition, there would be US teams attached to the commandos to liaise with US air support. Called Anglico teams, they would come with their own Humvee transport. The co-ordination and communication could easily have become a dog's dinner of confused responsibility and hazy chains of command.

Throughout January and February various table-top exercises were held to iron out potential conflict between units, and Gordon Messenger's Headquarters of 40 Commando participated in them. The exercise in the United Arab Emirates had resolved many physical problems with the helicopter force, but a mock-up of the oil facilities in the al-Faw peninsula had been erected in the Kuwaiti desert, which would offer valuable experience for the Commandos who would be landing on them, and the helicopter pilots who would have to make accurate low-level insertions in the dark.

Jon Pentreath had been made commander of the UK Air Mission, to co-ordinate the flights of the Sea Kings and the Chinooks. The SEALs would use their own specially equipped MH-53 helicopters, large, single-rotor machines with forward in-flight refuelling probes, special infrared night-vision systems and secure communications. After landing the SEALs on the metering station and the pipelines they would return to pick up the advance elements of 40 Commando and take them to the targets, then exfiltrate the SEALs. It was the most efficient use of the assets, but it meant that Pentreath spent a lot of time with the SEALs, co-ordinating communications procedures and getting to know them. As the plan developed, it seemed that there would be no pre-landing aerial bombardment, which bothered him. But the SEALs brought with them significant assets to make up for this.

The plan was that before the SEALs were due to land a B-52 from Diego Garcia would arrive over the area and drop sixteen joint direct-attack munitions (JDAMs), GPS-controlled bombs, on known enemy targets. Then a flight of A-10 tank-buster aircraft would patrol the area as the helicopters went in, and an AC-130 Spectre gunship would be ready to fire its cannon at any target. Jon Pentreath was most concerned about that, and scheduled several joint flying exercises with this fearsome plane so that the crew would not mistake a Sea King or Chinook helicopter for an Iraqi model and blast it out of the air. 'One of my key concerns was that they knew what one of our helicopters looked like from above in the dark.'

The first day of the landings was studied in the most intense detail. Daily intelligence reports, the latest reconnaissance photographs, were examined minutely to see if there was any change in the Iraqi forces, or any changes to the target that would affect the landing plan.

As all of these preparations were made, earlier concerns about helicopter assets, and the need for the marines to sustain themselves for at least twenty-four hours seemed insurmountable. Pentreath recalled, 'We had conducted two rehearsals in the Kuwait facility, and it became obvious that the assault would need to be land-based.' They had set up a helicopter base in the Kuwaiti desert, but sand and dust made landings extremely difficult. Pentreath wanted to pour oil over the ground but the idea was rejected for environmental reasons. TAA Viking was not an ideal place from which to operate but, as far as Gordon Messenger and Brigadier Dutton were concerned, it was unavoidable.

Colonel Messenger knew that a decision to launch the helicopter assault from Kuwait, not the ships at sea, would be contentious, because it would have far-reaching consequences for future defence plans and might influence decisions about the relevance of expensive ships like *Ocean* and *Ark Royal*. Gordon Messenger had to break the bad news to the task-force commanders. The sailors, or dark blue as they were known, would have their own views.

'There were issues of reputation, but nobody made a point of that. They argued their case as they saw it. The dark blue was absolutely right in the way that they approached it. The most overriding issue for us was the tempo for the first wave that we could generate. We could lift all helicopters off at once and it was frankly easier to control. It's ten times simpler to launch from a massive cleared site on the land.'

Many of the sailors on *Ocean* and *Ark Royal* felt that this decision was a mistake, but Messenger knew that the ships were vulnerable to attack by Iraqi shipwreck Seersucker missiles from the al-Faw peninsula, forcing *Ocean* and *Ark Royal* to cruise some fifty miles from the coast. This would impose too long a flight time on helicopters that would need to transit back and forth so the pace of the assault would be slowed. It was of paramount importance, in Gordon Messenger's mind, that his marines should land in as large a formation as possible.

Normally, taking off from a ship like *Ocean*, up to five Sea Kings could be accommodated on the flight deck and would take off one at a time, form up in the air, then head to their landing site. They would then have a lengthy round trip before they could bring in more troops. A land-based site made the journey time shorter, and more helicopters would be able to move more troops. Given that the targets were separate, and each one had to be occupied and captured at the same time, speed and maximum force were crucial. Gordon Messenger's second consideration was the role of the US Navy SEALs. Operating from land-based facilities would give 40 Commando situational awareness via the SEALs' live remote drone aircraft, Predator, which was capable of sending back coloured real-time television pictures of the targets as they were being captured. Those images wouldn't be available on the ships, and neither would other aspects of the SEALs' special communication or command and control facilities. If 40 Commando were based on the same landing zone ashore, they would be able to share them. Finally, the SEALs' eight MH-53 helicopters would be used by the first wave of Commandos anyway, so they would need to be on land.

Captain Johns's view on *Ocean* was different. 'My belief, my strong advice, at the time, was that we should do it all from the sea, because we were in a safe area. We were not subject to the same weather constraints that they had ashore, which was dust and heat and sandstorms. It did affect us at sea but we could avoid that. We were safe and assault-protected within the task group. We were safe from chemical attack as well. You have to decide where the balance of advantage lies and Jim Dutton decided that he wanted his Commando HQ next to him and he wanted the troops next to him as well.'

The Mother of All Rehearsals was held in daylight on 24 February, with a combined exercise, including night-time rehearsals, scheduled for 6 March. These seemed to support Captain Johns's opposition to the assault being launched from land. Severe sandstorms forced a cancellation, and the weather forecast remained poor. However, the sea was rough and visibility poor. The northern Arabian Gulf was extremely crowded, with Arab dhows conducting their trade from ports in Iraq, Iran and Kuwait, as they had done for centuries, prepared to give way to no one, with no radio, radar or other navigational aids. Scores of oil rigs and the vast number of warships congregating in the area made navigation hazardous. It was extremely important for *Ocean*, *Ark Royal* and their escorts to maintain a high level of awareness of the radar and surveillance picture, day and night. This 'relentless poise', as Captain Massey called it, took its toll on the crews, who were becoming fatigued. Compilation of the tactical surface picture was occasionally sloppy, and he recorded, 'It did nothing for my confidence to discover that an Iraqi vessel that we had ourselves not seen was heard reporting my ship's position to his authorities in Iraq.'

On 25 February, meetings took place with the US Navy to discuss the co-ordination of ship- and submarine-launched Tomahawk cruise missiles so that they did not collide with the helicopters taking 40 Commando into Iraq. Admiral Costello, the commander of Task Force 55, responsible for all the escort vessels including the Royal Navy destroyers and frigates, was still doubtful about the wisdom of some aspects of Brigadier Dutton's plans, and needed reassurance. The war approached with last-minute changes and doubts. As far as Admiral Snelson was concerned, an initial plan to deploy *Ark Royal* with a company of marines had been transformed. The Royal Navy had brought a fleet of twenty-five ships to the Gulf, with two cruise-missile-armed submarines. Two Commandos were in theatre with a Brigade Headquarters, artillery and helicopter force, and despite the speed with which they had been assembled, they were ready to go. It was a testament to the rigorous peace-time training of the Royal Navy. The armed forces are professional, fighting is their job, and the prospect of war was an opportunity to do what they were trained for.

Despite suppressed fears, they were, for the most part, keen to get on with it. All they had to wait for was the decision by Prime Minister Tony Blair and his cabinet, that they would invade Iraq. Nobody knew how long that decision would take.

5

42 COMMANDO FLIES IN

While the naval task group and 40 Commando were preparing to start the first set of exercises off Cyprus on their way to the northern Gulf, another unit from 3 Commando Brigade was preparing to make a more direct journey there.

The US CentCom's decision to make the Royal Marines responsible for clearing the al-Faw peninsula of Iraqi troops and securing the oil-exporting facilities meant that more than one Commando would be necessary. The US Marines would be responsible for taking and securing the port of Umm Qasr, to allow it to be used by ships bringing in emergency aid.

The question was which other Commando, 42 or 45, to send. At first 42 Commando seemed least likely to get the job. They had just completed a tour in Northern Ireland, which, in the words of its new operations officer, Oliver Lee, had required a fairly idiosyncratic force structure and mode of operating. They were about to start training to adjust to a new combat formation, and integrate heavy machine-guns. Their commanding officer, Colonel Buster Howes, was also new to the Commando, having taken up his post in November 2002. The officers of 42 Commando were eager to take part, and set up live firing exercises and manoeuvres to ensure that they would be considered. This paid off, and they were selected. Training was carried out in the rainy and windswept Brecon Beacons in south Wales, hardly appropriate for the desert of the Middle East, but it was all that was available. On 20 January the Commando boarded some chartered aircraft and flew to Kuwait. Buster Howes was with some of his men on a 747 jumbo jet. When they landed, he remembers the bizarre experience of being welcomed to Kuwait by the stewardess on board, wishing them a safe and productive stay.

After that things went downhill. They boarded buses and were driven into the desert, to Camp Gibraltar, which was beside the road that ran from Kuwait City to Basra. It had become known in 1991 as the Highway of Death, after a convoy of retreating Iraqi troops had been reduced to an inferno of fire, twisted metal and charred bodies by US warplanes. On the other side of the road there was a US Marines encampment, but 42 Commando found they had arrived before their tents had been put up. In a downpour at two in the morning, they had to construct their headquarters and accommodation. Perhaps the time spent in the Brecon Beacons had not been wasted.

Sergeant Dominic Collins, a platoon weapons instructor and trained sniper, was not impressed: 'We had been promised metal-framed bunks, electricity, running water and showers. All there was was a pile of tents.' Even when the tents were erected they were reminiscent of marquees at a wedding or country fête. There were upwards of a hundred men in each, with room for their sleeping mat and their Bergen backpack but nothing else. Food was in short supply. Sergeant Collins estimates that only two-thirds of what was needed was available, and the marines, who are not normally fat, were losing weight. This was a serious matter when they were so close to combat. The logistics couldn't cope, and at one point there was a severe shortage of rations for several days.

The task confronting 42 Commando was simpler in many ways than that of 40 Commando. While the oil pipelines and the metering stations were being secured, 42 Commando would provide a screening force to the north of 40 Commando, to prevent Iraqi forces from Basra mounting a counter-attack. The al-Faw peninsula was one of the most fought-over pieces of earth in the world; Colonel Howes and his

Commando planning group were aware that it had been the site of a shattering victory for Saddam Hussein's army against Iran.

The terrain was boggy, liable to rapid flooding when the Euphrates was in spate in the spring, and the only firm surfaces were roads that ran south along raised embankments. The western shores of the Shatt al-Arab were planted with dense palm groves, surrounding villages and settlements all along the riverbank. The trees provided concealment, and would prevent any rapid advance other than along the exposed roads.

The Iranian Army had crossed the waterway in strength early in the war and had occupied al-Faw town and most of the peninsula. Saddam had sent an armoured division south from Basra down the metalled roads in an assault on the occupying Iranian forces. At the same time he had outflanked them by mounting a helicopter assault along the coast. The Iranian division had been fixed at the end of the peninsula by the Iraqi use of mustard gas to the rear of their position, and they had been destroyed by shells containing a nerve agent. The combined operation had enabled Saddam to drive the Iranians out of the peninsula over the Shatt al-Arab. It had been one of the key strategic reversals that had eventually compelled the Iranians into negotiation with their enemy.

The situation was different now. Saddam's army

was in far worse shape than it had been in 1986, and the Iranians had never enjoyed the air power that the US could deploy. Also, the question of whether Saddam had stocks of chemical weapons and the means to use them was a matter of current political debate, and was the purported reason for the threat to invade. At the level of Brigade and Commando Headquarters, intelligence briefings told them that Saddam still possessed chemical weapons. The Iraqis had not used them in 1991 when the US had driven them out of Kuwait, but it was generally believed that a direct threat to Baghdad or to Saddam's power might trigger their use. Some experts, and one from the US Marine Corps, advised 42 Commando planning group while they were in Kuwait that chemicals might be used when coalition troops landed in Iraq – it might also be the moment at which Saddam would order the destruction of the oilfields and the deliberate pollution of the Gulf.

Iraqi forces had been trained in the Soviet school of fighting a war, in which almost every manoeuvre was predictable, and this known fact was used in the planning process. As Buster Howes explained, 'You do something called an intelligence preparation of the battlefield. It looks at the terrain; it looks at where you can walk, where you can drive a tank. Then you get an idea of where the avenues of approach are, and how fast people can advance and withdraw. Then you put on a threat overlay, which looks at the doctrinal template. In other words, if a Soviet motor rifle brigade was to advance between Basra and al-Faw, how would it do it? So, you can anticipate the Iraqis in rather a ragged way because they don't do it with the rigour that the Russians are perceived to do it. But that's how you work out what the enemy, in this case Iraq, will do.'

With intelligence reporting the presence of fifty or sixty Soviet-made T-80 tanks in Basra, 42 Commando's blocking force had a crucial role to play. It was also clear that to keep the element of surprise they would need to be in their positions at the same time as Messenger and his men went into action. 40 Commando had taken all of the available amphibious platforms in the Royal Navy's inventory, hence the need for 42 Commando to fly directly to Kuwait. As the planning taking place in HMS *Ocean* was beginning to reveal, 40 Commando's mission was also going to require more lift capacity than could be provided by *Ocean* and the *Ark Royal*. In order to achieve the necessary near-simultaneous landings of both Commandos, 42 Commando would have to rely on helicopters provided by the US Marine Corps.

They would need to start liaising quickly and training together. It was also vital to work out the best way to deploy 42 Commando's firepower. The task that Buster Howes was being asked to achieve was quite a tall order. With 800 or so men, armed with heavy machine-guns and portable anti-tank rockets mounted on stripped-down Land Rovers and tracked vehicles, he had to secure an area of operations of 400 square kilometres.

The size of the area meant that the basic military doctrine of concentration of forces went out of the window. Individual units would not be able to offer each other mutual support. The solution was to place heavy artillery on Bubiyan Island, a large, flat, muddy island north of Kuwait City and close to the border with the al-Faw peninsula. The guns' arc of fire covered most of Buster Howes's area, so the deciding factor in deploying the various units was the ability to provide artillery support if they came under attack, and for the units to fall back and redeploy if necessary. At the same time, to give as early a warning as possible of any Iraqi advance, a Brigade Reconnaissance Force (BRF) would be deployed on the forward edge of 42 Commando's area of operations.

The BRF is a specialized reconnaissance, intelligence and communications unit, lightly armed with heavy machine-guns mounted on stripped-down Land Rovers. The furthest forward elements of this force would be in vulnerable but discreet places where they could observe areas of territory. They would not be able to prevent Iraqi armour advancing, but could report its position and call in air strikes and artillery. Between this reconnaissance force and the next unit of 42 Commando there would be a large area designated as a killing zone, where artillery and aircraft would be free to target Iraqi tanks. M Company, under the command of Major 'Daisy' May, would be the next unit on the rear of the killing zone, armed with thirteen tracked vehicles mounting Milan anti-tank missiles.

The BRF and M Company would be the most forward of 42 Commando's units and the members of the BRF were slightly nervous about their position. So far forward, they would be at considerable risk. But they were trained to carry out these operations, they were experienced and highly qualified. What concerned them was the procedures adopted by US pilots, who might be called in to attack advancing Iraq armour or troops and the precautions they took to avoid targeting members of the Reconnaissance Force. The US forward air controllers wanted to impose a no-fire zone around predetermined map co-ordinates, where the BRF observation posts would be, but the marines were very uncomfortable with this. They might find a location selected from a map unsuitable when they had landed there – the terrain might not offer good sight lines or concealment. They wanted the flexibility to select their positions once they were on the ground, but the US air controllers didn't seem able to adjust to this. But it was a minor issue when compared to the lengthy process of working out, as 40 Commando had to do, the all-important details of which men and equipment would be carried by which aircraft and in what sequence they needed to take off and arrive at the various landing sites.

The US Marine Corps' helicopters were twin-rotor CH-46 Sea Knights and large, single-rotor CH-53 Super Stallions. The latter created so much dust that a significant interval had to occur between each take-off. The assault was planned using two waves of helicopters. M Company, the stand-off company armed with anti-tank weapons, would lift the thirteen tracked BV10s into position to its own separate landing site on the al-Faw peninsula so that it could quickly deploy as a forward anti-armour screen. Their commander, Major 'Daisy' May was poised with a stopwatch, timing how long it took a squad of men, with their equipment, to load everything on to a helicopter, then sling a BV10 under a Sea Knight and, at the other end, to pour down the ramp, board the vehicles and move to their positions. After several weeks he could say that he knew to the minute how long every manoeuvre took. The Royal Marines discovered that US Marine Corps pilots were less comprehensively trained than those of the RAF or the Royal Navy, who were expected to be proficient in most aspects of military flying, carrying underslung loads, operating at night and in varied climates before entering an operational squadron. Some US pilots had little experience of load-carrying, or night-time operations. A few members of 42 Commando felt that their landings on the training flights had occasionally been hairy. But there was a willingness to get things right.

At times Colonel Buster Howes and his planning group would work through the mission in eye-watering detail, knowing that good planning wouldn't guarantee success, but that a bad plan would invite disaster. There were thirty-seven supporting helicopters, which would take 42 Commando into Iraq. They would be flying through a complicated and crowded air space, with as many as 150 aircraft stacked in the air ready to launch support operations against Iraqi troop movements, or anti-aircraft positions. Buster Howes had decided that he would fly in a Huey helicopter and control the mission from the air, while Oliver Lee, his operations officer, would fly in a separate one in case Howes was shot down.

Every day the plan would be tested against the latest intelligence assessments, which kept changing. The Iraqis altered their troop dispositions: on one day a reconnaissance flight photographed a battery of eighteen artillery pieces dug in in the middle of the area of operations; four days after the planning had been done on how the threat would be neutralized a repeat reconnaissance mission revealed that the guns had been moved and now could not be found. It was a draining process. 'At the end of the day the buck stops with the commander so when I adjourned for six hours' kip I'd find myself wandering around in the desert just thinking, Hang on a minute, is this right?'

As well as the manoeuvres with the US Marine Corps helicopters there was an enormous amount of live-firing practice. A three-kilometre-long range was created for small-arms, rocket, missile and artillery firing, which gave everyone a sense that this was no longer just another exercise: war was approaching and the limits of peacetime could be abandoned. But there was the occasional reminder of what this might mean. The artillery was in position some kilometres away and would be firing over the heads of troops on the range – considered normal practice. Sergeant Dom Collins was with J Company on the range, training a platoon, when a 105-mm shell fell short, exploding barely a hundred yards away. The soft sand absorbed the shell and the blast. Another time, in another place, they might not be so lucky.

They were in the desert for seven weeks and, eventually, planning absorbs the amount of time available to do it. The operational orders for 42 Commando's assault on the al-Faw peninsula came to 120 pages, an enormous document, and despite the continued political uncertainty about whether they would take part in the invasion, they felt ready for it – were even eager for the conflict to begin. Sergeant Dom Collins had asked Colonel Buster Howes if he could leave his headquarters duties for a front-line position with his fellow snipers. He had been trained for this for seventeen years, he said, and did not want to miss the chance. 'It was like being a ballet dancer, training and training but never allowed to take the stage.' Buster Howes saw his point and let him go to J Company, where he would argue again, demanding to be sent forward. 'Boys and soldiers want to go to war, although once they have, they might think differently.'

By the middle of March, the only thing stopping them was the politicians. And some, like Major 'Daisy' May, felt this was a real possibility. 'You just did not believe that they would let this happen.'

6

THE EVE OF WAR

In the weeks leading up to the invasion of Iraq, the northern Arabian Gulf and the deserts of Kuwait and Saudi Arabia were the focus of an enormous concentration of military firepower assembled from across the globe. At sea there was a Royal Navy fleet, its two helicopter carriers, *Ark Royal* and *Ocean*, with their escorts. This was dwarfed by the five US Navy carrier battle groups, each nuclear-powered aircraft-carrier escorted by a guided-missile cruiser, two guided-missile destroyers and a frigate. Each American aircraft-carrier could carry up to eighty aircraft, but hundreds more were operating out of airfields in Kuwait, Saudi Arabia and Qatar. Patrolling E3 Sentry aircraft, with their huge radar dome mounted above the fuselage, probed as far as Cyprus in the Mediterranean, sending an electronic image of the battle space to every military computer

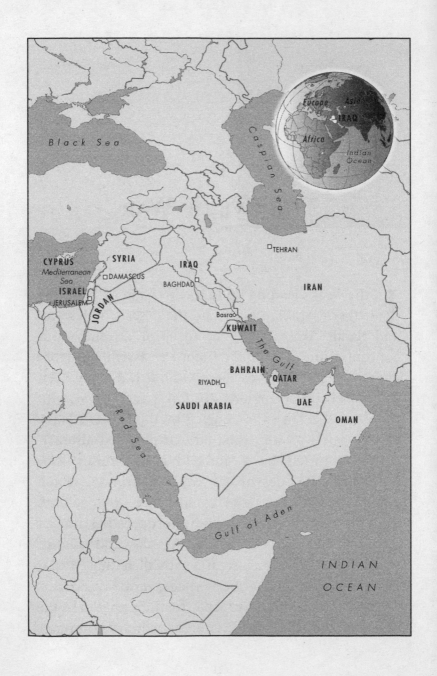

Black Sea

Caspian Sea

Europe Asia
IRAQ
Africa
Indian
Ocean

CYPRUS
Mediterranean
Sea
ISRAEL
JERUSALEM

SYRIA
☐DAMASCUS

IRAQ
BAGHDAD ☐

☐TEHRAN

IRAN

JORDAN

Basra☐

KUWAIT

The Gulf

BAHRAIN
RIYADH☐

QATAR

UAE

OMAN

SAUDI ARABIA

Red Sea

Gulf of Aden

INDIAN

OCEAN

screen in the coalition, the blue symbols representing Allied shipping, aircraft or military units so densely packed that they were impossible to identify.

British forces were tiny by comparison with their colleagues, but represented a significant national military effort and made up the second largest element of the coalition formed to overthrow Saddam Hussein. As well as the fleets, and the helicopter assets of the navy and the RAF, almost 40,000 troops had been deployed in Kuwait, the 1st Armoured Division, the 7th Armoured Brigade and the 16th Air Assault Brigade, as well as the Royal Marines. All were waiting for the diplomatic manoeuvres in the United Nations Security Council to reach their conclusion.

Admiral Snelson, and most other British military personnel in the northern Gulf, knew that despite the mobilization of a large part of Britain's armed forces, and the detailed negotiations that had integrated them into the US command structure, they would not go to war without the lawful authority of the British government, which, everyone supposed, would require the authority of the UN Security Council.

That had been the British government's position for several months. In March 2002, David Manning, the Foreign Office adviser to No. 10 Downing Street, reported back to the Prime Minister, Tony Blair, from a meeting he had had in Washington with Condoleezza Rice, the President's national security adviser, who supported the overthrow of Saddam Hussein – 'regime change', as it was known. It was clear from his conversation with her that there was still a debate about how to persuade international opinion that this was the right course of action. It was also clear that President Bush wanted the support of Tony Blair.

Blair said that any invasion of Iraq would only be acceptable with UN backing, and that the way to achieve this was to urge the UN to send its arms inspectors back into Iraq, with a mandate to carry out highly intrusive inspections. They would either find that Saddam Hussein had for years been in breach of his obligation to disarm, or would force him to expel them again. Either outcome would provide an excuse for military action.

There were two problems with this approach. It was not certain that the US administration would welcome a return to the UN. Neither, according to some military opinion, would a new team of inspectors come up with much more in the way of chemical weapons than the previous one had.

Tony Blair believed it was essential for Britain to stand side by side with the US. In a cabinet meeting he reiterated that not to support it in a matter of such importance would be to reverse fifty years of British foreign policy. Moreover, by supporting and keeping the US close it would be possible to influence its policy.

Blair went to visit George Bush at his ranch at Crawford, in Texas, on 6 April 2002 to discuss the options for dealing with Saddam Hussein. In private he told Bush that Britain would support regime change if there was an international coalition, and if all other options for international disarmament had been exhausted. In public he made a speech saying that the lesson of 9/11 was that threats had to be dealt with before they materialized and that Saddam Hussein was such a threat. He offered unconditional solidarity with the US in its fight for democratic values.

President Bush knew he could not alienate Blair, or ignore the conditions Blair had placed on his support.

In September 2007 Tony Blair paid another visit to President Bush, this time at his official country retreat at Camp David. He told him that several key questions needed to be answered to satisfy public opinion, the most important of which was, why now and why Saddam Hussein? These questions were important internationally, and he needed answers so that he could swing public opinion in the UK and bring his party behind the policy.

These arguments, put forward by the President's most consistent ally, carried considerable weight, and Bush announced at the end of the meeting that the US would be seeking a new Security Council resolution to tackle Saddam Hussein. It seemed a major victory for British diplomacy and a boost to Blair's prestige. There is a common military saying that no plan survives contact with the enemy: Tony Blair was about to discover that it could apply in other areas of human activity too.

There was only one ground on which the UN could authorize further action against Iraq, which was that Saddam Hussein had not complied with previous resolutions calling for the dismantling of Iraq's weapons of mass destruction. Once again the spotlight was directed on the Iraqis' range of chemical, biological and nuclear weapons that they had either used or attempted to produce during the 1980s. Hard information about what was left of these weapons was scarce. The Iraqi government refused to produce any figures; the United Nations Special Commission (UNSCOM), which had overseen the destruction of many such weapons after the Kuwaiti war, had eventually withdrawn in 1998 and was unable to say whether or not all of the stockpiles had been destroyed. Information about their existence was produced by exiled groups and defectors, who had a vested interest in exaggerating the threat, while forged documents and fraudulent claims circulated, alleging that there were a variety of continuing programmes but no real intelligence was coming out of Iraq.

One senior figure who had defected from Iraq in 1995 was General Hussein Kamel, Saddam's son-in-law and former director of Iraq's Military Industrial

Corporation, the government body responsible for much of the research into and procurement of chemical weapons. During his debriefing in Amman, in Jordan, he claimed he had ordered the destruction of all Iraq's chemical weapons in 1991. At the same time as he defected, the Iraqi government released a cache of documents that they claimed he had hidden on his farm in Iraq. These showed that there had been weaponized biological agents, and in 1990 a crash programme to produce a nuclear weapon. Kamel's evidence was never given the prominence or attention it perhaps deserved, and the assumption remained that chemical weapons were still to be found in Iraq. And by now it was too late to question him any further: in 1996, under a promise of amnesty, he had been persuaded to return to Baghdad, where he was tortured and killed.

The campaign to obtain support from the UN began, and the governments of Britain and the US started to gather what information there was to bolster their assertion that Iraq was in breach of UN resolutions. President Bush went to the UN General Assembly on Thursday, 12 September 2002, where he reminded the delegates how Saddam Hussein had defied the organization year after year, and pledged to work with the Security Council. If Iraq wished for peace it would immediately forswear, disclose and remove or destroy all weapons of mass destruction. It was an impressive appearance by a president who had exhibited such antipathy to the UN just a few months earlier. It marked the beginning of a discussion with Security Council members on a new resolution that continued through the next two months until, on 8 November, a resolution on Iraq, no. 1441, was passed by a unanimous vote. It deplored the fact that Iraq had not provided accurate and full disclosure of its programmes for weapons of mass destruction, decided that Iraq had been in material breach of its obligations, and gave Iraq one final opportunity to comply with its obligations and set up an enhanced inspection regime. It concluded with the warning that Iraq would face serious consequences as a result of certain violations of its obligations.

This further apparent victory for diplomacy had merely been a postponement of a difficult decision. The US and British governments had gone to the UN to avoid the US taking a unilateral decision to go to war, so forcing Britain to decide whether or not to support it. It also assumed that weapons of mass destruction would be found, or that the UN inspectors would be rebuffed, thereby justifying the use of force.

Britain published a document purporting to sum up the evidence of Iraq's continued breaches, ending with the somewhat dubious claim that the Iraqi armed forces could launch chemical weapons within forty-five minutes. It had been drawn up by Cabinet

Office staff and the Government Communication Service, and was found subsequently to have been based on a trawl through the Internet; substantial pieces of text had been lifted from an academic thesis. It was an own goal, and made the presentation of the government's policy that much harder. The anti-war mood in the country was growing. Tony Blair was under considerable political pressure from backbench MPs and some members of his cabinet, notably Robin Cook, formerly foreign secretary and now leader of the House, and Clare Short, minister for overseas development, not to go to war.

Then on 7 December the Iraqis handed to the United Nations Monitoring, Verification and Inspection Commission (UNMOVIC), the new body charged with inspecting Saddam's arsenal, 12,000 pages of documents which they claimed contained details of Iraq's stockpiles of weapons of mass destruction. Hans Blix, head of UNMOVIC, analysed them, and realized that, apart from some fresh information about developments in missile technology, they contained little that had not already been submitted to previous teams of inspectors working under UNSCOM's jurisdiction.

Meanwhile the inspection teams were diligently at work in Iraq, and discovering little. One team found a crate of empty warheads designed to be filled with chemical weapons. There was also some evidence that Iraq had imported and tested rocket engines with a range greater than the permitted 150 kilometres.

Hans Blix was scheduled to deliver a speech to the UN Security Council on 27 January to sum up his findings. He said that although Iraq had co-operated with the inspections, the regime had not come to an acceptance of the disarmament demanded of it. This was an odd statement to make because he went on to say that UNMOVIC's reports neither asserted nor excluded the possibility that weapons of mass destruction existed in Iraq. They merely, he said, pointed to a lack of evidence and raised questions that needed to be resolved. For those wanting a cast-iron reason to remove Saddam Hussein, it was an extremely damp squib, an equivocating compromise. It was clear that Hans Blix was not going to let the US and Britain off the hook. If there was war, it was not going to be his report that led to it.

The next day President Bush gave his State of the Union address to Congress, and raised the pressure on the UN with a reference to information received by British intelligence that Iraq had sought to obtain significant quantities of uranium from African countries. The evidence proved to have been a forged document, concerning a contract to supply 'yellowcake', unrefined uranium, but it signalled the start of an attempt to move the debate on.

On 5 February, the US secretary of state, Colin Powell, made a speech to the UN assembly that laid out the charges and presented evidence that Saddam

Hussein was in clear breach of both resolution 687, the original UN resolution calling for Iraq's disarmament, now more than ten years old, and the present 1441. It was an attempt to influence world opinion, and to show that the US leadership was united on the question of Saddam's breach of his international obligations, despite rumours to the contrary. He backed his argument with intelligence from spy satellites and intelligence intercepts and showed photographs of alleged mobile chemical laboratories, and details of unmanned aerial vehicles that could potentially be used for spraying nerve agent. It was not an impressive case, and many people felt so. Admiral Snelson, in the midst of his negotiations with the US Navy over the deployment of 3 Commando Brigade, was not at all convinced. In his diary he recorded that the presentation and the evidence it contained 'was no knock-out blow'.

The British government was becoming anxious. The UN ploy was not delivering the smoking gun and, anyway, as more and more observers were noting, resolution 1441 did not necessarily authorize the use of force in the event of a breach of its provisions by Iraq. It was clear that the French and the Russians were not happy about using 1441 as a pretext for war against Iraq. Blair was coming round to the view that a second UN resolution was needed to authorize force, postponing any action until it could be agreed, around the middle or end of March. He was engaged in endless meetings and telephone conversations, but opposition to war was mounting.

On 15 February there was a major demonstration against the war, reportedly the biggest ever seen in London, with two million people marching through the streets. The problem with a strategy of delay was that the pressing military timetable had a logic of its own. Maintaining the troops in place in an open-ended commitment was hugely expensive. It was also difficult to keep them poised for action indefinitely, without loss of morale and efficiency. The summer was approaching and fighting in intense heat would be wearing on the troops and their equipment. Time was running out, and Blair was becoming desperate. President Bush was supportive of him and promised he would attempt to get another resolution through the Security Council. However, reports were arriving in London that Rumsfeld and Vice President Dick Cheney were increasingly exasperated with the UN strategy, complaining to President Bush that it would never provide the justification for action that the US desired.

Tony Blair's problems were intensifying. On 9 March Clare Short, who portrayed herself as the left-wing conscience of the Labour government, announced that she would resign if Britain went to war without a second resolution.

On 13 March Jeremy Greenstock, Britain's

ambassador to the UN, tabled six tests that were to form part of a new resolution by the Security Council on Iraq. They called for a statement from Saddam admitting the concealment of weapons of mass destruction and undertaking not to retain or produce them in future; that at least thirty scientists and their families should be delivered for interview outside Iraq; the surrender of anthrax or evidence of its destruction to be provided; all Al Samoud missiles to be destroyed; all unmanned vehicles to be accounted for, including details of any aerial devices for spraying chemical and biological weapons; and all mobile biological production facilities to be surrendered.

Just how the Iraq regime would have responded to these demands will never be known. The UN strategy, which Blair had once seen as a way to provide the justification for removing Saddam Hussein, 'the political strategy to give the military plan the space to work', had put the military strategy itself in the hands of the Security Council. The French government, however, a permanent member of the Security Council, had its own views about war with Iraq and the alleged intelligence, and announced there was no question that they would approve a second resolution that would allow force. The draft second resolution was hastily withdrawn.

Captain Massey, following events on *Ark Royal*, succinctly summed up the situation: 'The pace of events has suddenly quickened in response to the collapse of the diplomatic process, and the withdrawal of the draft second resolution. This is the brink of war.' He further wrote, 'I am encouraging my team to examine issues and consciences one final time. There is no doubt in the ship that we are now approaching war ... I remain convinced of the moral correctness of this imminent war, but I also pray that we find all the evidence that we know is there.'

In Bahrain the drumbeat of approaching war had been obvious to Admiral Snelson. On 14 March General Tommy Franks, commander of CentCom, had called all the force commanders together at CentCom Headquarters in Qatar for a final briefing. It was an extraordinary meeting. The lights were lowered in the windowless CentCom command centre, but rather than the first slide of a PowerPoint presentation on the plan of attack, the giant screen at one end of the room showed an image of Russell Crowe, the film star.

Dumbfounded and amused in equal measure, Snelson watched the opening sequence of *Gladiator*, the Hollywood movie in which Russell Crowe stars as a Roman general in command of a legion attempting to subdue the Germanic tribes to the east of the Empire. The Roman soldiers are in a sprawling encampment in the forests of Germany ready for battle, but they have offered the native chieftains one last chance to seek peace. In a gruesome scene their offer is symbolically rejected as the severed head of the Roman emissary is hurled into their ranks. The legions prepare for war, and Crowe, the general, cries, 'On my command unleash hell.'

It was an unmistakable message but not a surprising one. Snelson had assumed for some time that, as far as the United States was concerned, war was inevitable.

The commanders' conference confirmed what they had all assumed for some time, that D-day, when Iraq would be hit by bombers and Tomahawk missiles, would be 21 March. Ground forces would invade on the twenty-second. President Bush was due to have a meeting in the Azores on the seventeenth with Tony Blair, José Maria Aznar, the Prime Minister of Spain, and José Manuel Barroso, the Portuguese Prime Minister. He would issue an ultimatum to Saddam Hussein to vacate Iraq with his family, the only way to avoid the coming war. Saddam would be allowed forty-eight hours to comply. In the absence of any further UN action, Snelson knew now that his orders would depend on a debate in Parliament that was scheduled to take place on the eighteenth. Not until then, and not before he had been sent the official orders, would British forces be allowed to take any hostile measures against Iraq.

Overnight on 16 and 17 March all members of 40 Commando, except D Company on *Ark Royal*, were transferred by landing craft to a beach in Kuwait.

Laden with heavy Bergens, they climbed aboard buses and were driven in darkness round Kuwait City to TAA Viking. They arrived on the morning of the seventeenth, and started to dig shell scrapes in the sand, cover them with tarpaulins and camouflage netting, then lay out their sleeping mats to make themselves as comfortable as possible. Those holes were their home for the next few days.

Talking to the planners in Company Headquarters, Major Matt Jackson formed the view that war was a matter of when, not if. It seemed to him that the biggest question mark was over the weather, which was forecast to be very poor over the next few days.

That evening the debate that took place in Westminster was watched around the world. It was of vital importance to President Bush and his cabinet. They knew that if Blair lost the vote, the Labour government might fall, and the US would lose their closest ally. The debate was also watched on TV screens in military camps and bases in Kuwait, in the CentCom headquarters, and Snelson's offices in Bahrain and on the ships of the task group steaming in the northern Arabian Gulf.

In the end Tony Blair's strategy had failed. Britain would not go to war with the authority of the UN. He had no other alternative than to seek a majority in the House of Commons for declaring war on a country that offered no immediate and present danger to the UK.

His opening address to the House claimed that Britain was acting to uphold the authority of the UN, although in seeking legal justification for the use of force he went back to the ten-year-old UN Resolution 678, 'which has revived and so continues today'. His speech underlined the importance of the debate: 'It will determine the way in which Britain and the world confront the central security threats of the twenty-first century, the development of the United Nations, the relationship between Europe and the United States, the relations within the European Union and the way in which the United States engages with the rest of the world. So it could hardly be more important. It will determine the pattern of international politics for the next generation.'

On the night of the eighteenth, watching the televised debate in his flat in Bahrain, Snelson had little doubt that the government would win. A short while after the vote was finally taken he received a telephone call on the special secure phone in his flat. General Reith, chief of Joint Operations, was at the other end of the line. Snelson was quietly informed that prime ministerial authority had been received for British forces to conduct hostile operations against Iraq. He knew that, a few minutes after he put the phone down, the conversation would be followed by a confirmatory signal from the Permanent Joint Headquarters in Northwood, the final step in the process of putting British forces on a war footing.

Then he would send similar back-up signals to the ships in the fleet, telling them of the change to their rules of engagement, and would signal the various CentCom commanders that they had been delegated executive authority over the various British units under their command. Even before he received the call he had rummaged through his files for the pre-pared signals, and had set up a video conference call with Captains Johns and Massey on *Ocean* and *Ark Royal* so that the orders could be quickly passed on. It was clear that they were abreast of events and ready to go. And so, without any drama, war was declared and a section of Her Majesty's Armed Forces was poised to invade another country.

There had been a crisis in the morning that had threatened to overturn the timetable. Reconnaissance photographs had shown that six or seven oil wells to the south of Baghdad had been set ablaze, and thick smoke was slowly spreading southwards. General Franks sent urgent signals seeking to know if the attacks on the oil facilities could be advanced by forty-eight hours. A decision to do so would have placed a question mark over the role of British forces, which were still under peacetime rules of engage-ment. But it was almost impossible now to change the overall air plan of the US forces, and General Franks decided to advance the land attack by a day, to occur before the main aerial bombardment on the twenty-first. If weather permitted, the commandos would move out on the twentieth.

The next day, 19 March, Admiral Snelson attended a video conference at Fifth Fleet Headquarters in Bahrain, where President George Bush, Condoleezza Rice and Donald Rumsfeld in the White House were introduced via a satellite link to General Franks and the component commanders in Bahrain, Camp Qatar and Doha, and were congratulated by the President on the great job they were doing. As each commander was introduced, they introduced their British deputy. President Bush then passed the written order to Donald Rumsfeld with the words, 'I now give the order to Secretary Rumsfeld and this operation starts.' David Snelson was introduced by his superior officer, Admiral Tim Keating, to the President at the beginning of the video conference, but some details of the collaboration between the navies of Britain and the United States were now becoming acrimonious. Relations between Brigadier Jim Dutton and the female senior officer of the US hovercraft unit were poor. Dutton believed that she was overly bureaucratic and nervous. He had landed on the Falklands, knew something about the dangers of invading an enemy beach and believed that risk was part of war fighting, and had to be accepted. The commander of the hovercraft didn't share this view. She was extremely concerned about the threat from mines, and would not make any approach to the beach unless it had been thoroughly cleared. The engineers who would accompany Matt Jackson and B Company would do what they could to clear a single marked channel up the beach, but it was impossible to assess how long it would take.

The only solution was to ask the US Navy to provide extra divers to supplement the Royal Marine engineers who would be clearing the beach. Also, three ships from the Royal Navy and one from the Australian Navy were assigned to provide gunfire in support of 40 Commando if they required it, but the vessels were part of a larger naval task force under the command of a US commodore – in his view they were planning to sail far too close to the Iraqi coastline, risking attack from Iraqi missiles and running aground in the shallow waters. He was unhappy, too, about the constant direct communications between the Royal Marines and the British ships, which he felt was threatening to bypass his authority. Brigadier Dutton thought it late in the day to start raising these problems, and angry emails were hurled back and forth. David Snelson's diplomatic balancing act wasn't over yet.

The Royal Marines of 40 Commando were unaware of these last-minute disagreements over the details of their mission. They would be the first conventional soldiers to invade Iraq, and the operation would hinge on their ability to achieve the maximum surprise, with a swift, decisive occupation of the oil-exporting machinery and the surrounding area on the al-Faw peninsula.

The first assault would be made by the special forces of the US Navy SEALs, who would be taken to the targets by their dedicated force of eight CH-53 helicopters.

They would secure the key machinery that allowed these facilities to function while their helicopters would return to TAA Viking, Kuwait, and load the first wave of 40 Commando. Colonel Messenger and his headquarters company – C Company, the Manoeuvre Support Group (MSG), under Captain Paul Lynch and B Company under Major Matt Jackson would fly in to capture the facilities and secure a perimeter, allowing the SEALs to pull out. C Company would provide security inside the perimeter of the metering station, which was bounded by a high barbed-wire fence and an earthwork, or berm.

The Manoeuvre Support Group would advance to the western edge of the metering station, where there was a main gate, a security bunker, and roads led to al-Faw town and the north. They would then advance to secure the edge of 40 Commando's area of responsibility and make sure that 42 Commando's landing site was clear of enemy troops. A group of SEALs from SEAL team 3 would already have secured the gate, and would be able to call in an AC-130 Spectre gunship to eradicate any Iraqi forces that might get in the MSG's way.

An hour later 40 Commando's A and D Companies would be flown in on Chinooks and Sea Kings. Four hours after the first helicopter had lifted off from Kuwait, 800 marines would be attempting to secure the oil facilities and clear the area, including al-Faw town, of any Iraqi troops. It was an audacious plan.

Intelligence about the Iraqi forces that might have to be dealt with was hard to come by. There was a large complex of buildings that looked like a series of bunkers to the north of the pipeline sites that B Company would have to take, a series of trenches and a barracks close to the MMS and a further set of bunkers to the west. RAF Tornadoes were flying reconnaissance flights daily but it was difficult to tell what forces occupied the buildings, or what else might be hidden in the palm groves along the banks of the Shatt al-Arab, or in the town of al-Faw.

The Iraqi 6th Armoured Division, equipped with around a hundred Russian-built T-55 tanks, was stationed to defend the approaches to Basra, and would pose a formidable threat. Brigadier Dutton had thought it prudent to strengthen 40 Commando, in case the 6th Armoured Division decided to intervene. But as far as Gordon Messenger was concerned, the main comfort was the presence of 42 Commando to his front, and his ability via embedded US fire-control teams, to call in air and artillery support if his position was coming under sustained attack. Having left *Ocean* and the landing ships, and living now in their small trenches in the desert at TAA Viking, 40 Commando were going through their last orders, physically and mentally making the final adjustments to the coming fight, and waiting.

Now the troops on the ground were impatient with the delay and the endless debate. They were in the desert, with weeks of training and planning behind them. In the words of Captain Paul Lynch, 'Right or wrong we just wanted to get on with it.'

7

D-DAY

The next night Admiral Snelson received another telephone call in his Bahrain flat. It wasn't from the UK's military chiefs in Northwood but from CentCom telling him that an attack was going to be made by stealth bombers and a large number of Tomahawk cruise missiles on an area of Baghdad. CIA agents in Iraq had received information that Saddam Hussein and members of his family were going to stay at a compound called Dora Farms in the south-west of the city. President Bush and his war cabinet had been informed that this was the perfect opportunity to remove the leadership of Iraq, a swift decapitating strike, with the possibility that the Ba'ath Party regime would then crumble and the armed forces would surrender.

There were risks associated with the attack, in particular that the coalition forces would lose the element of surprise and the Iraqi armed forces would be on full alert. Bush and his advisers thought that removing Saddam was worth it, so the strike was to go ahead.

Out in the Arabian Gulf, Captain Johns on *Ocean* saw some of the Tomahawks fly low overhead, and, fifteen minutes later, saw the explosions in Baghdad broadcast on television by CNN. It was a strange start to the war.

In his shell scrape in the Kuwaiti desert, Major Matt Jackson had been enduring a fierce sandstorm, in which it was impossible to see more than a few feet. He heard that the war had started in a bulletin from the BBC World Service, which said that the bombing of Baghdad was now possible, as was the insertion of special forces. At 2100 he attended a command meeting at which he was told there would be no movement that night, but to expect action on Friday.

The attack on Baghdad triggered a rapid response from Iraq, and throughout the day of 20 March a variety of missiles was launched at targets in Kuwait. Iraqi intelligence was good: they were aiming at the coalition's command centres. Seersucker anti-ship missiles were fired at Kuwait City; Scuds were launched at Camp Commando, the US Marines' divisional headquarters, and the assembly areas for the armoured divisions to the west of the city. They caused no casualties, but every time a missile went overhead the marines in TAA Viking had to seek shelter, to the amusement of those already in their shell scrapes. Major Justin Holt, commanding A Company, watched a marine agonize about whether to ignore the rocket warning or jump into a latrine trench. The latest intelligence, that a hundred T-72 tanks, from the Medina Division, had been deployed west of Basra, along the road from Safwan on the Kuwaiti border to Umm Qasr, was quietly digested. Then news came in that the landing was scheduled for that night.

The company commanders attended the final orders group at Commando Headquarters. There, Colonel Messenger asked everyone to describe their understanding of the scheme of manoeuvre, and their specific actions within it. Then he quizzed them about their own orders. This form of backwards-and-forwards interrogation was a mechanism to ensure that everyone in the unit fully understood the plan and how they fitted into it, that they all had a picture in their minds of how the action was meant to unfold. In the dark, in the heat of combat, there would be no time to consult maps or engage in lengthy communications. Areas and tactical objectives had easily remembered code names. The buildings in the metering station had been grouped in three clusters, and called Taunton, Arbroath and Plymouth, the three home bases of the Commandos. The main area where the pipeline machinery was located was Shell, the landing zone Poole, and the two main roads through the facility were Broadway and Main Street.

They were going to mount the first helicopter assault since Suez, the first opposed landing since the battle for the Falklands. Knowledge of the enemy forces they would face was scanty, and shifting all the time. They would be relying heavily on the fire from the air that would precede their assault. After that, Justin Holt wrote in his diary, 'The skill of the pilots would be tested to their limits in inserting and building up combat power in the face of the enemy we didn't know about.'

He went back to his company headquarters to brief his troop commanders and sergeants. Most of the marines in A Company were young and had never seen combat before. Major Holt knew that the effect of the aerial bombardment on the Iraqi soldiers might be catastrophic. He hoped it would be, but wondered how his men would react at their first sight of dead and maimed men.

When Gordon Messenger addressed 40 Commando, he emphasized that they were privileged to take part in this bold operation as members of a proud group of marines. This wasn't cheap rhetoric designed to persuade frightened men: he believed in what he said. He believed in the mission. What 40 Commando were about to do was what they existedfor, what they were paid to do, what they had trained for and what, ultimately, they had volunteered for. Major Jackson

and his fellow officers stuck patches on their vehicles
and clothes to identify themselves as friendly in the
night-vision goggles of the US airmen who would be
riding shotgun. As Jackson remarked to his second-
in-command Rob Ginn, 'It works at five paces. Not
so sure that the AC-130 and A-10 pilots will spot it at
ten thousand feet.'

As darkness fell hundreds of men, their faces
blackened, clustered in small groups, with the quiet
murmur of conversation. The paraffin smell of solid
fuel stoves mingled with the high-octane aviation fuel
from the helicopters. There was the metallic clink of
small arms and mess tins, the heavy diesel notes
of military vehicles moving forward along the
adjacent road, the incessant thump of helicopters in
and out of the landing site. Gordon Messenger
walked around the huge Assembly Area known as
Viking, talking to his troops. If there was fear, and
there had to be, he saw no sign of it.

Matt Jackson's B Company, C Company, under
Duncan Dewar, and Colonel Gordon Messenger would
be the first wave of troops into the al-Faw peninsula.
Their assembly time was 1730 Zulu (Greenwich
Mean Time) and as C Company filed past in the
darkness, the marines of A Company formed lines on
either side and gently applauded their comrades,
wishing them luck. The whole venture rested on
the ability of C Company, the MSG and B Company
to seize the initiative, and act with speed and

aggression in securing their objectives and establishing a beachhead. After that, the plan was flexible.

Major Holt's A Company was acting as a commando reserve, ready to respond to any contingency if the initial assault started to fail or to exploit the situation if it went well. He had been charged with nine separate tasks that he had to prepare the company to carry out, should the need arise. One was to consolidate an area for D Company, still on *Ark Royal*, to land on and move south to clear the tip of the al-Faw peninsula, relieving B Company in their enclave round the pipelines.

H-hour, when the helicopters were due to lift off from Kuwait with the marines on board, was set at 1900 Zulu, and 0200 local time. Long before that a B-52 bomber had taken off from Diego Garcia, an island just south of the equator in the Indian Ocean, loaded with sixteen JDAMs GPS-guided bombs targeted on the various bunkers around the oil facilities on the al-Faw peninsula.

The progress of the flight was monitored by Lieutenant Commander Pentreath, the air commander in 3 Commando Brigade's main headquarters in Kuwait. The B-52 was scheduled to drop its bombs seventeen minutes before the SEALs CH-53 helicopters were due on their target and the bombing run would take approximately ten minutes. The B-52 would depart, and seven minutes before the helicopters were due to land, two

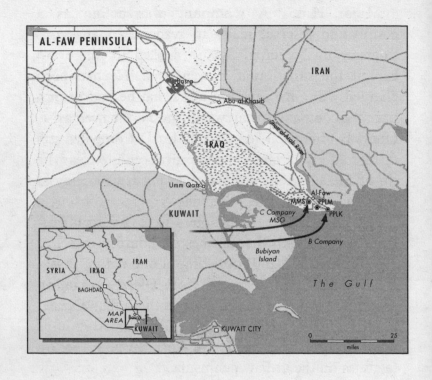

AL-FAW PENINSULA

IRAN

Basra

Abu al-Khasib

Shatt al-Arab River

IRAQ

Umm Qasr

Al-Faw

MMS   PPLM

KUWAIT

C Company   PPLK
MSG

B Company

Bubiyan
Island

The Gulf

SYRIA   IRAN

IRAQ

BAGHDAD

MAP
AREA   Basra

KUWAIT

KUWAIT CITY

0   25
miles

low-flying A-10 aircraft, loaded with bombs and with a massive rapid-firing rotating cannon mounted in the nose, would fly over the helicopter route to destroy any anti-aircraft guns or missiles that would threaten the special-forces insertion into the oil facilities. At the same time a Spectre gunship, a Hercules C-130 cargo plane, modified to carry searchlights and a variety of quick-firing cannon, would be circling overhead. It was a closely timed operation.

The B-52 arrived on time, and Pentreath in Brigade Headquarters heard the laconic, 'Weapons release', as the crew closed the switches in the cockpit, and sixteen 1000-pound bombs sliced through the air, exploding on dug-outs, bursting over trenches, creating a cataclysm of fire and shrapnel, spreading destruction with a violence that it is impossible to anticipate.

It departed as calmly as it had arrived, leaving death on the ground, but also clouds of blinding dust and sand, which hung in the air. The pilots of the A-10 ground-attack aircraft, arriving five minutes later, could see nothing of the route they were expected to follow, and radioed that they were going into a holding pattern until the dust cleared. It was the first delay.

At TAA Viking, B Company were organizing themselves into their various sticks in their pre-arranged spot, waiting for their helicopters to arrive.

Major Matt Jackson saw his helicopter hover in out of the dark and land with a flex of its undercarriage. His company was going in on three CH-53s. There was an enormous amount of activity in the darkness, dust whipped up by the rotors. He looked for the number of his helicopter, making sure it was the right one, and the loadmaster prepared to check them all off on his manifest as they entered.

For the pilots of the Sea Kings and Chinooks taking A and C Companies, this was their moment to launch into enemy territory. Approaching takeoff, it is impossible to ignore the fear of the unknown, however much training has gone into a mission. As the pilot hits the starter button, the thought inevitably rises that this might be the last flight he will make. He's going to face an enemy, hostile fire; people will try to kill him. Jon Pentreath had felt the fear: 'But your training kicks in, your professionalism, then as your guys appear, as if by magic and they're the right guys, you think, These guys are going to get it a lot more than me. And it's because you don't want to let them down you get focused. At this stage almost everyone is hiding their fear because you don't want to let your mates down. Other people next to you depend on your actions. It's an extremely powerful reason.'

Matt Jackson saw CH-53 No. 5 come in, which was his. Adrenalin surged and his heart pounded. In such circumstances, he remembered, nothing runs smoothly: 'Royal Marines try to stay clean and dry for as long as possible, because as soon as you get dirty and wet, life becomes more uncomfortable. And I remember thinking, Christ, I've just got to try and keep clean. And there was a massive problem with loading our quad bike up on to our helicopter. It got stuck in a sand berm, right in the helicopter downdraught, and I was pulling and pushing it to get it on to the helicopter with all the other guys, getting sand-blasted.'

Eventually they got it into the cabin, hot and sweaty and dusty before they had even started. Matt Jackson went to the cockpit and put on headphones so he could listen to the conversations between the marine who would guide them in, the other helicopters and the air controller at Brigade Headquarters. There seemed to be no trouble at any of the sites, and they agreed that the helicopters should lift off when they were ready.

Their route took them over Kuwait, and Bubiyan Island. Here, there was an emplacement of Royal Marines artillery and British Army self-propelled guns, ready to cover the deployment of 42 Commando and the move north. Shortly after 40 Commando had landed, the guns would open up a barrage at Iraqi artillery positions on the al-Faw peninsula. After a few minutes the helicopters would cross the border into Iraq. They kept low to maintain contact with the ground and remain below the flight path of Tomahawk cruise missiles.

Flying conditions were difficult, the inbound and outbound routes separated by three or four miles, and the pilots were flying on radar altimeters. They were wearing night-vision goggles, which limit their field of vision, and trying to keep in formation with the other helicopters heading for the same landing site, relying on their infrared lights. The AC-130 Spectre gunship, circling overhead, shone an infrared searchlight at the landing spot when the helicopters were about a mile away so that the pilots could orient themselves, then switched off for the final approach.

The landing would be quick, the helicopter engines left running; this was when everybody was most vulnerable – to machine-gun fire, a mortar or an RPG – and the most basic weapon could kill them all in an instant.

Jackson's CH-53 had the benefit of forward-looking infrared, and he could see the target approaching on the screen in the cockpit. The flight seemed interminable and he was hot and uncomfortable after his struggle with the quad bike. Oil was dripping off the cockpit roof, the cabin was crammed with thirty-eight marines, their Bergens and weapons, some standing because it was a short flight, others sitting on their backpacks. It was getting hotter, and the anxiety was building. Sweat was pouring down Matt Jackson's back.

The pilot gave the five-minute signal. They were on the approach. The quad-bike driver started its engine because it had to move out as fast as possible under its own power. The pilot said they had to do another circuit, they had to hold off. It was impossible to tell why. The insertions had gone well, but there were reports of sporadic firefights. What would they find when they landed – if they landed?

Once again they approached and were told to hold off. 'And this must have happened three or four times. I'm standing there with my Bergen on my back, in excess of a hundred pounds of kit, and all I could think was, I don't care whether there's the assembled masses of Genghis Khan, I just want to get off this bloody helicopter. Because it was so suffocatingly hot. When I stepped out into the cold air, I felt supremely cold because I was drenched with sweat. I might as well have just jumped in a bath full of water, I was just absolutely soaked. It was the weight and the oil and the smell and the avgas and, I suppose, fear, because you've got no idea what you're going to be greeted with when you charge off the ramp of a helicopter.'

The SEALs had secured the pipelines, but they had been in a firefight, which had caused the hold-up. They had shot and killed one Iraqi soldier and captured thirteen prisoners, who would become Matt Jackson's responsibility – the SEALs and their helicopter were leaving.

The two pipeline terminals, M and K, were separated by 1.5 kilometres, and Matt had landed on the westerly M. B Company's forces were initially split to create a defensive perimeter around M and K. Milan anti-tank missile-launchers and heavy machine-guns were deployed to give covering fire around each facility. At each terminal, two 48-inch pipelines emerged from the desert parallel with each other and separated by several feet. They ran for about twenty yards above the ground and were fitted with large hand-operated valves. Then the pipes curved down into the sand and disappeared out to sea. Between the pipes and the sea there was a hexagonal two-storey concrete bunker, and breeze blocks and another building with the reinforcing bars of a second storey poking into the sky. These two buildings were the highest points on which to place a lookout. Matt had to divide his forces and his six Milan launchers, five heavy machine-guns and three 51-mm mortars between the two facilities. His plan was to ultimately clear the area and move out so that his troops could create one larger perimeter round both pipelines. But he needed to wait for D Company to move into the area to the north.

About 2.5 kilometres away from him a bunker and a command post had not been seriously damaged in the B-52's bombing raid. Sporadic fire was now coming from it, and the heavy machine-guns and a Milan post at K fired back. Jackson radioed a request for fire suppression from the Spectre gunship circling overhead. It droned over and fired a lethal mixture of

40-mm cannon shells and 105-mm artillery shells at the bunkers. Then an F-18 was called in and two 1000- and two 500-pound bombs were dropped on the bunker. The flash and explosions split the night.

Jackson was unwilling to advance to meet the enemy. His main task was to secure the pipelines. He had no idea how many Iraqi forces were in the bunker, or what lay further behind it in the palm groves that stretched to the Shatt al-Arab and the border with Iran, so he decided to hold a defensive position until daybreak.

A group of Iraqi soldiers made an approach, but seemed uncertain what to do, and merely fired the occasional pot-shot from the limited cover between the pipelines and the bunker. Jackson didn't want to send out a patrol to deal with them because he couldn't support it effectively with his limited number of men and heavy machine-guns. At the same time the Iraqis seemed equally unwilling to make an assault on his position. Gradually they drifted off to the plantation to the north.

Through the next few hours, as the dawn light revealed the area, the report of heavy machine-guns and the explosion of Milan missiles fired from pipeline K, closest to the bunker, split the silence. At daybreak the bleak tidal mudflats of the al-Faw peninsula came into view. Matt had established a small Command post in the basement of the building he had captured, where they had found some bunks, a desk and several AK-47 assault rifles and ammunition.

The marine on the roof called down, 'There's something here you should have a look at.'

Matt Jackson went up with his binoculars and saw a group of enemy soldiers approaching their perimeter. He ordered the machine-gun section to open fire, which they did. One Iraqi was shot and the Spectre gunship, still circling, fired at the rest as they fled. They were killed. The man they had shot, though, was only injured, and was struggling on the ground. The medical assistant, Marine Sumner, volunteered to go out and assist him. Matt Jackson was doubtful: it was dangerous, because there were still Iraqi troops in the bunker to the north, and there was almost no cover. Finally, with the machine-gunners prepared to provide cover, Marine Sumner ran out and gave first aid to the wounded Iraqi soldier, who was brought back to the pipeline. He would eventually find himself at sea on one of the Royal Fleet Auxiliaries.

Two of the prisoners captured earlier seemed to be fairly senior officers, and one had a suitcase stuffed with Iraqi dinars, but B Company still hadn't been able to call in a helicopter to evacuate them. All thirteen men needed to be fed and given ponchos and blankets. None of the extra vehicles Jackson expected had arrived; neither had supplies of food, water and ammunition. The Milan missile stocks had been depleted by the night firing and what remained wouldn't last long if there was a daytime assault from the bunker complex. Another urgent task was to clear the beach next to pipeline M of mines so that the Scimitar tanks could be landed from the hovercraft. The engineers were slowly uncovering mines and other unexploded ordnance, but they had a large area to cover. It seemed to Matt that it was going to take a long time.

While Jackson had been struggling to push a quad bike out of the sand and up the ramp of his helicopter, C Company, Colonel Messenger and his Tactical Control team had been loading on to the five RAF Chinooks that would fly them into the monitoring and metering station, fifteen kilometres to the north-west of the pipelines.

The man who had stood in front of his men, charismatic, straight-backed, summoning their reserves of optimism and *esprit de corps* was tense and strained. He, perhaps, knew the risks better than most, and had planned for them. He had estimated that they might lose two helicopters to accidents or enemy fire, and the most difficult part of the planning had been loading the helicopters so that in the event of a major catastrophe the operation could continue: 'If you are in the back of the helicopter there is not much you can do to influence your fate. We were taking pre-treatment tablets against nerve agents. My mouth was so dry through nervousness that the pill just fizzled on my tongue throughout the flight. I couldn't swallow it.'

The cabins of the helicopters were packed with marines, all standing like passengers on a rush-hour train. Gordon Messenger was told there had been a delay and the pilot manoeuvred the Chinook in a slow circle. Their landing had been held up because, although the aerial reconnaissance photos had revealed the layout of the metering station, the roads running through it and the buildings, remote surveillance could not reveal the state of the ground. The SEALs' helicopter had immediately got bogged down in thick oily mud. It had taken them far longer than expected to find the machinery they wanted to secure. They had been lucky to avoid contact with Iraqi soldiers.

As the helicopter circled the men inside swayed, Gordon Messenger remarked, like water moving about in a fish tank. One Chinook had an ambulance slung beneath it, which was gyrating like a pendulum, making the helicopter pitch. The vehicle was rapidly ditched by the load master, allowed to plummet, its cable severed, into the mud of Bubiyan Island.

The Chinooks continued to circle, while Gordon's team discussed making a change to their landing scheme. They decided to land on the only guaranteed hard surface in the compound, the single tarmac road that ran through it, Broadway. When Colonel

Messenger's helicopter put down, he knew he was supposed to turn left out of the ramp and run towards a light where the commander of SEAL Team 3 would be waiting. Gordon Messenger found him and he confirmed there had been no enemy fire and prepared to leave. However, the road was lined with telegraph poles, which would have to be felled before the other Chinooks could land, and the leading demolition expert was still in the air. They improvised using small keyhole charges placed against the base of the poles to clear the landing area.

The original plan had been to land in the corners of the MMS, which was a walled compound about two kilometres square. In one sector there were oil storage tanks, in the middle along the road were some offices, a bunkhouse and workshops and the two oil pipelines running parallel to each other, with their valves and flow meters, for hundreds of metres along the road. The rest of the area was a flat expanse of drainage ponds and boggy wasteground.

Their first task was to clear the buildings and secure the area out to the perimeter, set up a head-quarters and select a landing site for A and D Companies. The cumulative delays had caused their planned turnaround time to stretch to several hours instead of the intended sixty minutes. Time was running out. Nobody wanted the helicopters landing in daylight, least of all their pilots and the marines inside them. C Company moved through the metering station, spreading out from the area controlled by the SEALs, looking for tripwires, snipers and mines. The crack of fire from a marine's assault rifle echoed from the buildings and storage tanks. Everyone who heard it knew immediately there had been contact with the enemy and went to their positions. Two Iraqi guards had been shot dead but now everyone was alert for more contacts. Another troop hurled grenades into a building in another section of the compound, and an assault team swept through it.

Then the helicopters left, sending a wave of grit-filled air into the marines' faces. As the harsh clatter of their rotors faded, there was an eerie silence. Colonel Messenger surveyed the surreal landscape of grey sand and moonlit, oil-stained buildings. It was strange to see the complex that had become so familiar through countless reconnaissance photographs and models. Because of the exercises, and the mock-ups in Kuwait, everybody knew exactly where they were.

It was important that, with A and D Companies following to land in the metering station, the area around it was cleared and secured. The strategic objectives, the MMS and pipelines M and K, had been captured, but Gordon Messenger's forces were split and isolated in three separate locations spread down the peninsula more than eighteen kilometres. If they didn't push out and expand their perimeter they might become fixed in their positions, forced on to the defensive.

Captain Paul Lynch and his Manoeuvre Support Group had landed 500 metres from the objective they were meant to secure. It was the task of the SEALs team to kill anyone they saw and call down fire from the Spectre gunship on Iraqi troops outside the perimeter so that the MSG could move through the SEALs' position to secure the key points of access from al-Faw town and the north. They would be the firm edge where 42 Commando was due to land and set up a more substantial blocking position. In Kuwait the MSG had rehearsed clearing an area of 200 to 300 metres from the gatehouse, securing a bunker that guarded it and setting up their heavy machine-guns with interlocking arcs to create a killing zone. The SEALs, however, had lost their vehicle in the mud, it had become immovable and they had been delayed. They did not have grenade-launchers with them or a heavy machine-gun, so had been unable to secure any areas outside the inner perimeter. The Manoeuvre Support Group marched to their objective with as much as they could carry, some with two Milan missiles each. They went forward with their SEAL co-ordinator who could talk to the Spectre gunship that was circling above them.

The last intelligence that Captain Paul Lynch had received was that there might be thirty people in trenches to the north of the gatehouse. Now he was informed that the Spectre gunship had located at least a hundred, perhaps 130, using its infrared sensors. Moreover, there was apparently another trench system that had not previously been spotted. He had just thirty-five men in his MSG.

He spoke to Colonel Messenger, and told him that he wasn't going forward to his objective. Gordon Messenger was stunned that there were so many Iraqi troops, that they had not been identified until now, and that they had survived through the intensely planned pre-assault fires from the B-52, the A-10s and the Spectre. However, he was adamant that they had to be cleared. Paul Lynch told the SEALs he was going forward to take that position.

According to Lynch, they were surprised that he could even think of doing it, but called back the Spectre gunship, which started to pour fire on the trenches.

Captain Lynch had never seen anything like it. The lumbering four-engined AC-130 blasted tracer and cannon shells into the ground, so close to him that he quickly pulled his men back to safety. In the background the divisional barrage from the artillery in Bubiyan Island was now landing further north and the thunder of distant explosions and the flash of shell-bursts lit the horizon. Behind him a Chinook was clattering in, landing at just the wrong moment, and the men in the trenches had started firing back. A motorbike was hit and burst into flames and a propane cylinder exploded. It was utter mayhem. Paul Lynch had studied *Julius Caesar* at school: 'I stood there, and thought, "Let slip the dogs of war." '

The Spectre gunship ceased fire because of the danger of hitting the marines, and ten men were ordered to secure the gatehouse bunker. Corporal Pete Watts went out, and radioed back that there were still people in the building and the trenches: 'What about the enemy on the roof? Can they be destroyed before we attack?'

Lynch replied: 'They are the enemy. We are here to kill the enemy. Now get on with it.'

Quickly a Milan post and three machine-guns were set up for covering fire, then the rest of the Manoeuvre Support Group ran out through the gates, moving up section by section, adopting the classic rule, no fire without advancing, no advance without firing. They moved forward, shooting Iraqis in the trenches and other buildings to the north.

The plan had been very optimistic. The marines did not have the numbers to expand outside the perimeter, but with overwhelming firepower and aggression they imposed themselves on a far superior enemy. For an hour they assaulted the Iraqi positions, moving north, even though they were outnumbered. Corporal Watts's section killed eight Iraqi soldiers and took twenty-five prisoners. Eventually they had to stop and secure a position, but they knew now there were still more than two hundred men in the trenches and the low-lying bunkers whose existence had come as a total surprise.

Some of the Iraqis gathered themselves to mount a defence, and mortar rounds started coming into the metering station, with the pop of AK-47s. It was clearly a two-way range: the targets were firing back. One of the exploding mortars created a cloud of smoke, and the cry, 'Gas', went up. One of the US special forces had forgotten his gas mask and ran back to retrieve it. Captain Lynch observed the US serviceman on his way back: he remained in good health. He assumed it was a false alarm.

More mortars rained in, but most of the defending Iraqi troops were demoralized by the initial Spectre gunfire and the marines' assault. Captain Lynch saw one Iraqi soldier raise himself out of his trench, his rifle in his hand. He shouted at the man in Arabic to put down his gun, but it made no difference. He was utterly confused, probably deafened by the gunfire and cannon shells exploding all around him. Several marines aimed at him, and there was a dreadful gut-wrenching pause. He was a tragic figure, clearly no threat to anybody. Nobody fired. He turned round and lay down in his trench.

There were less humane moments. As the firing stopped it became clear that one badly injured Iraqi was lying between the marines' position and the Iraqi trenches. His screams were audible and disturbing. Some marines approached Captain Lynch for permission to go to him with medical assistance and evacuate him, but he refused. He knew that 42 Commando would be landing shortly and the area would be shot up by Cobra helicopter gunships. He couldn't take the risk that they would be in the fire zone.

The Iraqi's cries continued for a long while. In the morning he was dead.

The Manoeuvre Support Group had advanced against much larger Iraqi forces than anyone had anticipated, but still faced an enemy who might be reinforced from al-Faw town. The second wave of Commandos was becoming crucial. A Company had lifted off from Viking and were on their way in. Major Justin Holt, the company commander, had already heard that the landings had been successful, but that at both the metering station and the pipelines they were meeting resistance from Iraqi forces. He had boarded his helicopter but didn't bother to put on the headphones that would allow him to listen to the conversation between the pilot and the marine air controller on the ground. He knew that nothing he could do would change anything, that nothing he heard would ease his anxiety. The Chinook banked and headed off into the darkness. It was luck and the skill of the pilots that would keep them alive now.

Their landing was hard and fast. The Chinook pilots didn't want to waste a second in their approach to a landing site that was taking incoming mortars, and where the night sky was streaked by tracer rounds. This was the second time they had been into this landing zone, and it was far more dangerous than it had been on the first. God knew what the third flight would be like. The marines of A Company raced out of the back of the helicopters, and Justin Holt ran over to Gordon Messenger. There was bad news: 42 Commando had taken casualties, and could not adopt their blocking position; 40 Commando were on their own; B Company was in two groups fifteen kilometres away in a sporadic fight with Iraqi forces in a complex of bunkers on their eastern perimeter. Mortars were landing in the metering stations, threatening to damage the high-pressure oil pipes and storage tanks that were the main strategic target of 40 Commando's assault but, fortunately, had caused no casualties so far.

A Company's original task was to head south and secure a line of departure, an area from which an assault could take place, for D Company, who were due to fly in from *Ark Royal*, and were going to advance on the bunkers in the south and take the pressure off Matt Jackson in B Company.

Now everything had changed and Gordon Messenger had other orders. Justin was to take his men and secure the northern perimeter, reinforce Captain Lynch and his marines, then go forward and clear the area. Justin raced back to his assembly point and passed on the orders to his troop commanders.

The company spread out, and the instructions were passed down the line as they moved through the metering station, ready to break out to take on the Iraqis in the trenches. Struggling through the mud, laden with ammunition and weapons, radios and batteries, they moved forward with almost no cover. Despite the imminence of conflict, the immediate call to action had energized them. Major Holt felt a wave of confidence in his men. He knew almost nothing about the situation that they were going to face but trusted that his men had the intelligence and confidence to deal with whatever they found.

Captain Lynch's men had come under fire from a complex of well-built and well-organized trenches and bunkers that had probably been constructed during the Iran–Iraq war. A Company moved forward through the perimeter to the trenches, killing the mortar squad with grenades and advancing, firing at any movement, but found that the whole complex had been pounded by the Spectre gunship.

Mutilated bodies lay everywhere, flesh, bone and blood mixed into the mud and smeared on the walls of the trenches. It was astonishing that any Iraqis had managed to organize themselves to get a mortar into action and fire at the advancing marines. They were clearly in a minority. Many had survived but they were in abject fear, shivering with shell-shock, crouched in a heap. Marines from A Company walked into the trenches and what was left of the bunkers, rounding up the survivors. They found two badly injured soldiers still alive on the perimeter road, with a number of dead. The company medic started prioritizing the wounded and giving what treatment he could. Without the ambulance, the marines formed stretcher parties to move the injured back to a regimental aid post, while the prisoners were taken to a holding area in the MMS.

A Company then moved further north to secure a landing zone for the arrival of 42 Commando, long delayed, before returning to Commando Main Head-quarters, which had been established in a building in the metering station. Their next task was to move south to establish a secure area for D Company, who had landed in the last wave and were going to assault an Iraqi command bunker.

Meanwhile, Captain Paul Lynch, now under less pressure with the arrival of A Company, had sent a group of his men in vehicles with the recce troop along a narrow coast road to the south, which would take them to pipelines M and K. After a few kilometres they came across a fortified position overlooking the sea.

They stopped and could see Iraqi soldiers in it. Under an overlooking machine-gun and Milan post, a section moved forward, and came under fire. They returned fire with their machine-guns while the advance section moved round and fired grenades. The Iraqi soldiers surrendered and another twenty prisoners were taken back to the MMS. These captives were equipped with night-vision goggles, more modern weapons and better-quality boots and uniforms. They also had a large sum of money, and it was assumed that they were special forces meant to guard against an amphibious landing.

Having cleared the road they returned to the metering station. Their initial task was over, and they had pursued it vigorously, with success, but other units had a lot more to do before the first phase of 40 Commando's mission was completed.

8

SECURING AL-FAW

D Company, under Major Matt Pierson, had never set foot in Kuwait, remaining at sea on *Ark Royal*. They were the only marines in 3 Commando Brigade to make a classic amphibious helicopter assault. They had not taken part in any of the training exercises in Kuwait because their landing site, in the monitoring and metering station (MMS), should have been secured before they took off. Their role in the occupation of the al-Faw peninsula was secondary, although they were to become engaged in some of the heaviest fighting further north.

D Company had been well cared for on *Ark Royal*, treated almost as special guests by many of the ship's crew, who knew the dangers of the marines' mission, and that some might not come back. On 20 March the tension on the ship had been almost palpable: they had gone to action stations and all the crew were dressed in white anti-flash hoods, bags round their waists with gas masks and anti-nerve-agent tablets.

At action stations, groups of sailors wait at damage-control centres and fire points around the ship; all watertight doors are closed, movement in the ship is restricted and the galleys are closed. The crew are fed in a process called action messing, when bacon sandwiches and water are passed round to the stations, or they're served a pot mess on a plastic plate which is eaten while standing up. The captain and his senior officers are in the control room, worrying about the depth of water, the wind speed, the heading and the status of the seas, ensuring that there are no threats in the vicinity. The sole purpose of the ship is to get the marines ashore without a mistake, on time, with no accidents or casualties. For their part the marines are mentally moving to another place that is less warm and safe, dark and very hostile.

Major Pierson had assembled his marines on the hangar deck for a final briefing, and had said that there would be no Henry V moment from him. He reiterated the plan, the details of the landing site, and urged them to trust each other. They lay in the hangar deck, faces blackened with camouflage paint, doing a quick, final, rigorous kit check, making sure that their weapons were secure and their gear was at hand, going through the final mental preparations for landing in a war zone. Through the noise of the air-conditioning and the beat of the ship's machinery they heard their Sea King helicopters landing above them on the flight deck.

Wrens, with illuminated wands, led each group of marines through the corridors and up the narrow companionways to their assembly point, their perfume an unsettling reminder of a human world that each marine was trying to put out of his mind. The marines climbed through the side doors of the helicopters and each Sea King was waved off from the flight deck.

Major Matt Pierson found that his headphones didn't work and that he had no communication with the pilot. Their route from *Ark Royal* took them straight over the sea to the coast of Iraq, but after they had been flying for ten minutes Major Pierson's helicopter banked, turned and headed away. He grabbed at the load master's earphones, nearly wrenching his jaw off and screamed at the pilot to find out what was happening. The only reply he received was 'The LZ's hot!'

The helicopter continued its journey and, to Pierson's concern, hovered over HMS *Ocean*, and landed on the flight deck. It was dark, and no one came out to the helicopters, except a refuelling crew. *Ocean* was closed down at action stations. The helicopters refuelled, and waited. Finally the all-clear came. There had been no gas attack: it was a false alarm after a mortar had exploded, releasing a cloud of smoke. The Sea Kings lifted off again, and headed once more for the Iraqi coast. All of the marines on board were by now sweaty, stiff, confused and thoroughly irritated. But they landed uneventfully, leaped out of the helicopters and formed up at the metering station. They were the final piece of the jigsaw in the complex scheme of manoeuvre, whose target was the seizure of the oil installations.

B Company had to create a single perimeter around pipelines M and K, but there remained the large complex of bunkers between them and al-Faw town, from which occasional probing patrols were made to B Company's perimeter. Machine-gun fire and the odd Milan missile kept them at bay, but the bunker needed to be cleared so that B Company could move out from its defensive position.

A Company, under Major Justin Holt, had cleared their way south-east from the metering station to create a line of departure within two kilometres of the bunkers, and it was D Company's task to advance from A Company's position, clear the bunker of enemy troops and join up with B Company.

D Company reached the line of departure. Pierson and Holt looked through their binoculars. There was a considerable amount of movement in the complex, with troops milling around, vehicles coming and going from the town of al-Faw. A frontal assault would be a lengthy, bloody battle. The marines would have to move through the buildings bunker by bunker, clearing each room, and there would possibly be a lot of casualties.

* * *

The JDAMs dropped in the pre-assault B-52 bombing raid appeared to have left the bunker unharmed. It might be possible to call down another bombing mission, but Matt Pierson knew there was a naval gun line in the Arabian Gulf of three Royal Navy ships and an Australian one. Their 4.5-inch guns could pour high-explosive shells on the bunkers, but that would inflict high casualties on the Iraqi forces. Matt Pierson wanted to utilize the naval gunfire, believing it more accurate and controllable than an air attack. He decided to ask for a barrage on an area of desert next to the barracks. Out in the Gulf, the four ships loaded their guns with a mixture of high-explosive and airburst shells. Then at eight-second intervals, the four guns started firing, sending their shells in an arcing trajectory to land fifteen miles away.

At D Company's tactical headquarters, they counted the seconds as the shells hurtled inland, but inside the bunker there was no warning. The earth exploded as the shells crashed in. Fountains of sand and mud flew high into the air, as blast after blast hit like giant hammer blows on the bodies and ears of the soldiers in the bunker, making them cry with fear and stress. After sixteen rounds the shelling stopped, leaving them paralysed, surrounded by the smell of blasted earth and cordite. Even Matt Pierson was shaken by what he had seen. He ordered his mortar troop to fire an illuminating round over the bunker, then a smoke charge, to emphasize that the next barrage would be on target. Slowly men emerged from the bunkers, hands up, some stripping off their uniforms, walking through the shell holes and rubble in their underwear. Three hundred surrendered, while others fled to the palm groves near the Shatt al-Arab.

D Company moved into the bunkers, where they found piles of weapons, ammunition, large amounts of food, other stores and accommodation for almost a battalion. If the Iraqi soldiers had chosen, they could easily have outnumbered and overrun B Company's positions around pipelines M and K. D Company cleared the bunkers and moved on to B Company to tell them they had been close to a large group of enemy soldiers.

Their position had been precarious. It was fortunate that the aggressive actions of B Company in securing the pipelines had intimidated the Iraqi troops, because there would be none of the reinforcements they had expected from the armoured squadron landing on the coast. The Royal Engineers, who had been trying to clear the beach of mines, had been defeated by the task. There were layers and layers of anti-personnel mines and other explosives on the beach, and the commander of the US Navy hovercraft carrying the Scimitar tanks of the Queen's Dragoon Guards had refused to land.

Major Matt Jackson had agreed with the decision

but might have been less willing to go along with it if he had known the size of the Iraqi forces encamped just a few kilometres to the north. So, the dispute between Brigadier Dutton and the hovercraft commander was resolved. Much publicity had been devoted to the intimate links between US and British units, where chains of command crossed nationality, but this collaboration had collapsed on the al-Faw peninsula at one of the most critical moments. There were others to come. The loss of the Scimitars increased the vulnerability of 40 Commando's position from the first day.

Colonel Gordon Messenger's men had secured their main targets, destroyed most of the military hard points in the area, and killed or taken prisoner a large number of Iraqi soldiers. Yet they were reliant on a continuous helicopter lift to the metering station for all their supplies. A stream of helicopters from HMS *Ocean* and HMS *Ark Royal* were still bringing vehicles and further supplies of ammunition, with the pilots working on a twelve-hours-on-twelve-hours-off shift system. There was a trade-off between equipment and other supplies, and the main focus was ammunition. Even during intense fighting the company tactical headquarters was signalling updates to Commando Main Headquarters of the state of their equipment and stores. With the shortage of transport, men were carrying most of their supplies on their backs and they were quickly going through their stocks of ammunition and batteries were depleting. The Commando had no reserves of food, and very little water. Some companies were running short of their personal stocks and Justin Holt recorded that, to a man, A Company was dehydrated and hungry.

Nevertheless, A Company was tasked to move to the south-east of al-Faw town, and set up a blocking position between it, the bunker and barracks that D Company had cleared. It was late afternoon, and everybody in the company, indeed everybody in 40 Commando, had had an extremely long period without proper rest. All had experienced the massive adrenalin surges of fear and excitement during the initial assault and the firefights after it. They had had almost no sleep since the night of 19 March, and had been constantly on the move.

They dug some trenches for protective cover, but often, with the flat, marsh-like nature of the ground, the shell scrapes filled with water. Some men just found a niche by a road. They set up their heavy machine-gun, lookout positions, and a headquarters to maintain radio watches for the night. Then they slept as best they could.

In the morning they established a blocking position. They were quite spread out over a kilometre, and their positions included two roadblocks. To their surprise, there was quite a lot of traffic, even though the area had seen a tremendous amount of violence over the past thirty-six hours. Al-Faw town, however, had remained untouched, and the oil facilities were undamaged.

Civilians from al-Faw were keen to get to work in the oil installations, although they wouldn't be allowed to, and they also wanted to get to the bunkers where they would help themselves to medical supplies and food. They were compliant and friendly at the checkpoints. Major Holt was unconcerned at the looting of the barracks – there was little he could do about it anyway – but he stopped those who were attempting to retrieve the assault rifles and rocket-propelled grenades cached in the cellars of the bunker. They were disarmed and told to go back to the town.

A Company had with them a tactical psychological operations team, who were operating a portable loudspeaker system that contained mini-disks with various messages in Arabic. As people approached the checkpoints the messages were played at them, telling them the coalition had come to overthrow Saddam Hussein, that they intended to help the Iraqi citizens recover their freedom and to go about their ordinary lives. A lot of Iraqi citizens spoke to the troops, and one said he had information about the town but needed to be arrested. He was hand-cuffed and dragged away to Company Headquarters where an Arabic-speaking member of the Joint Forces Interrogation Team could question him. His information was interesting and alarming. There was a Ba'ath Party headquarters in the town: the Party members were organizing sections of the Fedayeen Saddam, a regime-funded paramilitary organization set up after the Kuwait war, and were paying people to visit the bunkers to recover arms.

Major Holt had been given a list of nine things 'to be prepared to do' during the overall planning for the assault on the al-Faw peninsula. Low on the list was the clearing of al-Faw town, yet he was not surprised when he suddenly received orders to enter and secure it: they were understandable. Colonel Messenger had orders to seize not only the oil facilities but to clear his area of responsibility of all enemy resistance, which obviously included the town. 'There was no discussion. I just acknowledged his orders. We were only a single company of a hundred and five men entering a town with a population of around twenty-five thousand whose response could not be predicted. Conventional doctrine would recommend a ratio of nine to one for any military operation that could become engaged in urban warfare. We had a degree of momentum and initiative now working in our favour and therefore it was a calculated risk.'

Another Iraqi informer had pointed out on a map where the Ba'ath Party headquarters were so Holt sketched out the bare bones of a plan to enter the town. He wanted to go in with a highly visible, non-threatening posture, helmets off, and playing messages of reassurance on the loudspeakers. At the same time, a troop of soldiers under Second Lieutenant Buczkiewicz would approach along the side of the town, by the banks of the Shatt al-Arab waterway so that they would be in a position to isolate the Ba'ath Party headquarters if they met any resistance.

By late morning A Company had moved into the town. They were making careful but good progress, patrolling the busy streets, when they heard gunfire. They put on their helmets, and adopted a more aggressive posture, taking cover behind walls and buildings, but there was little to see. Major Holt asked that the message on the portable loudspeaker be changed, ordering everyone into their homes. The streets emptied.

The gunfire had come from the eastern side of the town. The troop moving along the waterway had entered an area of wasteland when fire from AK-47s rang out, and bullets ricocheted past them, thudding into walls. They had been ambushed, and the wasteland had been set up as a killing zone. The marines dived to take cover behind buildings and some were reduced to lying flat behind a pavement's kerbstones. It was hard to locate the snipers, as they dodged and changed position from rooftop to rooftop. One Iraqi turned a corner just six feet from the lead section of the troop and hosed the area with his assault rifle, but was shot by a corporal lying on the ground. Another

Iraqi charged into the wasteground using an old horse as cover, firing underneath it. The animal fell under a stream of bullets from several marines.

Small-arms fire was coming from houses on the troop's left flank, and a light machine-gun was firing from a frontal position. They needed to get the forward section back from the wasteground quickly and regroup. Mortars were fired into the buildings that seemed to house snipers, and the marines abandoned the non-existent protection of the kerbstones to retreat under the cover of fire from the rest of the troop.

As they pulled back, shots came into their position from Iranian border posts on the opposite bank of the Shatt al-Arab. Justin assumed it was a reflex response to gunfire, but it seriously complicated the marines' withdrawal. Running from cover to cover they retreated, and a final shot was fired at a sniper on a rooftop, which appeared to be fatal.

Remarkably, the marines had suffered no casualties, and had killed seven of their assailants, but the calculated risk had now transformed itself into an extremely grave situation. They had no idea of the numbers opposing them. They could continue to clear the town, but it seemed pointless. With everyone in the company so widely spread, hidden between buildings and moving quickly from cover to cover, they couldn't see each other, let alone the enemy. The civilian casualties that would result from an assault into the town were unacceptable. Even if Justin Holt was prepared to kill innocent civilians and destroy homes, he had only a hundred and five men, and couldn't secure those areas of the town that the company had already passed through. They might easily become surrounded. The plan to invade the al-Faw peninsula with so few troops had always looked audacious; it was now beginning to look as if it had been a serious miscalculation.

Colonel Messenger had no reserves left to pour into the town; in fact, he had received orders from Brigade Headquarters to prepare to move half his Commando north. He protested that his men were tired, hungry and low on ammunition, and that the clearance of al-Faw town was incomplete. He was told he hadn't understood. The message was blunt: 'Wind your neck back in, Shorty, and get a move on.' Gordon Messenger recollects that he talked to Justin Holt, and suggested he withdraw. It was not a job for a single company.

Justin Holt chose not to. He doesn't recall a suggestion to withdraw. Rather, he remembers Gordon Messenger asking if he needed help. He said it would be useful if some ambulances could be sent on standby. He also asked for two A-10 aircraft to do some overflights of the town to remind anyone who wanted to take them on that the Commandos were not alone. He then told Commando Headquarters that it was his intention to conduct an assault on the Ba'ath Party building.

'All the time I felt we were being watched and tested. In the whole campaign this was probably the first major incident to take place in an Iraqi town and I felt we had to prevail and set the conditions for others to clear similar-sized towns with the minimum risk to civilian lives and collateral damage. Therefore there would be no possibility of calling in indirect fire support from our own artillery or mortars. Nor would we be able to use our vastly superior air power to extricate ourselves from this situation. It was going to take individual riflemen and snipers with well-aimed shots to positively identify then kill the enemy at close quarters. It would take time and perseverance, not to mention considerable risk to us, to bring the fight into the Fedayeen's preferred ground. However, through every small gap and open window I could almost feel the gaze of those Iraqi townspeople watching us.' He knew that the Iraqi civilians and the Fedayeen were waiting to see what they were made of.

The afternoon wore on and in the heat and dust they sweated heavily under their assault loads of ammunition, which averaged 67.9 kilos per man. Justin Holt decided to form a strong defensive line through the centre of the town before nightfall and assault the Ba'ath Party headquarters after dark. He reasoned that it represented the seat of power in the town, the symbolic heart of Saddam's regime. It would allow his company to regain the initiative and re-emphasize that only supporters of the regime and loyalist militia would have anything to fear from the Commandos.

As soon as it was dark, 2 Troop took up a position in a fire station opposite the Ba'ath Party building to formulate their plan. It was clear that the building had been prepared as a defensive strongpoint and there was no way of telling what was inside. It also happened to be next door to the regional hospital and backed on to a residential area so there was no possibility that artillery or air strikes could be called in. It had to be taken by an assault. The opening phase had to be extremely violent to shock and paralyse the fighters inside the building, giving the marines the advantage of surprise. Major Holt also wanted the attack on the building to have a major impact on the town. He wanted to make plain to everybody in al-Faw that A Company had not been beaten, that they had once more gone on the offensive. They planned their assault quickly and meticulously. It would open with the two assault engineers attached to the company crossing the road and attaching explosives to blast open a wall in the building. As the charges exploded, three shoulder-launched anti-tank missiles would be fired at the main doors. With these two entrypoints open, a volley of small-arms and machine-gun fire would be poured into the building before troops entered with grenades and assault rifles.

The two engineers worked their way to the side of the building and attached the demolition charges. It was a strange atmosphere. There was no electricity and the town was completely dark. Nothing moved, and all that could be heard was dogs barking in the distance. When the engineers returned and crouched under cover, Justin Holt heard them giggling to themselves. He realized they had doubled the size of the charges. The explosives went off, and the missiles, fired with a whoosh, hit the doors. The noise was shattering. Holt said, 'Everybody in the town instantly knew that something big had gone down on the Ba'ath Party building.'

The assault teams charged across the road and entered the building, hurling grenades into each room, then hosing it with bullets, methodically turning each corridor and office into a lethal area. The flash and bang of exploding grenades and gunfire filled the night. As the assault team hit the last room, there was a huge detonation and three marines ran out of the building, their uniforms burning. A grenade had ignited a gas cylinder, which had blown out a corner of the roof and a wall. The rest of the section rushed to beat out the flames on their comrades, and evacuated the building, which was now on fire. The company signaller was already sending a casualty report.

Commando Headquarters decided to take the burned marines by ambulance back to the oil installation where a forward surgical team could stabilize them and assess the degree of their injuries. As the assault was complete and the building burned brightly in the darkness, with six dead Iraqis inside it, the stretcher-bearers took the three men to the edge of the town to transfer them to an ambulance for the two-minute drive to the regimental aid post.

Holt remembers, 'It felt sickening to have to treat our own and suffer the loss of three good men. That night we rested fitfully in each of the three defensive strongpoints we had established in buildings, keeping a watch. We had been resupplied finally and had water and rations.'

The next morning they continued with the operation to clear the town. Major Holt felt they would experience another series of firefights, and that this time they would not be so lucky. It was difficult to ask men deliberately to put themselves in danger again, but the company shook out quickly and stepped off in the same configuration as the day before to clear the northern half of the town. The sun was rising, the heat was building, and the town was stirring for a new day.

They had not reached far into the town when an evidently important figure approached them and was taken to the company headquarters. He pleaded for a ceasefire. The deaths of seven Fedayeen in their failed ambush the previous day and the violent assault by the marines on the Ba'ath Party building in the middle of the night had had the desired effect. The Fedayeen had evacuated the town, and the inhabitants were not looking for any more conflict. He showed them several arms caches, and there was no more gunfire.

They had achieved a victory.

At midday they retired to their company assembly area in the MMS. The al-Faw peninsula had been secured, with a remarkably small number of people and no fatalities. In Colonel Messenger's words, 'We were fucking lucky.'

9

NO PLAN SURVIVES CONTACT

42Commando had been living under canvas in the desert of Kuwait for five weeks and were becoming increasingly impatient to see some action. Their role in the overall scheme of manoeuvre of 3 Commando Brigade was simple. They were to land in the al-Faw peninsula and prevent any units of the Iraqi armed forces moving south in an attempt to dislodge 40 Commando from the oil installations they had captured.

This simple mission was made complicated by lack of hard intelligence about the nature of the threat they might face, and the large area of operations that they would have to control. Speed and surprise were of the essence, and their five weeks in Kuwait had been spent on the painstaking creation of a plan that would ensure all elements of 42 Commando were landed almost at the same time as 40 Commando, in the right places and with the right weapons to deal with anything, even the approach of tanks from Basra in the north. Four rehearsals had been held with the Marine Aircraft Group 39, part of the 3rd Marine Air Wing, whose CH-46 helicopters would fly them in. Colonel Buster Howes, commanding 42 Commando, and Captain Oliver Lee, the operations officer, were as certain as any human could be that every conceivable thing that could go wrong had been taken into account. Oliver Lee remembers that 'The day was the most profoundly affecting twenty-four hours of my career. I remember being absolutely terrified of making a mistake that cost people's lives and messed up the plan. I spent every waking hour in the whole day – I'm sure even my lips were moving, it was going through my head – just talking myself through everything I expected to happen.'

On 20 March, as the clock ticked inexorably towards the time for the helicopter assault to begin, impatience for action was tempered by fear of its imminent approach. The atmosphere of anticipation was fuelled by the growth in activity around the assembly area. For days the noise of convoys moving up the road that ran past the camp had grown louder and more persistent, kicking up clouds of dust that thickened the air. Helicopters came and went with increasing frequency, adding to the sense of a great juggernaut coming to life.

Captain Chris Haw would not take part in the

assault although he should have been in one of the first units to enter Iraq. He was the commanding officer of the Brigade Patrol Troop, a specialist unit responsible for the close forward reconnaissance of enemy positions, one of three troops in the Brigade Reconnaissance Force (BRF). This unit had been assigned to 42 Commando, under Buster Howes's command and would set up the very forward positions in the Commando's area of responsibility.

Chris Haw had been removed from the planning process to prepare instead for a covert operation in Umm Qasr, which had, disappointingly, come to nothing. He was now kicking his heels, jealous of his friends' opportunity to see action. He had been assigned to a Tactical Recovery Aviation Personnel (TRAP) team, who would supply first aid and security round a helicopter brought down by mechanical failure or enemy fire. He would be based in the landing zone while his friends and comrades took off for Iraq.

He was conscious of an air of foreboding among the troops at the assembly area: 'The overarching mood was of uncertainty. There were stories about T-80 tanks coming down from Basra, chemical weapons, things we had to be prepared for. So the uncertainty of what lay on the al-Faw peninsula and the build-up to it – "Are we going or are we not?" – didn't help. Then, suddenly, "It's here, this is it." Everyone was feeling a bit nervous.' As darkness fell he wandered around the landing zone. All the helicopters were on the ground with their engines shut down, but the vehicles to be carried in were assembled in their loading areas, and the commandos were waiting in their groups by their helicopters, sitting around and talking quietly. One of the first wave of helicopters in the assault, with the call sign Delta 3, would take in the headquarters team of the BRF, and Chris Haw went to say goodbye. He knew them all intimately – the commanding officer, Major Jason Ward, was a good friend of his, as was Warrant Officer Mark Stratford. The signaller, John Cecil, was Haw's signaller from his own troop, Sholto Hedenskog was his radio officer, and he knew both of the Artillery Regiment forward observation officers and Sergeant Les Hehir from 29 Commando Artillery. They shook hands and he wished them good luck. 'I'm always an optimist. I thought I'd see them later on, but you never know, do you?' He watched as they walked on to the twin-rotor CH-46 helicopters, their Bergens packed with ammunition and rations, radios and spare batteries. He wouldn't be carrying that weight tonight.

Captain Oliver Lee had found saying goodbye to those he had been sharing a tent with over the past five weeks quite emotional. 'I remember feeling pretty apprehensive but confident. I thought the plan was good and I thought we were good enough to discharge it effectively. You almost feel a sense of love for those around you, and you shake hands with a degree of trepidation. As we got to the landing site, there were some very nervous people there.'

The engines whined into motion, and the rotors turned slowly, then faster as the pilots waited for full power. Their pitch changed, the fuselage shook and they lifted off.

The first of a giant airborne armada, the largest helicopter assault since the Vietnam War, took off. Captain Lee had checked all of the men into their helicopters; all the right call signs were received as each took off. He felt that this was now all working, so practised and seamless had it become, and now they were flying and were away, taking up their position in the lead formation of six helicopters.

Four Cobra gunships would fly in advance of the first wave, to make sure that the route had been cleared of anti-aircraft and artillery positions. Then two Huey helicopters would follow, acting as airborne command posts. Buster Howes was in one with the US Marines air-mission controller. The second carried Lee as a back-up controller, in case Howes's helicopter crashed or had to put down.

The four CH-46s of the first wave followed, at two hundred feet above the ground. They headed out over the desert, all wearing night-vision goggles, flying through dust and haze, with no moon or stars. Shortly after takeoff the air-mission controller's helicopter developed a fault in its torque meter, which tells the pilot how much power the engines are putting out, and went back to the landing zone to change to a reserve helicopter, the second Huey returning with him. Buster Howes and the air-mission controller changed aircraft, then put into the air again. By this time Major 'Daisy' May, commanding M Company, in the second wave of helicopters, had boarded his CH-46, the cabin lights had gone out, the engines started and he waited for lift off.

The two Hueys, which should have been in the lead, were now seven miles behind the first formation of four helicopters, and the air-mission controller was concerned about visibility. There had been a build-up of dust in the atmosphere at the landing site over the past two days, and smoke from fires south of Baghdad had reached the area. In addition, the CH-46s in front were contributing to the dust that the Hueys were now flying through. Captain Lee was looking through his night-vision goggles at what seemed like a television set that had not been properly tuned: all he could see was lights dancing around. The air-mission controller, codenamed Swamp Fox, had a conversation with the air wing commander about the deteriorating conditions, and decided to abort the mission because of the poor visibility. He called on the radio network for the helicopters to head back to the landing site.

At the same time the lead CH-46 helicopters had reached the waypoint at which they were due to make a turn to follow the route into Iraq. They turned, and Dash 3, the helicopter carrying the Brigade Reconnaissance Force, was seen by the pilot of Dash 4 to pitch and adopt a nose-down attitude. It didn't recover – at such low altitude it was unlikely that there was time to do anything – and the helicopter, with its crew and passengers, flew at 100 knots nose first into the desert. It exploded in a ball of flame and flying rotor blades, debris spinning off into the dark for hundreds of yards. The blast shook Dash 4 violently, but the pilot kept control and completed his turn.

Chris Haw was in the TRAP team's helicopter back at the landing site, listening to the radio traffic on his headphones. The pilot was the first to understand the message from Dash 4, and said to Haw, 'There's a bird down. It's in flames.' This was the signal for the TRAP team to spring into action, and Chris Haw told his men they were going. The pilot started his engine, and Haw climbed with his men into the cabin. But the helicopter stayed on the ground. Haw asked the pilot to confirm that a helicopter was down, and he did. Chris said 'Are we going then or what?' The pilot turned off the engine, 'It's exploded. There's nothing left of it. There's no point in us going.'

It dawned on the TRAP team that people had died in the accident, and that there were no survivors. Chris Haw was still in denial: 'But, like I've been saying all along, I immediately thought, No, it won't be any of our lot. It's a shame. I wonder which 42 lads it was.' Then the helicopters came back, and the truth hit them. The helicopter that had gone down, disintegrating in an exploding fireball, had carried the command structure of the BRF. Within minutes of the three remaining CH-46 helicopters and the two Hueys arriving back at the landing zone, 42 Commando was engulfed in a multi-layered crisis. The men who had died in the crash were well known and popular. Their deaths were a shock to Chris Haw, Oliver Lee and others. Chris thought not only of his close friend Jason Ward but of Ward's wife in England, ignorant of her husband's death. Buster Howes was also a personal friend of three of the dead men, whom he'd known for thirty years.

People were stunned, and no one knew quite what to do. The BRF was a key component of the blocking manoeuvre that 42 Commando was charged with establishing on the al-Faw peninsula. With its leadership wiped out, another set of officers, with the same communications and targeting skills, had to be put together and briefed. There would be time later to remember the dead, but 40 Commando was in place, and 42 Commando Headquarters had received reports that they were in contact with the enemy. There was not a moment to lose.

Then came the second and, to some, more damaging event. The commander of the US Marine Air Wing decided to cancel the mission. Their helicopters would not carry 42 Commando on to the al-Faw peninsula. 'Now, this was the biggest shock of all because at the very start the US Marine Corps commandant general had said, "We'll be there to support you all the way." I thought, You just don't do this.' Buster Howes remembers that the crash seemed to demoralize the aircrew. 'They'd already lost four of their guys and it was becoming very bureaucratic for them, trying to make a decision what to do next. They were sitting around as the sun came up and there was a certain amount of argy-bargy. My attitude was "For fuck sake, we've got to get on with this."'

The problem for the US Marine Air Wing was that they were scheduled to divert to another mission after landing 42 Commando on the al-Faw peninsula, and their system was too inflexible to accommodate any sudden change of plan.

Buster Howes, Oliver Lee, and Rob McGowan, 42 Commando's second-in-command, now had to solve the overlapping problems and get themselves into position as quickly as possible. The major requirement was to find alternative helicopters. They had told Brigadier Dutton, at Brigade Headquarters, that the mission had been aborted because of poor weather. They now had to inform him that the mission could not be completed at all unless Brigade, and it was only they who had the power, could organize substitute aircraft. Leaving that bridge to be crossed by Brigade Headquarters, 42 Commando's senior officers had to address the issue of morale.

There was shock at the death of eight officers, but most people could not understand why they had not continued with the mission. They were pumped up with adrenalin, still focused on the need to get involved in the fight, feeling impatient and frustrated, rather than demoralized by the deaths.

The next vital requirement was to reconstitute the BRF, because they were the eyes and ears, the early-warning system of the Commando once it was deployed. Chris Haw was identified as the man to lead it, yet he was ignorant of the planning behind 42 Commando's scheme of manoeuvre. That wasn't so important, however, because the plan itself would now have to be reworked. His most important task was to rebuild the BRF around him.

He remembers how he became aware that the task would be his. 'The second-in-command came over and said, "Right, Officer Commanding BRF", and all of a sudden that was me. Someone had decided I was taking over. I didn't know where anyone was supposed to be on the ground, what the capabilities were, what the killing areas were, so it was pretty intense. Fortunately we had enough redundancy of capabilities like forward air controllers, indirect fire controllers in the organization that I could recruit. But the reason all this worked was because I knew the guys and had worked with all of them before, and they were extremely competent operators.' He and Captain Oliver Lee spread a map over the bonnet of a Land Rover and, holding a torch, started to fix the details of the scheme of manoeuvre in his mind.

Meanwhile, Colonel Howes was assessing how much of the plan could still be implemented. An enormous amount had changed in the last few hours. As well as the US Marine CH-46 transports, the escorts of Cobra gunships were no longer available. This meant that the landing sites and routes into them would not have been surveyed and sanitized. The landings would have to take place in daylight, so there would be much higher risk from anti-aircraft fire, and artillery targeting the landing sites. Buster Howes had to make some quick calculations about how far north he was prepared to order people to fly into enemy areas without any idea of where the enemy was, risking helicopters being shot down. To reduce that threat he decided that the marines would have to march further than originally anticipated, even though they would be carrying very heavy loads.

By now it had become clear that the only available transports were the Puma helicopters and Chinooks of the Joint Helicopter Command, whose crews had already been flying into Iraq with 40 Commando. Negotiations were taking place with the US Marine Corps to move their helicopters away from the landing zone so that the Chinooks could land. But the loading scheme for the helicopters would of necessity be different. There were fewer of them, and they carried different numbers of troops and vehicles.

People were trying frantically to make calculations about what vehicles could be loaded, what endurance the helicopters had and where they could refuel. The plan that had been carefully and painstakingly worked out over five weeks was, Buster Howes felt, 'shot to smithereens'. It was, but for Captain Lee the time spent on it was now crucial. 'We all understood the plan implicitly, we all understood everything about it, and as things changed, we were able to amend it quickly.' They were coming under considerable pressure to do so.

Chris Haw went to Commando Headquarters where Buster Howes was on the radio to Brigadier Dutton: 'I could hear him saying to Buster, "Get your Commando on to the al-Faw peninsula." There was no question about it, you know. Obviously he saw 40 Commando sitting there about to be attacked by something coming down from Basra. That was what forced us into doing a daylight manoeuvre. There was a huge risk but the risk had to be taken because there were guys who were vulnerable.'

The Chinooks arrived. They had been flying through the night, since the first wave of 40 Commando had gone into the attack. The pilots were 'on the bare bones of their arse', as Buster Howes said. They knew the risks were now high, that they were going to fly at daylight into unreconnoitred landing sites, and must have realized they had a good chance of taking casualties. Haw and the reconstituted BRF boarded their helicopter. The plan was still changing as they did so, and Lee walked beside Haw, explaining some last-minute complications until it was too late for anything more and the doors of the helicopter closed.

Forces like the Royal Marine Commandos place a premium on the intelligence and initiative of their men. They have to be able to take decisions on the spur of the moment, and it makes sense for them to be aware of the planning for operations that they are taking part in at least two levels of decision-making above their own unit.

This was clearly not going to be the case for 42 Commando's landing on the al-Faw peninsula. All 800 men knew that they were intended to provide a blocking screen for 40 Commando, but the detail of how that would be accomplished had been destroyed in the aftermath of the destruction of the CH-46 Sea Knight helicopter, whose shattered wreckage they saw on the desert beneath them as they flew over it. But they had little time to spend on contemplation, because even in the air they were receiving changes to the plan.

On the radio Chris Haw was told that he would be landed close to the front edge of 40 Commando's area, and would march to his position from there. He tried to brief his team, clustered round a WMIK Land Rover in the cabin of the Chinook as they thundered over the Kuwaiti desert, across the Khawr 'Abd Allah waterway and into Iraqi territory.

Landing on the front edge of 40 Commando's area was potentially dangerous for the men on the Chinook, and certainly bad news for the pilots. They were flying into the contact area between British and Iraqi forces, where there was every likelihood that a battle would take place. It also meant that once the BRF had landed, they would be in the wrong position to carry out their task, and would have to move forward about fifteen kilometres to set up their blocking formation.

The pilot put the Chinook down at the new landing site, and the wheels sank into thick mud. He kept the helicopter hovering and the commandos leaped out, their Bergens on their backs, carrying heavy machine-guns, missile man-packs and their own personal weapons, and stepped into mud up to their knees. The Land Rovers were driven off the ramp and also got bogged down; the marines struggled to free them and get them to firmer ground.

When the second wave of helicopters arrived, they landed in positions that put the BRF at the rear of the formation. L Company and the BRF found they had to move through each other's lines, which was potentially dangerous with the possibility of a friendly-fire incident. The change-over operation was accomplished and the BRF started to march to the north to set up the front edge of 42 Commando's position.

M Company, under Major May, landed to the left of L Company, and found that, like the BRF, they would not have the number of vehicles they had originally planned for. They had just two instead of the thirteen they needed. It meant that the heavy machine-guns, spare barrels, tripods and ammunition would be carried on somebody's back. They spread out over a line of two kilometres, and were just about mutually supporting. Iraqi artillery was in place and managing to shell many of the landing sites, although it was never sustained enough to do any real damage. K Company was shelled, and Second Lieutenant Rob Jones recalled, 'The first shell landed about seventy metres away, and we took cover as shrapnel flew past. But it soon became apparent that unless the round landed on you and you were in decent cover it wouldn't actually do anything.' He found that when he took cover with his radio operator they were both laughing, as the tension that had been building up dissolved now that they were under fire.

J Company arrived on their original landing site, and found it had been attacked by a Spectre gunship as part of the pre-assault plan for the operation. They were pleased that it had, because they found it was overlooked by an enemy position with troops and heavy machine-guns in place. The Iraqi troops were dead, and the ground around the trenches and sand-bags had been churned up by the gunship's bullets. As the company moved out from their landing site, alongside the palms that fringed the Shatt al-Arab, they observed a ZU-23-2, a Russian-built mobile anti-aircraft machine-gun, which appeared unmanned. The commanding officer of the manoeuvre support troop wanted to fire a Milan anti-tank missile at it, which seemed excessive to the CO of J Company. Major Kevin Oliver reasoned that a show of arms might encourage enemy forces in the shelter of the plantation to surrender. The rocket sped to its target and exploded. The gun's crew were hiding among the palms, but didn't surrender. They fired on Sergeant Dom Collins's sniper unit moving up in advance of the company. The snipers returned fire, killing one of the soldiers, at which the other surrendered.

Meanwhile the BRF had been marching to take up its forward position. It was heavy going, and they had to stick to the roads because it was hard to make progress through the mud. In any case, it was possible that areas off the roads had been mined. It was approaching midday, with temperatures around 40 degrees centigrade, they were wearing helmets, body armour, and struggling to reach their positions as quickly as possible. They moved along the road, hot and sweating, feeling exposed and nervous. One of the team commanders was called Gaz Veecock. Someone shouted, 'Gaz!' and down everyone went into the ditch at the side of the road, fumbling for their gas masks. They realized the verge was most likely mined and rolled out again on to the tarmac, unbalanced by their Bergens, stuffed with ammunition. 'I shouted, "Who called that? Did anyone call that?"' recalled Haw. 'He said, "No, I called *Gaz*."'

They were the most forward Allied troops in the al-Faw peninsula and grasped how vulnerable they were when a US Cobra gunship flew over them from their rear and banked to inspect them. Chris Haw thought initially that the Cobra was patrolling the al-Faw, which, of course, it was, and wondered how far it would go forward when he realized that the pilot would have no information about their position and might mistake them for Iraqis. Another surge of adrenalin shot through him as he saw the Cobra adopt a nose-down attitude, a sign that it was clearing an arc of fire for its nose cannon. He shouted to his forward air controller to get on to the UHF network and warn the gunship to 'Check fire, check your fire!'

As he heard the controller shout the words into the mouthpiece he saw the nose of the Cobra lift and the pilot pulled away. The BRF was spread out about five kilometres on either side of Haw's post and he heard another man on the radio saying he was being circled by an A-10 aircraft, a ground-attack machine armed with bombs, rockets and massive rapid-firing rotary cannon in its nose. It, too, was warned off at the last minute. Haw said, 'I was shouting back to

42 Commando HQ, saying, "Sort this fucking air out because they need to know where we are, I've given you all our positions." But the air network is massive, and the observation posts are moving around, and for every single pilot to have a map on his knee of every single position of where these OPs are is never going to happen.' Meanwhile, large-calibre shells were whistling over the heads of the BRF towards Commando Headquarters.

Colonel Buster Howes and the Commando Tactical Headquarters had established themselves alongside the regimental aid post adjacent to J Company's position. No sooner had they done this than they came under fire from Iraqi 152-mm artillery, which they found alarming. It caused Buster Howes to wonder, 'What else is hiding in the area that we don't know about?' The shells were coming in from a battery within the commandos' area of operations. The headquarters was fairly conspicuous with its large array of aerials, and various companies had observed white SUVs driving, some thought suicidally, through the battle area. It was noticeable after a while that the shelling often followed the arrival of the vehicles. It dawned on Chris Haw, and 'Daisy' May and others that they were spotting for the artillery and were legitimate targets. The next time they were seen, two Milan missiles were fired at them, killing the occupants, and the shelling stopped. Commando Headquarters had called up a Cobra gunship to destroy the artillery battery, and it attacked the howitzers with rockets.

J Company had also been targeted by artillery, and as they moved north came under fire from a T-55 tank and a troop of Iraqi infantry. Sergeant Collins was in the lead and returned fire. As the tank was firing, Iranian border guards on the east bank of the Shatt al-Arab were shooting across the waterway, bringing the British troops under fire from two directions. Buster Howes surmised later that it must have been an instinctive response and fear of what looked like the Third World War breaking out across the water. There was little anyone could do about this, as their rules of engagement did not allow them to take on the Iranians, and Howes thought President Bush wouldn't thank him for starting a war on another front. But it made manoeuvring more difficult and dangerous.

Dom Collins knew he had to eliminate the Iraqi tank quickly. He called his section back, then asked on the radio for artillery fire to get rid of it. The Commando Headquarters Royal Artillery controller directed the gunfire, and the tank was hit in a barrage of shells. Collins called in the signal, 'Fire mission finished', and moved forward. Twenty minutes later another round landed with an enormous explosion 100 metres from Collins, who had walked away to relieve himself. The humour of the situation wasn't lost on J Company, but didn't amuse Dom, who had been lucky to survive a similar incident of friendly fire during a training exercise in Kuwait. He was beginning to wonder who was more of a threat: the Iraqis or his own artillery.

There were sporadic encounters throughout the day, with occasional shelling from artillery batteries further up the al-Faw peninsula. Collins noted that the regular Iraqi soldiers had no will to fight: they were often observed stripping off their uniforms and leaving the battlefield or surrendering. Buster Howes wrote later, 'It was strange in many cases when you closed on the location where you identified the enemy to be, you either found nobody or a pile of discarded uniforms. Even more surreally you would then come across groups of men in their underwear, as if it was normal to be standing around in their Y-fronts.'

The presence of civilian vehicles now often presaged artillery fire and a firefight might end when the Iraqis just disappeared. The fighting was not what they had expected or prepared for. Dom Collins knew they were now involved in a counter-insurgency war. The enemy had quickly become 'asymmetric'.

Whatever threat this held for the future, the first thirty-six hours had seen a successful completion of the first phase of the Commandos' tasks. The oil facilities had been captured, the town of al-Faw had been secured, and a defensive position had been established several kilometres towards Basra. The withdrawal of the hovercraft carrying the Scimitar tanks, the loss of the BRF, and the potentially crippling withdrawal of the US Marines' helicopters at the last moment had all been overcome.

Now orders were being prepared for 40 Commando to move forward and exploit its situation by heading rapidly up the peninsula towards Basra. Brigade Headquarters had another surprise in store for 42 Commando.

10

TAKING UMM QASR

When Admiral Snelson had arrived in Bahrain eight months before, the principal task of the Royal Navy was the clearance of the Khawr 'Abd Allah waterway of mines so that humanitarian relief could be shipped into the port of Umm Qasr. Once a village set some way back from the western bank of the waterway, the old port of Umm Qasr was a maze of densely inhabited streets and buildings, housing large numbers of workers. The port's role had grown during the Iran–Iraq war, taking over from Basra because of the threat to that city from Iranian forces.

When Iraq had been expelled from Kuwait at the end of the first Gulf war in 1991 Basra had been the centre of a rebellion by the Shia population of the south against Saddam Hussein; as a punishment to the city he had continued to favour the development of Umm Qasr. It now had a modern port about a mile from the old town, with a large dock and channel that had been kept dredged to take ocean-going ships, with fifteen towering mobile cranes that ran on rail tracks along the dockside to unload cargo and containers. It handled around 3500 tonnes of food and humanitarian aid every day under the UN-organized oil-for-food operations after the Kuwait war.

An industrial area to the north contained cement works and warehouses, and there was the railhead of a railway line to Basra.

With the Royal Marines' presence at brigade strength, the task of capturing and securing the port at Umm Qasr had been assigned to the United States 15th Marine Expeditionary Unit, under the command of Brigadier Jim Dutton, 3 Commando Brigade. On 21 March, US and British forces had crossed into Iraq from the Kuwaiti border, which ran close to Umm Qasr. The invasion had been well pre-pared, with a thirty-minute artillery barrage and a unit of US Marines laying out mine-cleared pathways through the giant berms that marked the frontier between Kuwait and Iraq. There had been some last-minute intelligence that Iraq T-72 tanks from the Republican Guard, Medina Division, had been seen moving down the road to cut off Umm Qasr from the main road to Basra from Safwan; the US Marines had detached an armoured unit to act as a block in case the intelligence was correct.

The initial assault was in company with the British 26th Armoured Engineer Squadron. The US Marines' convoy of twenty vehicles was met with small-arms fire, but then mortars started landing in the sand around the line of vehicles. The lead company called up supporting fire from the Royal Artillery, and the shells hit the mortar position, silencing it, but there was a general and hurried retreat as the marines realized they were too close to the target area. After three or four hours, this time with reinforcements from two US Abrams main battle tanks, 15th Marine Expeditionary Unit started once more up the road to Umm Qasr.

This time their advance was successful and they entered the old town and spread out towards the port area. There were occasional shots from Iraqi soldiers firing AK-47s, but no organized resistance, and around two hundred Iraqi troops quickly surrendered. The Stars and Stripes was raised, but quickly lowered again. A strict edict had been sent to all the troops not to fly flags and other symbols that might suggest the coalition was an occupying force. On Friday there was increased sniping and a US Marine was killed. Later that day the US secretary of defence, Donald Rumsfeld, announced at a press conference in the Pentagon that the port of Umm Qasr was secure.

It wasn't.

On Saturday 22 March the US Marines believed

that there was no further resistance in the old town and moved to the port area. They took some time to clear the railway lines and industrial area, having to search fifty empty disused port buildings for enemy forces. They were not comfortable with this type of footborne operation. They preferred to deploy in armoured vehicles and rely on tanks and aircraft to clear obstacles in front of them. Their reliance on overwhelming firepower meant that they never came into direct contact with the enemy: they couldn't make an accurate assessment of his forces, or his intentions, and never became familiar with the terrain in which they were fighting. They were never in a position to take the fight to the enemy. Also, they knew that their task was to secure the port as quickly as they could before joining the main thrust to Baghdad. The planning for Operation Iraqi Freedom had stressed speed and the downfall of the regime by taking the capital, not the steady securing of territory behind a line of advance.

On the morning of 23 March, a US patrol near the old town was once again fired on by snipers. While they were returning fire, they thought they saw a group of Iraqi forces moving into one of the warehouses on the edge of the industrial area. The patrol took up a defensive position and called in some tanks, which fired on the buildings that had been identified as possibly harbouring Iraqi soldiers. A fierce firefight broke out, with gunfire directed at the US

Marines' position, which prevented them moving forward to identify their target. They were coming under machine-gun fire, and rocket-propelled grenades were being aimed at the tanks. It was impossible for the marines to spot where the enemy was, and they called in air support.

Two RAF Harriers flew low over the town. The first bombing run resulted in one aircraft releasing a bomb on a building that disappeared in a cloud of smoke, but did not stop the enemy fire. The second aircraft was more successful, its bombs bringing the heavy machine-gun fire to a halt, but more sniper fire started to come out of the town and there was an impasse. Fighting continued into the night and the marines were unable to make any progress towards the Iraqi fighters.

It seemed to Brigadier Dutton that the 15th Marine Expeditionary Unit would need time to secure Umm Qasr, but they were scheduled to join up with the 1st Marine Expeditionary Force within the next two days. He decided that they should be relieved by another unit and that 42 Commando could take over. He gave orders that the BRF and another company would remain in their positions; be passed to 40 Commando's commander, Colonel Gordon Messenger. The remainder of 42 Commando would be rolled up and sent to Umm Qasr to take over from the US Marines. In the middle of the night, 42 Commando's operations officer was called by the watch-keeper from his shell scrape in the desert to the small command tent. He had to issue orders to the company commanders to re-form at various landing sites and road points in preparation to return to TAA Viking in Kuwait. They would restock with ammunition and other kit, then be driven the short distance to the crossing point on the Iraqi border close to Umm Qasr.

Meanwhile Colonel Howes and the command group would fly to Umm Qasr that night for a face-to-face briefing from Colonel Waldhouser, commanding officer of the 15th Marine Expeditionary Force, to discuss the handover.

It had required considerable effort for the members of 42 Commando to reach their positions on the peninsula and create the blocking line to guard 40 Commando. The collapse of the US Marines airlift had meant that they had had to walk several miles through the desert heat. The signal that they were to re-form and prepare to head out was met with disbelief: 'I had a message back from every company commander saying, "Are you serious?" ' recalled Captain Oliver Lee.

He was, of course. Early that morning, Buster Howes and Oliver Lee arrived at the US Marine Corps Company Headquarters, which had been set up in a factory in the port area of the town. Relieving a force in place where fighting is still continuing is always a difficult manoeuvre, as there is an inherent danger of confusion and conflict between friendly forces. The dangers would be particularly acute in an area like Umm Qasr where there were no maps and the old part of the town was a patchwork of narrow streets, alleyways and ancient compounds.

Buster Howes went into the colonel's office and saw on the wall a large aerial photograph of the town almost two metres by one metre square. 'Can I hang on to that?' he asked. The colonel made no objection and Buster took it off the wall.

Howes and Lee proceeded to treat it as a map, marking each street and compound with codenames and numbers. Recalling their last posting in Belfast, they named streets after those of the Northern Irish city, and other strongpoint and reporting lines after Native American tribes, until the whole photograph was crisscrossed with red and white pencil lines.

This map would be the blueprint for the replace-ment of the marines by the British Commandos, and would form the basis for the operation to seize control of the town the next day. Poring over it in the dim light of the abandoned and partly derelict factory, they worked out the procedure for the advance through the lines of US Marines. Using a common radio frequency, the British Commandos would move up from reporting line to reporting line, at each one, called Apache or Geronimo, relieving the section of US Marines stationed there. As the

Americans moved out the next reporting line would be the focus of attention, until at a certain point a particular call sign would be given, and the British forces would know that they had control of the area and did not have to worry about firing on friendly forces. They would also know where each company's areas of responsibility were.

Another problem with relieving an occupying force is that the enemy will quickly become aware of what is happening and seize the opportunity to exploit the temporary vacuum caused by the withdrawal, and the lack of local awareness of the new incoming forces. In Umm Qasr this was all possible because the US Marines had made no attempt to expand their presence into the old town and the areas around the port facilities. They had relied on remote fires, artillery or aircraft to kill the enemy, and as a consequence they were unclear about whom they were fighting, whether Republican Guard or locally based Fedayeen, or where they were based. This was a serious handicap for 42 Commando, who had to secure the town but would be doing so against an enemy that had set up its killing zones, its arcs of fire and arms caches, and would have at least limited support from a civilian population that had been antagonized by the indiscriminate use of artillery shells and bombs by US and British forces.

42 Commando set up their headquarters in an old UN barracks that had been occupied until quite

recently by a group of Bangladeshi soldiers as part of the UN monitoring force. Like any vacant building in Iraq, it had been systematically looted and, according to Sergeant Dom Collins, 'shot to shit'. But it could be defended and parts were reasonably weatherproof.

The companies that had been taken to Viking had had about eighteen hours' rest and replenishment. They had been driven into Iraq and rendezvoused at the UN building in Umm Qasr. The company commanders gathered round the photograph that Colonel Howes had turned into a map, and made their own drawings of the report lines and sectors that their command and the US colonel had agreed on. Buster Howes was convinced that the period of transition between US and British forces was the time to be bold, to throw the enemy on to the back foot and prevent them seizing the initiative. There was also, he believed, a small period of time when the population would wait to see what a new force was capable of and what it might do. The key was to get intelligence, get a hold on the areas that so far had not seen a coalition presence and to dominate the town not with long-distance weapons but with the physical presence of troops. 'You've got to get troops in among the people.' But there was a serious risk. 'Once you're among them you don't have much warning time and you're down to small-arms range.'

As the company commanders stood round the aerial reconnaissance photo of the old town and the port, they were told they were to regroup in the formations they had used in Northern Ireland and mount patrols into the town as quickly as possible. It was two o'clock in the afternoon when they arrived, and Buster Howes told Major May, 'I want you in there by half past three.'

Major 'Daisy' May, the commander of M Company, was not immediately impressed. He thought they were taking a huge risk. They had had no intelligence back from the US Marines, and were attempting to dominate a town of around 43,000 inhabitants. Dom Collins, who had been allowed to accompany Major May, felt they could expect casualties. In a classic urban-environment combat, there could be nothing else. Buster Howes didn't pull any punches in his description of the town. He told May how dangerous the place was – 'seething with hatred', as newspaper reports at the time had stated.

Major May knew what the pressures were. 'I had to get the town secure so that the ships could come alongside and start dishing out baby food and so on. We all knew what it was about.'

They went out. There were no lights, no street signs. A few marines had quad bikes, but most were on foot. Their Bergens were left in the barracks but they took plenty of ammunition, water and field dressings in day packs. A hasty mortar line was established so that in a major conflict they would be able to call on some indirect fire for support. The US

Marines were still in control of the main gate and asked the British where they were going. Dom Collins told them, and the response was 'You can't do that. It's dangerous.'

Large groups of people were gathered on the street corners, and the commandos went slowly and cautiously through the town. There was occasional rifle fire, but the Iraqis didn't clear the streets, and the shots didn't seem to be aimed particularly at the troops. They identified a Ba'ath Party headquarters in the centre of town and made for it: 'We said, "Let's go and have a look and see if anything happens,"' recalled 'Daisy' May. They approached it, but little happened. According to Major May, the atmosphere was 'relatively benign'. The patrol lasted three or four hours, and they suffered no casualties before they returned to their base in the former UN building.

The next day they went into the town just before daybreak as people were starting to go about their business. As they walked through the streets it was obvious that a lot of thought had gone into defending the town. There were no booby-traps but there were lots of defensive positions with clearly worked-out arcs of fire, trenches and arms caches, mainly of ammunition, mortars and RPGs. Potentially the Iraqis had very strong defensive positions and could have put up a strong fight if they had chosen to. Instead they had decided to abandon the town.

Buster Howes understood the risk he had asked his

men to run, but believed it had been the correct thing to do. 'One of the big dangers of an environment like the old town of Umm Qasr is that when fighting does start the advantage can quickly shift to those who know the layout, the short-cuts and the best vantage points. They have the advantage of situational awareness. So it was extremely important to create a situation where any potential enemy had to think, We're not sure where the front is. We seem to be surrounded, there are hundreds of troops, are we going to fight to the death? Are we going to give up? Are we going to filter away and look for an environment where we can continue fighting with less risk?' He thinks they chose the latter course. Within a short while, contacts were made with local civilians and, acting on their information, Howes and his men winkled out without a fight the remnants of some regular army forces that had remained hidden in the town. But the whole operation in Umm Qasr had been a gamble.

Sergeant Collins had returned to Commando Headquarters that night. Since the mission to the al-Faw peninsula had been aborted and reconstituted with a completely different plan, he had had barely any sleep. Like most of 42 Commando, he was extremely tired. He unrolled his sleeping mat and crashed out. When he woke up a Lynx helicopter was tethered close by. He was so exhausted that even the racket of its landing hadn't woken him.

* * *

Two days later, orders came for 42 Commando to start clearance operations to the north, filling in once more behind the US Marines. A particular objective was a water-treatment plant in the town of Umm Khayyal, midway between Umm Qasr and Basra. The plant needed repairing, and the plan was to send in a team of engineers so that it could supply fresh water to Umm Khayyal and the next large town of Az Zubayr. One of the key objectives in securing the town was the Ba'ath Party headquarters.

A section from J Company was directed to take the building, and they moved cautiously through the streets, trying to locate it. They had started their assault in the early morning, but had not found it by first light. The map they were working from was not very clear. Eventually they identified the building, by observing it through the scope of a sniper rifle. As they reoriented themselves and prepared to make their way to it, machine-gun fire with red tracer thudded against the walls they were standing beside. They dived for cover behind walls and buildings. The fire was intense, coming from a roof 300 metres away.

The section corporal decided to call for fire support from the mortar section, and called 3 Troop back because they were barely 200 metres from the target. They declined. The mortar rounds came in, extremely close but not hitting the target, so the troop called in corrections. The next salvo hit the roof and the firing stopped.

Now the section prepared for an assault on the building, moving forward from cover to cover while fire was directed at the windows and doors. A marine moved forward with an explosive charge and blew a hole in the wall. They hadn't observed any enemy movement for some time, so the troop commander said they were to enter the building in a 'green' state – in other words, without firing unless fired upon.

Feeling vulnerable, the troop went in through the hole in the wall and the main doors. There were no enemy left, except two soldiers who had both been injured. They were taken to the regimental aid post for treatment.

Meanwhile Company Headquarters had also come under fire. Sergeant Collins was in the Commando Headquarters in Umm Qasr, carrying out his normal duty of radio watch-keeper when news of the contact was received. He asked to be relieved and return to J Company to assist, and Buster Howes gave him the OK. He rounded up another sniper, and a member of J Company, who wanted to get back to his company, and they roared off to Umm Khayyal on a quad bike.

Company Headquarters was based in an old barracks and was under assault-rifle and RPG fire from a large block of flats that overlooked the compound. Collins and the others entered the compound, where the situation was chaotic. 3 Troop, who had returned from their firefight near the Ba'ath Party headquarters, had come under fire as they approached the barracks, and had had to find a way in that was not covered by Iraqi forces. This was the entrance Collins had used on his quad bike. It seemed it was the only way in or out of the barracks. They were effectively pinned down. The block of flats had to be taken.

Heavy fire from machine-guns was directed at it, and a section moved out of the compound to the side of the building with several LAW anti-tank rockets. They fired them, breaching an entrypoint in a wall, and moved in, with grenades and assault rifles clearing floor after floor. There was nobody in the building. The ability of the Fedayeen to mount sudden assaults and disappear in the time it took the Commandos to make their assault was remarkable.

Dom Collins joined the sniper section and they set up a secure perimeter round the barracks with 360-degree cover from the fixed sniper posts. They set up two posts on the six-storey block of flats that they had cleared, and from there they could monitor access to the buildings around the barracks, prevent any Iraqi forces assembling to mount another attack and provide cover for foot patrols. The town was quiet but there was still a lot of sniping and grenade attacks.

Two days after their initial entry to the town, Collins saw a white Nissan pickup truck drive down a road close to the barracks. His spotter said that a similar truck had been seen near the flats during the attack. Collins fired, and the bullet went through the driver's door, and hit the driver, but the vehicle did not stop. He shifted his aim and put a bullet through the engine. The truck slowed and rolled into a ditch. The driver fell out, and tumbled under the cab. The passenger also got out and stayed behind the vehicle.

Collins's partner had a more powerful rifle, a 0.338-inch calibre gun, and said he could fire through the back of the truck and kill the passenger. Collins spotted for him and they judged the range was about 850 metres. He fired, and the bullet went into the back of the pickup. Later, when they investigated, they found it had passed through the vehicle, killed the passenger and penetrated the wall of the building behind it.

They continued to survey the area and Collins saw through his binoculars someone observing them, who was dressed in the black robes and green scarf of the Fedayeen. He was crouched low on the roof of another building, also using binoculars; the glint of sunlight off the lenses had captured Dom Collins's attention. They fired two shots and the man disappeared.

They broke off their observation to discuss with

42 Commando's second-in-command what was happening, and to give their estimate of the situation, which they believed they controlled.

On returning to their position they saw a crowd round the white pickup, and a man carrying a white flag started to drag one of the occupants from under the vehicle. It was the driver. The man dragged him along the ground by his legs, leaving a long trail of blood.

Collins could not see any weapons in the crowd and held his fire. He stayed in the sniper positions at Umm Khayyal for another two days, but there were no other major incidents, although the occasional sniper fire and random fire from AK-47s never completely ended.

Collins returned to Commando Headquarters in Umm Qasr and discovered that the man he had shot, who had been dragged away under a white flag, was not dead. He had been bundled into a car and driven to the regimental aid post for treatment, where, despite having two high-velocity sniper rounds enter his body, he survived. Dom Collins met the man again, when he was being questioned about his involvement with the Fedayeen. He had to identify him as the man he had shot. When the Iraqi was informed that the commando standing in front of him was the man who had shot him he reacted, thought Collins, 'like he had been tasered.

I think he thought I had come back to finish off the job.'

40 and 42 Commandos had yet to suffer any casualty inflicted by the enemy. The Royal Navy ships were still in the northern Arabian Gulf, and the captain of HMS *Ark Royal* and his crew were relieved that D Company had been landed safely, that the most important part of their mission had been carried out without a hitch. The Sea Kings and the Chinooks were now occupied with resupplying the marines from war stocks carried on *Ark Royal* and *Ocean*, and the helicopters also returned to the ships for periodic maintenance.

Ark Royal was also operating the early-warning Sea King 7s of 849 Squadron. They were flying on a rota that kept at least one Sea King on station above the al-Faw peninsula throughout the twenty-four hours of the day. Circling at a height of around 5000 feet their Searchwater radar could search as far as Basra, and monitor the roads in and out of the city for unusual movements, tracking suspicious vehicles and passing details of these contacts via the Link 16 combined forces computer net for further investigation by Predator unmanned spy planes. It was a valuable resource that had already monitored the movement of artillery and armoured vehicles.

Each crew's time in the air was three hours, including thirty-minute airborne handovers. With seven full flying crews in the squadron, each would fly at least once a day and three crews would fly twice. A typical routine for a crew would be eight hours on watch, including three hours airborne. The watch would include briefing, debriefing and the flight. This would be followed by at least a ten-hour-off-watch period, in which the crew could get some sleep.

The sea and air space in the northern Gulf was crowded, and in the very early morning of 22 March *Ark Royal* was patrolling in a pattern that brought it close to the al-Faw peninsula. One of the problems for the crews operating from *Ark Royal* were the Tomahawk cruise missiles being launched from US warships and submarines that were further south in the Gulf. The missiles' flight paths crossed the operating area of *Ocean* and *Ark Royal,* and it was necessary to impose restrictions on flying. Helicopters approaching or leaving *Ark Royal* had to stay below 250 feet. The Sea King 7s flew at this height until they were in a safe box of air space where they were free of restriction and could climb to their operating altitude. At 0400, local time, a Sea King 7 was on *Ark Royal*'s flight deck, scheduled to take off to relieve one on station. There should normally be a handover of data in the air in the safe box. As the time for departure approached, however, one of the crew realized that a problem had developed in uploading the data link software that allowed the helicopter to transmit their radar picture to *Ark Royal* and, more importantly, to 3 Commando Brigade Headquarters and the British Divisional Headquarters in Kuwait. It was still dark, a faint hint of light on the port side heralding dawn, but the helicopter technicians on the flight deck worked by artificial light. Captain Massey was asleep in his cabin in the stern. The Sea King in the air had descended to its transit height to return to the *Ark Royal* because it was low on fuel and in contact with flight control on the aircraft-carrier. By 0420 the technical problem had been fixed. The gas turbine of the Sea King had whined up to full power, and it lifted off.

Both pilots reported that they had visual contact with each other, but then at 0424 there was a massive fireball low in the sky about four kilometres off *Ark Royal*'s bow. HMS *Liverpool*, her escort ship, immediately signalled that there had been an explosion. The phone rang in Captain Massey's cabin, and a voice said, 'We have a snag, sir. We might have lost one of our helicopters.'

Massey raced to the bridge. By then *Ark Royal* had moved slowly to the site of the explosion, and it was already clear that communication with both helicopters had been lost. 'As I got to the bridge, dawn came up and there were bits of helicopter everywhere. It was just, well, pretty bloody ghastly. It suddenly went quiet and I looked round and, sure enough, every bastard was looking at me.'

The Sea Kings had collided almost head-on, at a combined speed of about 160 knots. They were utterly destroyed and seven crew members were dead. Captain Massey ordered salvage operations to start immediately, then toured the ship. The impact on the young crew was serious. Most of them, men and women, had had no experience of combat, and the sudden deaths of seven people they knew was a severe blow. Massey was acutely aware that morale, up to this moment so good, could plummet, and he stressed that the ship still had a mission to carry out, that marines on land were still fighting and expected their support. 'Sure enough, after a couple of hours everyone was back up, and working well.'

Warrant Officer Mack McKenzie, 849 Squadron's commanding officer, was horrified, but sought refuge, like so many, in the immediate problems of keeping the operation going. He had lost half of the squadron's complement of helicopters, and a third of its aircrew. He called the remainder to the wardroom, and told them bluntly the details of the incident. He remembered painfully what he had said to them during training in the Mediterranean: that they were possibly going to war and he could not guarantee that he could bring them all back alive. The truth of that statement had been vividly brought home ... But he had not assembled the crews to dwell on the loss of their friends. There was a mission to keep running. At the moment there were no helicopters in the air, and he called for volunteers to take up the standby aircraft, and resume operations. They all stepped forward. There was some disquiet about the rules for flying during Tomahawk missile launches, but they saw that little could be done about it. Within the hour another Sea King 7 was powering away from *Ark Royal*, and the two Sea Kings maintained their surveillance patrols for the next week.

On 23 March McKenzie was in the air when his radar operator announced a series of interesting contacts to the south-east of Basra. They turned out to be three self-propelled howitzers, two T-55 tanks and an armoured personnel-carrier, heading down Highway 6 to 40 Commando's position. They never made it.

42 Commando's effort to secure the port of Umm Qasr was not enough to allow ships to use it again. The original concern had been that the waterway's banks should be cleared of enemy forces before ships could travel up it; 40 and 42 Commandos had done that, but it was also necessary to make sure that the Khawr 'Abd Allah wasn't mined. If a relief ship was holed and sunk, the port would be completely blocked and a salvage operation could take weeks.

The first mine-sweeper into the waterway was HMS *Brocklesby*. She had the lowest sonar and magnetic signature of all the mine-sweepers and was least likely to detonate a mine. She found eighty Manta mines laid in a row close to the shipping lane. They were destroyed in a controlled detonation, but after this discovery any strange object on the seabed – there were lots dating from the Iran–Iraq war and the invasion of Kuwait – had to be investigated. The US Navy had flown in their Mammals Unit, trained dolphins that would leave electronic tags close to suspicious objects; with the animals and Royal Naval Clearance divers, the channel was eventually declared safe.

The dolphins had been flown in from their base in Tampa, Florida, slung in hammocks made of sheepskin constantly sprayed with water. They were a constant attraction to visiting officers from Kuwait and the task group at sea, and Admiral Snelson made an effort to see them on his first visit to Umm Qasr.

The first relief ship to tie up in the port of Umm Qasr was the Royal fleet auxiliary *Sir Galahad*, which finally docked on 28 March some days later than expected. There was an enormous amount of publicity, but in fact aid had been getting into Iraq via several routes for days. The capture of Umm Khayyal had secured a route from Kuwait via Safwan. But various aid agencies now started to mobilize resources, and the liberation of Umm Qasr had delivered a propaganda victory.

The initial tasks of 40 and 42 Commandos had

been completed. The oil facilities had been secured, al-Faw town and the peninsula had been cleared of enemy troops and Iraq's deep-water port had been made available to the coalition for the delivery of civilian aid and military supplies. Remarkably, there had been no casualties to enemy action.

However, the rest of the peninsula, and the city of Basra lay to the north. Basra had never been part of 3 Commando Brigade's list of confirmed objectives, but Colonel Gordon Messenger was already considering what he could do next. In part this hinged on how quickly the US could advance north to Baghdad. But a large swathe of country between al-Faw and Basra had to be secured, irrespective of whether or not the regime surrendered, and any forces moving up it would quickly get a feel for the intentions of the city's defenders. As the tasks were ticked off, Basra would inevitably start moving up the list.

11

OPERATION LEAH – FINDING THE SHAPE OF THE ENEMY

Colonel Gordon Messenger was tired, but he knew that most of the men he commanded in 40 Commando, Royal Marines, were far more exhausted than he was. The fear and the adrenalin rush of their night assault into Iraq would have made huge demands on their physical and mental resources. But before that, in shell scrapes in the Kuwaiti desert, their sleep had been disturbed by the constant gas alarms as incoming Scud missiles roared over them. Now there were still intermittent firefights with the Iraqi military and other irregular forces.

From the perspective of a commanding officer, the assault by 40 Commando had gone well, with no casualties except the burns victims from al-Faw town. Even the period of extreme vulnerability in the immediate hours of their landing had passed without significant efforts by Iraqi forces to drive them off the peninsula, or to fix them in their landing sites unable to move forward and secure the area. Gordon Messenger was aware, however, that the most sporadic firefights were stressful for the marines involved in them. Isolated some kilometres away from Commando Main Headquarters, guarding a remote position on the edge of the sea at a pipeline terminal, even the threat of a small-arms, mortar or RPG attack would deprive most sections involved of anything but snatched moments of sleep.

Some companies were also suffering from a shortage of water and lacked the transport that their plans had been based around. Major Matt Jackson's B Company had kitted out their machine-gun-fitted Land Rovers with camouflage netting, fuel and reflective identification panels in the hours before their assault on the pipeline terminals, and had never seen them again. Their sole means of movement was by six quad bikes. Messenger had argued that 40 Commando needed a pause to consolidate its position, and finish securing al-Faw town, removing any armed elements of the regime who might still be lodged there, but he had lost that one.

With 42 Commando moved to complete the capture of Umm Qasr and the port, it now fell to 40 Commando to press forward and secure the whole of the al-Faw peninsula. The eastern boundary followed the Shatt al-Arab waterway, the international border with Iran and through which the Tigris and

Euphrates rivers emptied into the Gulf. Along the bank there was a strip about a kilometre wide of dense vegetation, palm groves and houses, broken up by canals and irrigation channels, with small jetties and docks lined with craft of all types; the Shatt al-Arab provided fishing and transport for those who lived along the banks. It had been a major waterway to Basra at one time, but now the wrecks of large ships sunk in the Iran–Iraq war still blocked the channel, their bows sticking high out of the water, or lying on their side, slowly corroding. Inland was a road that followed the western line of the vegetation and beyond. Further to the west was a straight road, Highway 6, raised on a bank that cut north across the mudflats. Anything travelling along this road would be highly visible, and would have no room to manoeuvre, because each side of the road had been either mined or was waterlogged. Travelling north along the eastern road also presented problems because in parts the vegetation was impenetrable to reconnaissance flights and other surveillance, and could easily conceal Iraqi forces.

Moving north had not been among 40 Commando's original objectives. The possibility of expanding from the initial area of responsibility had been loosely discussed, but with the withdrawal of 42 Commando there was now a need to fill the vacuum on the peninsula. General Robin Brims, the Commander, UK Division was telling 3 Commando Brigade

Headquarters to move north and be seen to do so, keeping a clear line of advance in parallel with the other forces of the UK's main effort in the south.

Apart from 3 Commando Brigade, those other units that formed the British 1st Armoured Division were the 7th Armoured Brigade, the 16th Air Assault Brigade and the 102nd Logistics Brigade. With more than a hundred Challenger tanks and 130 armoured vehicles, the 7th Armoured Brigade was a significant addition to the coalition's tank forces in Iraq, and they had the main task of spearheading the drive towards Basra, sprinting the seventy miles to the outskirts of the city. As yet there was no firm plan for how the city would be taken, but with the advance of the 7th Armoured, the al-Faw peninsula had also to be cleared to prevent an Iraqi counter-attack moving south to attack their right flank.

The Brigade Reconnaissance Force (BRF) under Captain Chris Haw stayed in place and was transferred to 40 Commando under Colonel Messenger. Combined with 40 Commando's own Reconnaissance Troop and the Manoeuvre Support Group (MSG) under Captain Paul Lynch they were to form the advance guard of the Commando's move forward. They were highly mobile, and comparatively well armed. All of their vehicles had been helicoptered into the monitoring and metering station (MMS) as part of the second wave, and the combined force was composed of around thirty vehicles. The MSG had seven – three Pinzgauer 4×4s mounting two Milan anti-tank missile systems with one on top ready to fire, and another three Pinzgauers designed to carry two general-purpose machine-guns in the sustained-fire role. There was a Land Rover fitted with radio and signals equipment, the headquarters and communications vehicle, and a US Humvee, which carried the US Marine Corps ANGLICO – Air Naval Gunfire Liaison Company – team for calling in US air support, plus other Land Rovers, with the forward observer officer party to direct the Commandos' own heavy mortar and artillery fire.

The vehicles, which had started their transformation on board *Ocean* and *Ark Royal*, were now unrecognizable. They were covered with mud, sacking covered their headlights to avoid reflections, body panels and roofs stripped off, weapon mounts had been welded on, and the vehicles were draped with camouflage netting to break up their silhouettes. They were festooned with day sacks, bedrolls, spare missile tubes and the marines, boots muddy, wearing body armour and carrying ammunition pouches, grenades, radios and ration packs looked equally rough and ready.

From their assembly point at the MMS, they headed north along the road. They were going to set up a series of defensive anti-armour blocks, and probe through the inhabited, densely cultivated area along the Shatt al-Arab. As Captain Chris Haw described it: 'We were to locate the targets, try not to get decisively engaged, go round them and pass the targets on to the guys behind, who were the Manoeuvre Support Group.' They expected an Iraqi counter-attack soon, and it would be useful to have some idea of what shape the enemy forces were in before they arrived. 'We thought, to start with, there would be a significant sort of military line on the ground. Then we thought, Well, if it's not the case and they're not doing deliberate attacks on us, we'll meet small groups of insurgents or military. We were expecting to get ambushed. That's what the score was.'

The Iraqi armed forces had fought an enormously long and bloody war against the Iranians during the 1980s, then had been defeated in Kuwait by the US and its allies. They ought to have been battle-hardened and experienced. However, they had been seriously weakened by the nature of the regime they served.

Iraqi society had been fundamentally affected by the Ba'ath Party's dictatorship. It had taken power through a military coup in 1968. Saddam Hussein was a senior figure in the Party leadership, respons-ible for organizing the secret police. He had used this power not only to create a reign of terror that permeated Iraqi society, but also to build his own power base within the Party. In 1979 he felt strong enough to stage an internal coup, then assumed absolute power. The way he achieved this showed the unique skills he would continue to deploy to ensure that he retained his grip on power. In a meeting of senior Ba'ath Party leaders Saddam plotted with his supporters to denounce sixty delegates for planning to overthrow the leadership. The hapless victims were led out of the conference hall and immediately shot, allegedly by other delegates whom Saddam would appoint government ministers. From then on, he played faction off against faction, with the ever-present threat of death and torture. Any dissent was dealt with mercilessly and Iraq became cut off from the outside world. Travel was restricted, surveillance omnipresent; newspapers and magazines became propaganda outlets, and access to the Internet, fax machines and satellite services was heavily controlled. The regime of fear had a profound effect on the military preparedness of the Iraqi armed forces. Those who criticized policy, or brought bad news, were dealt with harshly: senior military figures were jailed for trying to warn of deficiencies in equipment or training, or to raise the alarm about US intentions.

Everyone lied to everyone else for their own safety. Despite the defeat in Kuwait at the hands of the coalition in 1991, the myth was generated that, given the overwhelming superiority of the US and its allies, since there had been no invasion of Iraq, and the Republican Guard had survived almost intact, the war had been a victory. This was attributed to Saddam's superior wisdom and strategic thinking. The conclusions he drew from the first Gulf war were not the same as those of Western observers.

To Saddam it was apparent that the biggest threat to his survival lay not in an invasion by the US and other Western states but in an uprising of Shias and Kurds. The coalition's refusal to invade Iraq in 1991 proved to him that the US was unwilling to risk significant casualties in a land war, and would hesitate to send troops into Iraq.

He became obsessed with the internal threat to his power. In 1998 Iraq was divided into four administrative regions, governed by four trusted senior members of the Ba'ath Party, who were also in overall command of the military units in their regions. They reported directly to Saddam, bypassing the Ministry of Defence and Iraqi intelligence.

Ever conscious of how he himself had come to power, Saddam was always suspicious that the armed forces might be plotting a coup to dispose of him. Officers were not allowed to meet to discuss matters of common concern, restrictions were placed on the movement of the army, and the most sycophantic commanders were promoted. In addition, Saddam devoted enormous resources to internal security, creating a system of secret agencies to spy on the various defence and security organizations. His suspicion extended even to the Republican Guard, a specially trained and equipped unit of the army that had been set up to defend the regime at the end of the Iran–Iraq war. They were supplied with the most modern arms, were better paid and housed than other army groups. Another even more elite Unit had been created, the Special Republican Guard whose sole task was to defend Saddam. While the Republican Guard was stationed around Baghdad, to defend the regime, only the Special Republican Guard was authorized to enter the city itself, and they formed a large personal bodyguard for the dictator.

Even the Special Republican Guard was riddled with informers and spies from the security and intelligence organizations, of which there were so many that spies from several different agencies attended military committees and conferences. By 2002 there was the Special Security Office, the Iraqi Intelligence Service, the Directorate of General Security and the General Directorate of Military Intelligence. There was also a Republican Guard Security Office. Such was the level of paranoia that no military commander dared to start a meeting without every spy being present, in case one agency or another accused him of holding secret meetings. Many of the intelligence and security services had developed their own military-style capabilities, often at the expense of the Iraqi Army and the Republican Guard. It was said that Republican Guard commanders were not trusted to conduct any exercise or even start a tank without permission.

Two other politically based militias were called into existence after the Kuwait war, the most important being the Ba'ath Party militia and the Fedayeen Saddam volunteers. The latter was set up in October 1994, as a response to the uprisings when it became clear to Saddam that the local Ba'ath Party branches were incapable of suppressing dissent without assistance, and the army was too cumbersome to act with sufficient speed. Uday, Saddam's eldest son, was appointed to lead it.

The Fedayeen Saddam opened its own para-military training camps for volunteers, training more than seven thousand in the first year alone. In the build-up to the allied invasion, courses were acceler-ated under the guidance of the General Directorate of Military Intelligence. The volunteers attended thirty-day courses in physical training, weapons training and communications. Their programme of activities focused on small arms, and small-unit tactics, sabotage techniques and reconnaissance. A strong disciplinary code was enforced, with severe punishments for military failure.

In 2003, as the prospect of war drew closer, the regime made preparations aimed at sustaining the Fedayeen and Ba'ath Party militia. Weapons and ammunition were moved out of the main arsenals while Ba'ath Party officials and militia leaders were asked to establish food, fuel and ammunition caches.

They were distributed to places that the regime would be able to maintain control of, such as schools, mosques or local Party centres.

The Ba'ath Party militia was also told to make its own preparations. In Az Zubayr town, for example, the Party headquarters was called on to set up a meeting for local tribal chiefs, families and religious leaders to work out the best way to defend against invasion. Tabletop exercises were arranged for Party groups, protective shelters built on main roads and at junctions. In many cities and towns it was the responsibility of the Ba'ath Party to set up strongpoints and dig trenches. But despite these preparations, Iraqi defences swung into action only at the last moment.

Plans had been drawn up for the defence of Basra at the beginning of 2003, and some of these documents were captured after the war. The city lay in the southern region under the command of Ali Hassan al-Majid, Saddam's cousin, a member of the Revolutionary Command Council and notorious for his masterminding of the chemical-weapons attacks on the Kurds.

The defensive plan called on regular army units such as the III and IV Corps of the regular army, elements of the General Directorate of Military Intelligence and units of the Fedayeen Saddam, so incorporated layers of both regular armed forces and militias. Fixed strongpoints throughout the area were guarded by defensive screens based on obstacles such as bunkers and dug-in tanks.

The chief objective was to force the enemy into exposed positions, delay his forward movement and seek to divert him into killing zones where major losses could be inflicted. This would be achieved with minefields, and the creation of small fortified positions. It was intended that self-sufficient infantry companies, reinforced with a variety of anti-tank and anti-aircraft weapons, would hinder the movement of enemy forces that were being channelled via the minefields and strong-points. These companies could also call on tanks and armoured cars. The enemy, once they were driven into prepared killing grounds in this way, would be destroyed by an armoured battle group, firing from cover, assisted by pre-positioned artillery batteries. This process would be repeated as the heavier units would fall back to prepared positions. The plan recognized that the artillery and the main strike forces of tanks would need to be adequately defended with anti-aircraft weapons, and to seek cover from aerial reconnaissance and attack. Finally, it was expected that groups of Fedayeen Saddam would operate in front of the lead artillery units. Any retreat would be punishable by execution.

That was the plan. In reality, there were serious weaknesses with the army's equipment. The road to Basra from Umm Qasr was guarded by the 6th Armoured Division, the 18th Infantry Division and the 51st Mechanized Division, but of the 250 tanks that should have been available, 220 were usable, and only about 145 were in good repair. Spare parts were hard to come by and the usable tanks were, at best, capable of operating at around 75 per cent efficiency. Morale was low and the regular forces were not prepared to put up much resistance. Opposition from the Iraqi Army guarding the oil installations had been slow and uncoordinated, and the Royal Marine Commandos had benefited from the severity of the initial fire that had rained down on the defences prior to the assault, and the speed and determination they had shown when they landed. After their initial success against the regular forces, it was the irregular Fedayeen Saddam who had regrouped and organized stiff resistance in Umm Qasr – where, clearly, they had reinfiltrated the town after the initial contact between the US Marines and the Iraqi Army – and in urban areas such as al-Faw town.

One worrying factor for Colonel Gordon Messenger was that the intelligence picture assembled before 20 March had proved inaccurate. 40 Commando had been outnumbered by the Iraqis based in the al-Faw peninsula, but their low morale and lack of commitment had contributed to their defeat. If they had been better organized, the initial landing on the oil facilities might not have been the success that it was, and 40 Commando might have suffered severe casualties.

The war was now several days old, and Saddam's regime had had time to set up resistance. The question that needed answering was whether more Iraqi forces were concealed in the terrain along the Shatt al-Arab, and whether their defensive planning was capable of being put into action.

Now 40 Commando were tasked to move up the al-Faw peninsula, and seek answers. They would discover the extent to which Iraqi defences were becoming stronger the closer they got to Basra. This advance was given the name Operation Leah.

The squadron of twelve Scimitar armoured vehicles from the Queen's Dragoon Guards should, in the original plan, have joined up with 40 Commando shortly after they had landed. Instead they had remained afloat on USS *Rushmore*, their dock landing ship, until their landing on the al-Faw peninsula close to Major Jackson's B Company had been aborted. Then they had returned to Kuwait and were transported north to the Iraqi border. They passed Umm Qasr and crossed the Khawr 'Abd Allah waterway by landing craft. Even this far inland the inlet was affected by tides and one Scimitar's crew, caught out by a misreading of the tide tables, had to be evacuated as their vehicle slowly disappeared, stern first, into the muddy waters. Ironically, as the tide receded, those trying to recover the Scimitar to tow it to safety realized that the bank they were negotiating had also been mined, and was potentially as dangerous as the beach on which the US Navy hovercraft commander had refused to land two days earlier.

The bulk of the squadron had entered Iraq safely, and travelled along the southern coast road of the al-Faw peninsula, then headed north to join up with 40 Commando. They rendezvoused early on the morning of 24 March, and made contact with the BRF. There, they split, and one troop of Scimitars moved forward to set up observation posts, while another moved north along Highway 6 with Chris Haw and the BRF. It was a strange terrain. Captain Haw remembers that 'To our right flank was a whole load of date palms, trees and houses, with narrow roads going down to the river. If you looked to your left you could see for miles, just berms and roads and electricity pylons. The way I worked it was to send the Scimitars up the main road to see if they got engaged because they had armour, albeit very thin, and we would make our way through the more complex terrain and the roads in between.'

When the plans for 40 and 42 Commandos' scheme of manoeuvre were being drawn up, one of the main threats was thought to be the presence of an armoured brigade based in Basra. There had been no sign of this in the days following the landing. Now the threat seemed to be emerging.

The forward observation posts that the Scimitars had established started to detect activity by Iraqi

Army trucks moving along a highway in the dark. The assumption was that they were moving troops into positions to block access to Basra. The next morning the Scimitars saw even more activity. To the east infantry were being moved to a prepared defensive line north of Highway 6, supported by T-55 tanks, dug in to provide arcs of fire to the south, covering the main approaches. Helicopters from 847 Squadron found the tanks difficult to spot as they were hidden in a plantation, and the pilots were unwilling to attack them because they were close to civilian houses. In the west there was more tank movement and a Scimitar from another squadron was fired on by a T-55. A Striker, a Scimitar that mounted an anti-tank missile, was called up and destroyed the T-55, then attacked the bunker system and watchtower.

Brigade Headquarters also received a report that an Iraqi tank battalion made up of fifty T-55s had been seen advancing out of Basra towards the al-Faw peninsula. One of the brigade's signals intelligence units intercepted some Iraqi radio traffic and was able to gain some assessment of the form-up position of the tanks. Several options were open to the Brigade, and they decided to wait till morning before making a final decision about how best to deal with it. Then, during the night of 24 March, Gordon Messenger was informed on the communications net that a brigade of sixty T-55s was approaching his positions. 'I was moving forward when I was told that potentially we were going to be attacked by up to sixty tanks. I asked my anti-tank officer what our stocks were of Milan missiles. His reply that in total in the Commando we had fifty-eight didn't help to calm my nerves.'

The Scimitars of C Squadron had also received signals about enemy tank movement, and at daybreak they saw a company of four T-55s moving from east to west. An aviation patrol of Lynx and Gazelle helicopters from HMS *Ocean*, tasked to carry out anti-armour patrols, was fired on, then the tanks directed their main armament at the Scimitars. At first the shells fell short, but it would be only a matter of time before they found their target. The 105-mm shell from the T-55's main gun would easily penetrate the aluminium armour of a Scimitar, and the 30-mm cannon in the Scimitar's turret could not penetrate the T-55's armour. Outgunned, the Scimitars pulled back and requested aircraft support. Two A-10 aircraft were directed into the attack and, with their bombs and rapid-firing cannons, quickly destroyed the T-55s.

The Iraqis continued to send armour, tanks and armoured personnel-carriers into the area throughout the day, and the forward air controller based with C Squadron continued to call F-18 and A-10 aircraft to attack the vehicles and the bunker systems they were moving to reinforce.

The main concentration of T-55s that had been

pinpointed by signals intelligence, and whose estimated size had so alarmed Gordon Messenger, had not advanced but remained in place in the area south of Basra, still potentially threatening 40 Commando. 3 Commando Brigade decided it was best dealt with using artillery and aircraft. A Company under Major Justin Holt had received preliminary orders to be prepared to deploy from their company position in the metering station by helicopter as a quick-reaction force if the Brigade Reconnaissance Forces and the Manoeuvre Support Group met any significant resistance while clearing the banks of the Shatt al-Arab. Instead, on the afternoon of 24 March they were told to make themselves ready to go forward in six Sea King helicopters to form a guard for 8 Battery 29 Commando, Royal Artillery, who would be moved forward to carry out an artillery raid, firing a barrage of 105-mm shells on to the T-55s.

The afternoon wore on, and eventually, confirming Justin's belief that any order involving more than thirty men and helicopters would be a mess, two Chinooks arrived. They were lifted, in three waves, to a position halfway up the al-Faw peninsula. They landed; it took some time to collect the company together as darkness had fallen by the time the last of the six Chinook flights had arrived and the manoeuvre was complete. They occupied a defensive line, dug in and kept radio watches. The night was cold and the company wore their NBC suits to keep themselves warm.

The devastating gunfire from 8 Battery and attacks from F-18s and A-10 aircraft destroyed twenty T-55s, and the rest retreated back to Basra. The tank threat had been deflected for the time being. The artillery battery was lifted by helicopter to their former position, leaving A Company isolated in the desert.

D Company had also re-formed in the metering station, having cleared the military installations on the peninsula and joined up with B Company on the pipelines. Their commanding officer, Major Matt Pierson, was expecting to stay and continue with the occupation of al-Faw town when he received orders to dig out the maps for seventy kilometres north. He pushed up behind the BRF and the MSG, moving through the palm groves, meeting little opposition. Where they came across a stronghold or other resistance he would order his mortar troop to fire some illuminating rounds over the enemy positions, then use the psychological-warfare officer and his loudspeaker to call on the troops to surrender or move away. In all the incidents they encountered, Matt Pierson found that, given the opportunity, the regular Iraqi soldiers, conscripts for the most part, would abandon their posts. He was happy with this: 'I didn't want to go chalking up the kills.'

By 25 March the weather was deteriorating. A storm was expected, and Colonel Messenger knew this would limit the availability of air cover. The threat of enemy tanks had receded, but he knew it could appear again quite quickly. A Company was very far forward and, unlike the BRF and the MSG, were dependent on helicopters for mobility. If they were attacked by enemy armour, it would be a replay of Custer's last stand. Gordon Messenger's forces were spread out over twenty-five kilometres and even his mobile anti-tank forces in the BRF and the MSG were no match for a serious encounter with heavy armour. He felt vulnerable, and continued to do so for the next two days.

A Company were told to set up an anti-armour block across the road that stretches across the mud-flats heading to Basra. Justin Holt moved 2 and 3 Troops astride the road below the raised levee, where they dug in, but the storm that they had observed on the horizon had advanced, and rain turned the area into a quagmire. There was also a strong wind, which was growing in intensity. Major Holt called for the troops' Bergens to be brought forward because they needed waterproof clothing. It was hours before a truck arrived, and then the working party unloading them was blown off their feet by the storm. The truck they were unloading started to slide across the road. Everyone took shelter where they could, Major Holt crouching behind a pile of rations, and waited for the storm to blow itself out.

With the first light of dawn, the rain had stopped but A Company were in a sorry state. 3 Troop was in an area that had been completely flooded; their shell scrapes were filled with water and they were huddled together for warmth. They moved up on to the raised road, which was drier but provided no cover. There was, however, no sign of the enemy and the morning sun gave everyone the chance to dry out, and clean the mud off weapons and kit.

Later that day Holt received a message telling him that A Company would be making another move, this time ten kilometres west, to take up another blocking position on a main route. He located a defensive position that appeared to be a hangover from the Iran–Iraq war, and decided to occupy it. This time a fleet of requisitioned Iraqi eight-ton trucks moved them to their new position, about thirty kilometres east of Basra. There, they were instructed to stand firm.

On the same day, 26 March, Colonel Messenger was told by Brigade that twelve Challenger II main battle tanks from C Squadron, the Scots Dragoon Guards, had been detached from the British 7th Armoured Brigade and would be deployed with 40 Commando. They were on their way to help clear the Commando's northern limit of advance. The Commando was now growing in strength, and Gordon Messenger's anxieties were diminishing. The Challengers could not come a moment too soon. As they moved forward on 27 March another Iraqi armoured thrust was launched against 40 Commando's area. A group of fourteen T-55s moved south, but were met and engaged by the Challengers. It was no contest: the Challengers' armour was better, their guns were bigger and more accurate, with a greater rate of fire, and their laser range-finders meant they could range and lock on to a target while the tank was being manoeuvred at speed. All the T-55s were hit and destroyed, without any significant damage to the Challengers.

That morning, which was cold and shivery, A Company was trying to make itself comfortable in its northern outpost. They were told that the Challengers should be upon them soon, and that also the artillery to the west had destroyed another ten Iraqi armoured personnel-carriers. The Challengers came through A Company's position and stopped to refuel. They were going forward to clear some enemy infantry positions, and the sight of them made everyone in A Company feel considerably less exposed.

To the east Captains Chris Haw and Paul Lynch had moved aggressively forward in their mobile column, followed by D Company. As they made their way up the al-Faw peninsula, various troops had minor encounters with armed Fedayeen in the palm groves, but the contacts never developed into lengthy fighting. There was as much shooting from the Iranian guards on the other side of the Shatt al-Arab as there was from Iraqi forces. Most of the time, as they worked their way along the road and sent patrols into the settlements along the river, they found abandoned positions and piles of uniforms. But all the time the Iraqis were aware of where they were. 'We were not encountering pockets of enemy soldiers as we expected, we were actually engaging these artillery spotters. We could see they had uniforms on but they were driving white civilian SUVs, and there would be the occasional gunfight with them.' Their progress was rapid, until they reached their final reporting line and were ordered to remain in position, 'to go firm'.

The Brigade Reconnaissance Force was also now in a potentially vulnerable position. Chris Haw was unhappy. 'We found ourselves with a couple of anti-tank missiles and all the vehicles lined up along the side of the road, and I was thinking, We're just a sitting duck, really. We couldn't go any further, we couldn't go back, and we couldn't go sideways because of mines. We had to wait there for two to three days, thinking that any minute something could just go off.'

40 Commando had reached the limit of its area of operation, and had to wait for further orders. Their advance had been rapid, and they were in position on a line that stretched west, almost two-thirds of the way from al-Faw town to Basra. Soon they would enter the suburbs, industrial docks and fishing ports that stretched along the west bank of the Shatt al-Arab from the edge of the city.

But the palm groves and fishing villages along the Shatt al-Arab remained calm. Night was the deep black of a countryside without electric lights, silence, except for stray dogs barking or a shout that could be heard for half a mile. The population went to bed at dusk and woke at dawn. So far, there had been no major enemy formations concealed among the palms, and the Iraqi forces, whether regular army or armed militia, had not made a stand. Would they? And if so, when and where?

12

KICKING DOWN THE DOOR

The bulk of 40 Commando had reached its objectives in the move up the al-Faw peninsula and was fixed in place to the south of Basra, having covered almost sixty kilometres in just a few days. It had the support of a squadron of Scimitar tracked vehicles, from the Queen's Dragoon Guards, and a much more comforting squadron of Challenger main battle tanks from the Royal Scots Dragoon Guards, capable of fighting off any armour the Iraqis possessed. Colonel Gordon Messenger felt more comfortable in his forward position than he had for some days.

Basra, the second city of Iraq, was now threatened from the south and west by the marines and the 7th Armoured Brigade. The UK's land forces commander, General Robin Brims, knew that the US CentCom commander, General Tommy Franks, was coming under pressure from Washington to deliver some rapid results in the battle for Baghdad, which had not fallen as quickly as the war's main cheerleaders had prophesied.

The activity of the Fedayeen, their asymmetric guerrilla tactics – setting ambushes, employing hit-and-run attacks in areas that US forces had already passed through – had come as a surprise and had prompted US commanders on the battlefield to reconsider their plans. The US general in command of land forces in southern Iraq, Lieutenant General David McKiernan, wanted to delay the thrust to Baghdad until the towns and villages they had bypassed had been properly cleared – to complete the job that 42 Commando had carried out in Umm Qasr and Az Zubayr, thereby removing the threat to supply lines and rear-echelon forces. He consulted the commanders of the US Marine Corps and the US V Armored Corps and decided on 27 March that there would be a pause in the advance to Baghdad. They had little choice, as the advance of V Corps over the Euphrates had already been blocked by strong fighting from Fedayeen forces.

He put the idea to Franks, who was unhappy: he knew that it would not play well with Donald Rumsfeld and the other hawks in the Pentagon. There was political pressure for a quick victory, evidence that would show the world that the war would be short and successful.

The decision to pause the advance on Baghdad highlighted what should be done about Basra. Originally the plan had been to bypass it, but the appearance of the Fedayeen as a military force suggested that this might not be an adequate strategy. Also, Basra was an important city, and a defeat here for the Iraqi Army might trigger a collapse across the country. Moreover, its fall into the hands of the coalition forces would be the victory that President Bush and Tony Blair needed in the first week of the war.

General Brims was aware of the influences on the changing strategy towards Basra. General McKiernan, his US commanding officer, had now told him to take Basra, but he would not be railroaded into an assault on such a large city. Basra had a population of around 1.5 million, according to the official statistics, but if the experience of the Commandos in towns like al-Faw and Umm Qasr was anything to go by, it seriously understated the true size of the population.

Taking a city of that size was a forbidding prospect. House-to-house fighting was costly in men, time and casualties, all of which could be avoided by subjecting the city to a massive artillery and air bombardment, but that was out of the question. Thousands of civilians would be killed or made homeless, and an important part of the Iraqi economy would have been destroyed for decades. Even if this was politically acceptable, which it wasn't, Brims would have found it reprehensible.

At the end of the Kuwait war the area around Basra had been the scene of a major uprising against Saddam Hussein. It had been bloodily suppressed. On the evening of 24 March reports had been received that a similar uprising had started in the city, which seemed to have been suppressed by the Republican Guard and the Ba'ath Party militia. These organizations were under the command of Ali Hassan al-Majid, who had orchestrated the use of chemical weapons against the Iranians and Kurds during the Iran–Iraq war. 'Chemical Ali', as he was known, was Saddam Hussein's representative, the regime's organizer in the city and the area now occupied by the British.

There was no sign that the Ba'ath Party had lost its grip on Basra so, rather than make an assault on the city, Brims preferred to get the Iraqi forces to leave it. He left a route open to the north, so that food and supplies could enter while Iraqi forces retreated. He played a waiting game, making a few exploratory raids into the outskirts of the city with armoured vehicles, testing the defences and gathering intelligence. If the fighting around Baghdad and in the rest of Iraq brought down the regime before he had to invade Basra, so much the better.

3 Commando Brigade Reconnaissance Force (BRF) were positioned at the leading edge of 40 Commando's area of responsibility, facing a suburb

of Basra, Abu al-Khasib, that stretched south for several kilometres between a major road and the Shatt al-Arab waterway. The area looked as though it had been fortified, and the BRF, with D Company, had been carrying out their own exploratory attacks on the town. The first major objective was a bridge across a waterway that cut off access to the town from the east. If there was going to be any attempt to capture Abu al-Khasib then the bridge, code-named Sennen, would be vital in allowing the marines to enter the town along the banks of the Shatt al-Arab.

The first raid was carried out by a company-sized squad, mounted on WMIK Land Rovers and Pinzgauers, carrying machine-guns and 51-mm mortars. There was no attempt to take prisoners or seize control of territory; the raids were purely intended as harassment. Machine-gun fire would be directed at any Iraqis firing, and illumination rounds were fired from the 51-mm mortars, which seemed effective in silencing the opposition. 'We discovered through talking to people we had taken prisoner that as soon as the illuminating rounds went up the enemy were so scared that they just ran away,' recalls Captain Chris Haw.

The next raid was slightly more aggressive, and much better armed. It was designed to destroy two suspected gun positions that were defending the approaches to the bridge. Four WMIKs, carrying

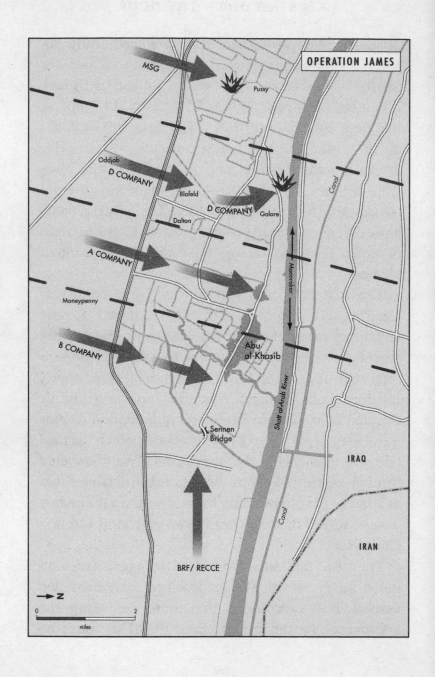

eight general-purpose machine-guns, were the base-line offensive weapons. The troop also carried mortars, anti-tank rockets, and their hand-held machine-guns. The raid would be supported by artillery fire if it was requested by the forward observation officer. It was a phenomenal amount of firepower. Captain Haw came up with a plan to put in a blocking force, then 'The WMIKs would drive up the road bold as brass and engage these two positions, and once they'd been destroyed we would then recover back to the location.' It was an extremely simple plan but it worked. Captain Haw was proud of this: 'It was the first direct action that my organization, the BRF, had done since the Falklands in 1982 when the Mountain Arctic Warfare cadre attacked Top Marlow House and killed some Argentinian special forces in there. As a reconnaissance force we're not normally in contact getting the rounds down.'

These escalating raids were designed partly to test the defences, to gauge what level of reinforcements the Iraqis were able to bring up, and whether they would stand and fight or melt into the built-up areas and palm groves at the first contact. They also helped to create a pattern of behaviour so that when the marines did embark on a serious attack the Iraqi defenders would not immediately recognize it as anything different from a night raid and similar to one that had gone before.

Colonel Gordon Messenger thought it would be

possible to take the suburb, paving the way for an assault on Basra. The Commando planning team looked at their options and went with a rough outline to Brigadier Dutton, at Commando Headquarters in a disused factory outside Az Zubayr. The team looked at the assumptions and the scheme of manoeuvre, which was called Operation James, after Colonel Messenger's son. The operation was seen as the perfect way to put pressure on the forces in Basra, but without committing to a major assault on the city.

After some discussions between Brigadier Dutton and General Brims, Gordon Messenger was given preliminary approval. He had the bulk of 40 Commando at his disposal, and the BRF was in place, conducting raids against their immediate objective, the bridge codenamed Sennen that was a main route into Abu al-Khasib. C Company, which had landed on the monitoring and metering station (MMS) in the al-Faw peninsula, had been left there to hold the oil infrastructure and the town of al-Faw. Five troops from C Company had been detached to B Company to strengthen it, while A and D Companies were also available.

The company commanders met at the sprawling 40 Commando Headquarters, in some old school buildings, on 28 March for their orders group for Operation James. From that meeting Major Matt Jackson formed the impression that Brigade Headquarters was reluctant to give the final go-ahead, but Gordon Messenger believed that, with the US main effort now held back, there would be a move to consolidate the coalition forces before entering south-east Basra, and that the operation would take place in three or four days. The orders group had been called in anticipation of this. Matt Jackson's memory is true in one sense: Brigade had not passed the Execute order to the Commando Main HQ to implement the operation.

The scheme of manoeuvre that Colonel Messenger outlined was complicated. There were a lot of moving parts, because intelligence was sparse. It would be an advance to contact. Commando Headquarters knew that there were T-55 tanks, both mobile and dug-in, hull down, stationed around the periphery of the area, and that the city had been fortified with large numbers of troops. But there was little information about the exact location of the Iraqis, and there was some doubt about the reliability of the intelligence. Much had come from the local civilian population who had been passing through the marines' checkpoints over the past few days and it was not easy to tell if the information was accurate or, perhaps, deliberately misleading.

In short, as Gordon Messenger summed up: 'The plan was to kick the ants' nest, and see what came out.'

In phase one of the operation two troops of a

squadron of Challenger II tanks from the Scots Dragoon Guards moved down the main road and established a blocking position at a point called TAKU, which controlled an important crossroads along Highway 6 to Basra and Baghdad, and a road that went to the left flank of Abu al-Khasib and down to the water. At the same time the BRF, under Captain Haw, would carry out an attack on Sennen, at the western or right flank of the area. This time they had been ordered to capture the bridge, secure the small village on the far bank of the canal over which it passed and link up with other marines, who would be approaching from the west. This would ensure a safe route for supplies from the rear areas.

While the attack on the bridge was taking place, four other 40 Commando units were to make their way to a line of departure to the south, which would be secured and defended by Scimitars from C Squadron, the Queen's Dragoon Guards. The marines would advance from here and head north to capture Abu al-Khasib and a small port, then secure the area up to the banks of the Shatt al-Arab. B Company were on the right, furthest to the east, and would join up with the BRF at Sennen. A Company was to their left, and had a metalled road in their area of operations that ran into Abu al-Khasib. This would be their main line of advance and they would be accompanied by four Challenger II tanks.

D Company and the Manoeuvre Support Group (MSG), under Captain Paul Lynch, were on the far left flank, closest to Basra, and were moving north, parallel to the other units. There was no reserve, although Gordon Messenger had asked Brigadier Dutton to free up L Company of 42 Commando and have them ready to helicopter in if 40 Commando met stiffer resistance than he anticipated. The plan was relatively straightforward, but the timings of the advance on Sennen, and the Challenger tanks' movement up the highway to TAKU had to be closely co-ordinated.

An extra complication was that before the marines arrived at their line of departure a rolling artillery barrage would clear the way for their advance. There would be some anti-armour support from the helicopter air patrols of 847 Squadron from HMS *Ocean*. Unlike the invasion of the al-Faw peninsula a few days earlier, Operation James would be a combined-forces operation, and wholly British.

After the orders group, the company commanders felt that they had some time to absorb the plan before drawing up their own orders for their section leaders. Major Justin Holt needed it, and remembers remarking to his forward observation officer that his brain hurt because the scheme of manoeuvre was so complicated. He had to go back to his company to think about it. But a short while after he had returned, he received a signal that the operation had been brought forward: the order to execute had been received from Brigade and Operation James would start in twenty-four hours' time.

There was a rush to put everything into action. Holt had to translate the complicated scheme of manoeuvre into specific orders for his section leaders, while the corporals constructed a model of the target and objectives and the sergeants checked ammunition, supplies and organized the platoons. It would have been better for the company commanders to return to Commando Main where they could go through a tabletop rehearsal, but Colonel Messenger thought this would take up too much time.

At 1900 on the evening of 29 March the men of A Company were climbing aboard requisitioned Iraqi trucks to move forward to the assembly point for the start of the advance that would take place a few minutes into 30 March. It was Mothering Sunday.

Major Matt Jackson's B Company had taken little part in Operation Leah, consigned to a rearguard role. They had struggled to move out of the pipeline terminal area and form up at the metering station. With just six quad bikes, the lads in the company had had to carry almost everything. 'The equipment is very heavy. Canisters of a hundred rounds of heavy machine-gun rounds, Milan missile tubes – we had to carry a shedload of equipment. The heavy machine-guns went on the quad bikes with the men walking beside them.' However, when they regrouped on 28 March at the MMS they were allocated a variety of vehicles – some requisitioned Iraqi trucks and two Land Rovers and a Humvee for fire control and communications – and soon arrived at Commando Main Headquarters.

It was huge and bustling, and everyone took the opportunity to clean up. A laundry had been set up and uniforms and socks were washed in old kerosene drums.

Matt Jackson attended the orders group, and was making arrangements to move his company head-quarters to a location a short distance away from the old school buildings when he was told that B Company would replace 42 Commando's Unit Manoeuvre Support Troop (their equivalent of the MSG), currently occupying a defensive position. The move would be made the next day, so B Company stayed at Main Headquarters overnight.

Early in the morning of 29 March Matt Jackson prepared to move his company and execute his order to relieve the UMST. He loaded his heavy weapons, stores, ammunition and guns on to the trucks to conserve his quad bikes.

The replacement of the 42 Commando unit had just been completed successfully, the Milan and heavy machine-gun troops distributed around the position, when a signal came through: Operation James had been given the go-ahead for that night. Matt realized he needed to write down some formal orders – and quickly. The company command team met, and prepared to make the move to their positions for the operation later that night. Then, Matt pithily remembers, 'The clusterfuck began.'

Once again, despite his efforts, Major Jackson was to be frustrated by a lack of transport. He had been told that he would have three Pinzgauers, a flatbed BV10 and a cabbed BV10 to move his company, their weapons and ammunition to their assembly area, but what arrived was a four-ton truck and one BV10 tracked vehicle, which was totally inadequate. He had no idea what to do with the marines' Bergens and other equipment.

After he had sent several messages to Commando Headquarters, which were ignored, he decided to start shuttling the Bergens to a 7th Battery artillery position, about a kilometre down the road. By 1900 he had managed to move just thirty and had realized he didn't have time to move them all as well as shuttle the company to its drop-off point, about five kilometres from the line of departure. He ordered the company to march the nine kilometres to their drop-off point at 2030, knowing they had to be at their reporting point, two and a half kilometres from their line of departure, at 2350.

Along the way, because the truck had got bogged down in mud, he instructed the driver of the ANGLICO Humvee, the radio and communications

Land Rover and the two forward-observation Land Rovers to find a different route. They had still not arrived by the time B Company was due to report in via radio to Commando Headquarters that they had reached their drop-off point. Matt found that the drop-off point was a frenzy of marines from various companies unloading arms and stores and attempting to organize themselves into their pre-assault formations. Jackson made radio contact with the crews of two Scimitar armoured vehicles that were securing B Company's line of departure; they confirmed that it seemed to be clear. The company waited for an hour before moving off to its stop-short position, and just before they did, finally, the gunfire co-ordinator and the forward observer arrived. This was a stroke of luck because the latter was meant to be moving forward with 4 Troop to direct mortar fire to provide a smokescreen for B Company's advance to their first objective of the night, a bridge and road junction at a point codenamed Dalmatian, the breed of Jackson's dog at home.

B Company were not the only marines to have trouble with transport that night. A Company had been given two extra vehicles for their forward-observation team and were expecting to be completely mobile for their move to their form-up point. The weight restrictions imposed by the first helicopter assault meant that, from day one, vehicles had been in short supply, and the Commando had been requisitioning Iraqi vehicles as they leapfrogged up the peninsula. A Company's troop-carrying vehicles turned out to be Chinese-made eight-tonne trucks, but they worked and were better than walking. With the marines crouched on the back the trucks moved slowly forward over the potholed desert road, lights extinguished, the badly maintained engines labouring and spewing fumes from the poor-quality diesel. They rattled and jolted over rubble until suddenly the bolts on one of the tailgates gave way, pitching four men backwards, head first, on to the road. The trucks lurched to a stop.

It was obvious that the men were badly hurt. Sergeant Bob Toomey had broken ribs and a damaged spine, Marine Glanfield had a suspected broken neck and the two others had concussion. They were all key men, from the mortar troop and the sniper section, but they needed urgent medical attention. It was impossible for them to continue the advance with A Company. Ambulances came forward to stretcher the casualties off. It was not a great start, and Captain Justin Holt, of A Company, found it unsettling.

A Company reached the form-up position, where they made contact with the Scimitar that would provide some over-watch for them as they advanced, the crew poised to open fire with its rapid-firing 30-mm cannon to send shells ripping into buildings or bunkers that housed Iraqi fighters. The path to the line of departure had been marked by the

Scimitar crew with coloured tape. The marines moved silently forward, still in darkness. Behind them they heard the rumble and clatter of the Challengers as they advanced up the road to secure position TAKU. The last three slowed and wheeled right, tracks clanking, the big diesel engines reverberating as they advanced slowly to form up with A Company. They would be taking the road on a line of advance called 'Scarlet' with 1 Troop, while to the left were 2 Troop; 3 Troop were to the right, next to B Company's left edge.

The instructions for the advance were complicated. They had to go forward for two kilometres to the line of departure, but halt at one kilometre until the artillery barrage had stopped. A Company, however, was so strung out that the head of the column had reached the line of departure before Justin had reached the one-kilometre mark. He wasn't happy. Nobody in A Company was happy. There was almost clear ground for a kilometre in front of them, then dense palm groves, which continued to the edges of the Shatt al-Arab. To Justin it seemed obvious: 'The enemy was going to be in the palm groves and we were going to advance through the killing ground towards them. It was early morning, and we would be advancing into the rising sun. The enemy had all the advantages. There was some nervousness as we approached the line of departure.'

It was a classic understatement. He might have

added that there were other reasons to be apprehensive. In the days since the marines had swarmed on to the oil facilities, and brazenly entered al-Faw town without warning, the Iraqi Army and the Fedayeen had had time to make preparations. The Scimitars of the Queen's Dragoon Guards and the air patrols of 845 Squadron had observed plenty of activity around Basra; tanks had been seen moving into position and convoys of troops had been deployed. The innocuously named Operation James was shaping up to be the toughest battle they had yet faced in Iraq.

The Brigade Reconnaissance Force (BRF) and the Reconnaissance Troop of 40 Commando were on the eastern edge of the battle space ready to be first into action to secure Sennen. Captain Haw, now commanding, was hankering for the days when he was a troop leader, close to the action, the adrenalin rush of contact with the enemy; when motivation, intelligence and training could defeat a better-armed and better-positioned enemy. He had no problems with the BRF's firepower: as well as the WMIKs and anti-tank missiles he'd deployed in his previous raids against the Iraqi positions that guarded the bridge, he had a troop of Scimitars from the Queen's Dragoon Guards to help clear the way in.

As the Challenger tanks moved up to TAKU, the BRF moved forward, the recce troop advancing through the palms on the Shatt al-Arab to take possession of some wharves where they could put snipers on to cranes to provide covering fire. The marines cleared through a small area of houses and approached the bridge. It was quiet. There had been little opposition. As a machine-gun troop lay in the dark, crouching by the corner of a building covering another troop of marines lying on the ground in front of them, they could see no sign of tanks or enemy fighters. They heard the explosions of the artillery barrage landing on the southern edge a few kilometres away.

Before a bridge is taken, engineers need to advance on it and inspect it for demolition charges, and also, if it hasn't been done before, to assess its weight-bearing characteristics. They are experts in explosives, but are lightly armed and need good covering fire before they can do their job. The lead troop went solid on the approaches to the bridge, tense and expectant, but saw nothing. They called the engineers forward. As they approached the nearest end of the bridge, which was quite wide, with low, white-painted metal railings on either side, a massive wall of gunfire exploded around them from the far bank. Their eyes were blinded by gun flashes, and the noise of high-velocity bullets filled their ears. Twenty or thirty Iraqi soldiers, dug in on the far side of the canal, were hosing the area with fire from machine-guns and AK-47 assault rifles.

The engineers dropped flat, and the marines took whatever cover they could in the reeds or by buildings.

Bullets thudded against walls, and ricocheted off the bridge's metal railings. It had kicked off with a vengeance, and it was difficult to see what was going on in the dark. But the engineers knew they needed to check the bridge before any advance could be made over it. The marines now started firing back with general-purpose machine-guns. The mortar section opened up with 51-mm mortars at the far bank. The enemy fire diminished but didn't stop, yet the two engineers raced on to the bridge to check for demolition charges. Keeping low and braving the fire snapping at the railings and whirring above their heads they checked the supporting beams and columns for any charges or tell-tale detonation cord. The bridge was clear, and they manoeuvred hurriedly back to cover, while mortars and machine-gun fire blitzed the Iraqis on the far side. Gradually the marines edged forward, targeting individual gun flashes, and the opposition fire slackened.

By daybreak, the Iraqi soldiers had been killed or had retreated, and the lead troop was able to cross the bridge unopposed. Chris Haw signalled to Colonel Messenger that the first objective of Operation James had been achieved. But the Iraqis had been waiting for them. Was this an indication of what lay in store for 40 Commando?

A few kilometres away, at 0120 on Sunday, 30 March, B Company started to move slowly towards their line of departure. The company's order of march was a close-combat troop, 4 Troop, accompanying the forward observation officers, followed by a stand-off troop, armed with Milan anti-tank missiles and heavy machine-guns. They were going to move forward together up the westerly route that led into the company's area of responsibility. The eastern route would be taken by 5 Troop and a second stand-off troop, then the Tactical Communications Unit, and Company Headquarters staff would follow with the third close-combat troop in reserve. Major Matt Jackson had told his troop commanders that their orders were to stop short of the line of departure about two hundred metres, then advance at 0150. The leading troop reached their stop-short point, but Jackson and his command team were delayed slightly because a quad bike had broken down.

As he and the rear echelon moved to catch up with 4 Troop, their world was split apart by devastating explosions. They seemed to Matt to be landing directly on 4 Troop. He was deafened by the shell bursts, shrapnel whistled past him and shock waves tugged at his helmet. Huge gouts of mud and earth were flung into the air, and artillery shells detonated in the sky above, with a crack like thunder. The marines at the front were completely stunned by the tumult directly before and above them, instinctively crouching low, willing themselves into the earth. They were surrounded by death.

Matt Jackson thought they were under enemy fire: 'It was the most frightening thing I have ever experienced, having shells explode in front of your face. Even now I flinch at loud noises.' It was traumatic for the members of 4 Troop directly in the line of fire. In shock, Matt stupidly ran towards them, but his mortar fire controller had a slightly better grasp of reality, grabbed his radio and shouted to Brigade to check fire. He was right: the shells landing on them were a barrage of airburst and high-explosive 105-mm shells, the prearranged barrage from two batteries of eight guns, ordered to deliver two minutes' fire for effect.

It was designed to clear the way for the advance of the marines, and the Challengers, but in the rush to bring the assault forward by twenty-four hours, the timing of the barrage, and the stop-short of a thousand metres had not been communicated to B Company.

Now eight marines were lying on the ground amid the shell-shocked frightened men of 4 and 5 Troops. Astonishingly, thanks mainly to the body armour they were wearing, there were no fatalities, but two marines were seriously wounded, one with a punctured lung and another with part of his arm torn out. Medical assistant Marine Sumner rushed forward and helped to stabilize them while the call went back for ambulances. At Commando Main the orders went out for a halt to the advance. An hour later the ambulances arrived, and the casualties were evacuated.

Then Matt Jackson had to pull himself and everyone else together. They were in the middle of a war and Colonel Messenger was on the radio, pressing him to prepare to start the assault. Matt remembers one marine, probably high on adrenalin, claiming that he was 'ready to go' even though he had a large piece of shrapnel in his buttock.

Jackson called his men to gather round, then stressed the importance of the mission and their role in it. It was the first time 40 Commando had taken part in a direct assault since the Second World War, he emphasized, and they couldn't fail now. There would be time for an inquest later but right now the light was coming up and they had to go. B Company's fire-observation team had been wiped out by the shelling, but a new team had fortuitously come forward, naval gunfire forward observers, who had been with D Company on the al-Faw peninsula. They merged with 4 Troop, and Jackson reconfigured the advance, with 4 Troop and their combat team heading out along the western side of B Company's area of responsibility, with 5 Troop now moving along the eastern, or right, flank.

4 Troop's first objective was the bridge into the outskirts of Abu al-Khasib, codenamed Dalmatian. As they moved forward down the road, a cry of 'Mines!' rang out. The wasteland to the west of the road was

littered with anti-tank mines, which were fortunately on the surface, but it was clear that the Iraqis wanted to channel their advance up the road, and they were probably heading into an ambush. As they went from cover to cover, they observed movement in the windows of two houses and fired LAW anti-tank missiles into them. There was no response, so they moved on to the bridge. There was no opposition, and they set up defensive positions around it.

5 Troop had also advanced towards their objectives, some buildings known as Labrador. Their advance was also uneventful, and they turned left and met up with 4 Troop. The company now together, they moved forward. A heavy machine-gun, manned by Corporal Beswick and three others, was mounted on the roof of a nearby building, giving cover to the advance of the rest of the company. Not far up the road the lead section encountered some barbed wire laid across the road. Not sure what to make of the tentative barricade they crossed it, and immediately came under fire from a building further up the road. The marines returned the fire, and while 1 Section kept it up, 2 Section moved rapidly across the road. They cleared a building with machine-gun fire and a grenade, then climbed up to the roof. A LAW missile was fired that crashed into the side of the house where the gunfire was coming from and the marines advanced on it.

Running at full tilt, a marine flung a grenade

through a window. It was followed by automatic rifle fire and they entered the building. There were no men inside but next door a woman and two children were totally petrified, screaming in fear. The marines bundled them out, but both houses were empty, although they found an RPG and some AK-47s.

The marines of B Company were now completely charged up. They had been shelled, and now they were getting shot at, but they were in action, the adrenalin was flowing and they were working in perfect co-ordination. An Iraqi came round a corner on a bicycle with an AK-47 slung over his shoulder. Seeing the marines, he reached for his gun and two bullets went through him, killing him instantly.

4 and 5 Troops separated again and moved forward down two axes. 4 Troop made contact with two more Iraqi soldiers, and again they were shot, the heavy machine-gun on the roof near Dalmatian adding its high-pitched bark to the firefight.

Their next major objective was another bridge, Collie, lying east to west about three kilometres along the road from Sennen. In order to approach it, another smaller bridge had to be secured on the westerly line of advance called Route Blue. As they crossed this bridge they were fired on from a building on the other side of the river within a palm grove, cutting off the lead section from the main body of 5 Troop. They hit the ground, getting covering fire going. The combat team fired smoke grenades and the lead section made it back over the bridge. The enemy fire was consistent, and well spaced.

The marines were in danger of being pinned down, but B Company was on a roll. Marines Wheldon and Brennan unloaded the second heavy machine-gun from the quad bike and, under heavy fire, picked it up by the legs of its tripod and ran with it, followed by Marine Forman with a heavy box of ammunition. Ignoring the continuous Iraqi fire they set up the machine-gun, and soon had the half-inch-calibre bullets pumping into the houses.

Under this cover, the stand-off troop brought up a LAW and fired at one of the buildings, where it exploded, silencing the gunfire from the Iraqis inside.

Now another set of Iraqi soldiers opened up on their position, from the vicinity of Collie: four Iraqis were firing down the road. There was little cover, and an assault up the road would be suicidal. Second Lieutenant Coryton, commanding 5 Troop, asked for a sniper volunteer, and Marine Cullen, with Marine Scorah as his spotter, ran across the road, again under fire, seeking cover behind a pile of earth barely a foot high. His position had been spotted and the range was around three hundred metres. He got a shot off, but so heavy was the fire from the automatic rifles that he had to get his head down quickly. Biding his time he fired again, this time close enough to the four Iraqis that they felt compelled to move. Three went left and one went right across the bridge.

The sniper rifle had been cocked again, and Marine Cullen sent a .338-inch high-velocity round at the soldier who had broken to the right, and he fell, shot through the chest. Cullen told 5 Troop that three Iraqis had gone into the palms on the riverbank. There was no escape: an underslung grenade-launcher mounted on an assault rifle fired round after round into the bank, hurling mud and branches into the air. There was no more fire from the enemy, but the heavy machine-gun poured some final rounds into the bank, and the buildings from which the initial firing had come.

The close-combat team advanced to the bridge, and continued for another two hundred metres before going firm on their position at the western edge of B Company's area of responsibility. Combat Team 1 then went towards the eastern edge to meet up with the BRF. As they went along the road, the inhabitants started to come out of their houses, waving and apparently friendly. The fighting, it seemed, was over after an intensely stressful and violent day. The marines fanned out, and moved through the narrow streets and low houses that lined the banks of the waterway. An old school building was taken over for a company base, guards and defensive positions were set up, and patrols sent out into the area.

Major Matt Jackson sent the following sitrep to Colonel Gordon Messenger, at Commando Main: 'Paradoxical day experiencing the highs and lows of warfare. The results of today's friendly fire incident may manifest itself over the next few days. I plan to stave this off with a bit of a get-together tomorrow. On the other hand, when we got going the lads were truly magnificent doing what they do best. Have cleared enemy within boundaries to best of our ability but don't suppose all will have gone. Civilian population in general friendly pro us, but simultaneously guarded. Plan for 1st patrol to depart 310100Z. [31 March, 0100 Greenwich Mean Time].'

It was just ten days since Matt Jackson, the new young commanding officer of B Company, had sweated into his boots as the US SEALs' helicopter had swooped low over the al-Faw peninsula and he had tried to control the fear and anticipation of rushing down the ramp into live fire. It seemed years ago. He had worried about how he would behave and, more importantly, how the men under him would judge his performance when any leadership failure might prove fatal. They were not tolerant of weakness in those above them. That night he slept the sleep of utter exhaustion, and woke to find he had missed his watch-keeping duty. Two of the signalmen had done a double duty and let him sleep. Nothing was said but he knew that he had passed the test.

The shells falling on B Company early that morning had delayed the advance for the whole of 40 Commando, but this merely gave Major Justin

Holt, commanding A Company, the opportunity to consolidate his company's position after losing eight of his men in an accident driving up to the assembly point. Their advance would be along an axis of a main road that led straight into the town of Abu al-Khasib. Reconnaissance flights by UAVs (unmanned aerial vehicles) and observation from air patrols flown by the Lynx and Gazelle helicopters of 84 squadron had shown that the route down which A Company were expected to advance was protected by T-55 tanks and armoured personnel-carriers.

Some of the Iraqi tanks were dug in hull down, where depressions had been excavated in the ground and the tank had reversed into it. Effectively this turned it into a fixed artillery hardpoint. It reduced the tank's mobility, but protected the hull and made it a much harder target to hit. As a counter to these defences, A Company would be accompanied by a squadron of Challenger IIs, from the Royal Scots Dragoon Guards.

Four of these sixty-three-tonne monsters would accompany 1 Troop, A Company, down the main axis of their area of responsibility. Second Lieutenant Buczkiewicz was nonplussed when he first discovered this: 'It conjured up images of the troops advancing behind tanks in a scene from *Full Metal Jacket*. It turned out that this was exactly what the tank commander wanted us to do.'

As A Company reached their stop-short position,

the shells landing on B Company to their left caused chaos in the advance. They were instructed to move back five hundred metres, behind some cover. Dawn was breaking as they finally crossed their line of departure. Any cover from the night had dissipated, but the weakness of their tactical position, crossing open ground into the breaking daylight, was more than made up for by the presence of the Challengers. No sooner had the lead tank advanced a few yards than it opened fire on a building on the left flank, to the sudden shock and alarm of the leading troop of marines. The tanks moved quickly, and 1 Troop found they had to work hard to keep up, and remain keenly aware of the sudden manoeuvres of the clanking tracks close to them. The air was full of the sound of Perkins diesel engines and the explosion of tank fire. The Challengers were fully engaged in taking out any bunker, T-55 or other military equipment they could legitimately target.

Major Justin Holt recorded a scene of 'utter destruction. We steamrollered our way up the axis, past burning and exploding tank hulks. Plumes of dense black smoke rose in the morning air.' The advancing marines now faced another threat as the shells in the burning T-55 tanks started to 'cook off', and detonate randomly. At the same time the company was calling down artillery fire on to enemy bunkers and positions.

As the marines approached to start clearing them

Iraqi soldiers, terrified, ran out with their hands in the air clutching any piece of white material they could find. A Company seemed to be running on rails through a scene of carnage.

Justin Holt became concerned that 3 Troop were being overly thorough in their clearance of bunkers and trenches, and the line of advance across the whole Commando was in danger of being split. The tanks, with 1 Troop in the centre, had their own momentum and created a significant bulge in the front edge, seizing a major junction, codenamed Coco, that cut off any retreat to the west and Basra. But the enemy was incapable of taking any advantage of A Company's fragmented advance. The Challengers' policy of destroying all Iraqi armoured vehicles they came across, and their seeming invulnerability to any opposition, quite naturally shredded the Iraqis' will to fight. Despite their numerical advantage they were in retreat. Justin Holt wanted to seize the moment and rush forward with a small force to capture a military barracks that lay just one and a half kilometres in front of A Company's lead troop. He could see that the Iraqi soldiers who were supposed to be defending it were rapidly retreating, and he thought it was important to take as many of them prisoner as he could. But his marines were on foot, and it would have been a reckless effort.

The company kept to its original plan. This was to move up to a T-junction, whilst 3 Troop started on a route east to meet up with B Company. When the main bulk of the company arrived at the T-junction, they would also move east, taking them through the centre of Abu al-Khasib. Holt waited until another squadron of Challengers, their call sign 'panzer two zero', newly assigned to him by Commando Headquarters, arrived, then the combined force started to clear the centre of the town towards B Company's area. There, they took some prisoners, mainly soldiers who were retreating from the east and B Company's area. There was opposition now, but it was small-arms and RPG attacks, which had no effect on the Challengers and their crews, who just kept coming, cutting down any Iraqis who got in their way.

The situation was becoming confusing and individual marines were now in danger of becoming exposed to sniper fire. Justin's radio was playing up, and intermittent communication with his troop commanders was dangerous in an urban environment. He made the decision to halt, and withdraw the company to a secure base at the abandoned military barracks.

They started to make arrangements for transferring the large number of prisoners they had taken, including a major and a lieutenant colonel who had been fleeing towards Basra. The exhausted marines had been awake for more than twenty-four hours, and had advanced almost seventeen kilometres, mostly on foot, since they had last slept. 'We were bollocksed,' recalled Justin.

Captain Paul Lynch (*centre*) and 40 Commandos Manoeuvre Support Group (*above*) saw some hard fighting on the first day. Two days later they formed up again and headed north along the al-Faw peninsula as part of Operation Leah (*below*).

Operation James was a major assault on Iraqi positions in Abu al-Khasib. Challenger tanks gave support to A Company (*above*), destroying Iraqi T55s (*above top right*), and A Company took a lot of prisoners (*above right*).

The Manoeuvre Support Group had the hardest fight. Corporal Thomas won the MC (*top left*) for manning a machine gun for fifteen minutes while his comrades regrouped and fought their way out of a trap (*middle and bottom*).

Captain Matt Pierson (*right*) and D Company had to clear Objective Blofeld (*below right*) after they were engaged in a firefight during which they killed several Iraqi soldiers and took others prisoner (*sequence below*). They went on to advance through their area of operations.

40 Commando
tried to deliver
aid and win
the hearts and
minds of the
local population
(*above* and *right*).

Refugees tried to flee Basra, the second largest city in Iraq (*left*), which was under the brutal control of Saddam Hussein's henchmen. The British maintained a loose cordon, searching vehicles as they entered and left the city (*bottom left*).

While the members of A Company put up posters (*right*), the rest of 40 Commando tried to replace the Ba'ath Party administration of Abu al-Khasib and other towns on the al-Faw peninsula.

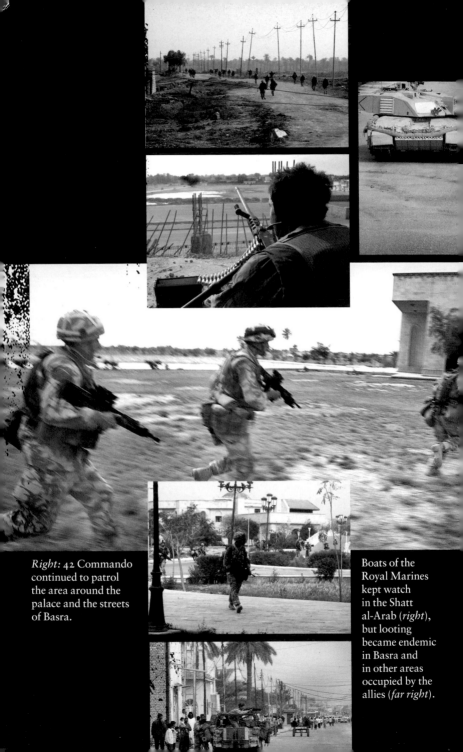

Right: 42 Commando continued to patrol the area around the palace and the streets of Basra.

Boats of the Royal Marines kept watch in the Shatt al-Arab (*right*), but looting became endemic in Basra and in other areas occupied by the allies (*far right*).

While 42 Commando made their assault on Basra, accompanied by Challenger tanks (*left*), the assault of J Company on the presidential palace was swift, and they rapidly secured this enormous complex on the river (*main pictures*).

A statue of Saddam Hussein is toppled by a British tank. Symbolic actions such as this were viewed by the media around the world as marking the downfall of the Iraqi regime and a successful end to the fighting. The reality over the next few years was to prove far more complex, and far bloodier, as the Ba'ath Party regime was replaced by anarchy.

The barracks had only just been abandoned: there was food on a table and coffee still warm on a stove, although the place was filthy. The marines set about making it more habitable. They established a defensive area, and foot patrols were sent into the town to make their presence felt. Iraqi civilians emerged from their houses to assess the damage, and the nature of the invaders.

At the end of 30 March, the eastern part of 40 Commando's operational area had been successfully secured. Both A and B Companies, despite their difficult starts, had overcome any opposition, had secured Company Headquarters and, with the BRF on the eastern edge, were patrolling their individual areas of operations.

The western area, closest to Basra, was the responsibility of D Company, and 40 Commando's MSG, and they, too, formed up at their assembly point at 2359, the last minute of Saturday, 29 March. Their fight would be quite different.

Major Matt Pierson, commanding D Company, had to give some last-minute orders about Operation James at the form-up point because one of his troops had been deployed elsewhere, and their return had been so badly delayed that they had missed the previous day's orders group. The checkpoint through which they had to go to the line of departure was a large compound that had once been an artillery depot but had been attacked either by artillery or in an air raid. It was on fire. To Matt Pierson it looked like a vision of hell, something from Dante's *Inferno*, with burning debris, and stacks of artillery cases being licked by flames, ready to cook off. It was not a place to hang around, but he had been delayed in moving forward because of the friendly artillery fire that landed on B Company's lead troop. He spoke to Colonel Messenger in Commando Main and told him it was impossible for him to line out; in other words, because of the fire and the danger at his checkpoint he was unable to form up on his line of departure. Gordon Messenger told him to find his own ground.

As D Company exited the artillery-supply compound, a large building stood straight in front of them, Blofeld on the scheme of manoeuvre, after one of the villains in the James Bond novel *Thunderball*. It was a very large modern six-storey office block, with several accommodation blocks behind it. On the map it had looked like an ordinary housing complex, but in reality it dominated D Company's line of departure.

As the lead troop advanced they immediately came under fire from the building. Adopting their standard procedure of fire and manoeuvre, the marines quickly advanced on a troop of ten Iraqi soldiers lodged in the building; four were killed, the rest surrendered. When the marines got to them they had already started to take off their uniforms, and one was so terrified, so fearful, that he was trying to bury himself in the mud. He believed he would be shot out of hand and, kneeling, shaking with fear next to the face-down body of one his comrades, whose dark red blood was soaking into the mud, it was easy to see why. All six prisoners were passed back down the line of advance for questioning by teams of human-intelligence officers who had joined 40 Commando's rear echelon.

The firing had ceased, but the vast building complex had to be cleared, and it was several hours before D Company could advance once more. Because of the delay a squadron of Challenger tanks was assigned to help them clear their next objective, code-named Dalton. There was no opposition and D Company continued, now clearing small villages set among palm groves, moving closer and closer to the Shatt al-Arab. The tanks had by now been reassigned to A Company, and the footborne troops of D Company were having a hard day in the searing heat, carrying large amounts of ammunition, water and chemical-warfare protective kit.

They cleared to the banks of the river, in a relatively uneventful assault on an area of operations that was perhaps five kilometres deep. Then Commando Headquarters was on the radio and Pierson was ordered to send a combat teamto the west of D Company's area of responsibility to help the MSG which had become bogged down in a firefight. They were on the left flank of the battle area, to the west of D Company, pinned down and facing stiff resistance in a district called al-Jahyidia.

Combat Team 1, under Sergeant Capewell, was tasked by Matt Pierson to push west and help secure the MSG's area. Meanwhile the rest of the company set about foot patrols of their area, searching out a site for a company headquarters. Minutes later the radio crackled into life, with the urgent command, 'Contact. Wait out!'

The combat team was in a firefight. They had been ambushed on their way to the Manoeuvre Support Group.

As the combat team's Pinzgauers had turned a corner in the road leading to where the MSG was fighting, they came upon a group of Fedayeen who had just finished setting up an ambush. It was hard to say who was most surprised or who pulled the trigger first. Small-arms fire and RPGs came flying from all directions, and a car with four Iraqis as passengers tried to accelerate away from the leading Commando vehicle. The car had gone barely thirty yards before it was riddled with bullets and slewed to a halt, its occupants toppling out lifeless on to the ground.

The marines of Combat Team 1 had a phenomenal amount of luck. An RPG hit the leading Pinzgauer, but stuck in the radiator grille and failed to explode. Another flew towards the front observer of the second Pinzgauer, Corporal Blackman, who had placed his day sack, filled with ammunition, water and rations in front of him. The warhead of the RPG hit the daysack and ricocheted over him, missing his head by inches. Bullets ripped though the vehicles, around the heads and bodies of the marines, and they burst out of them, into whatever cover they could find.

To Matt Pierson it was obvious that the ambush had been planned. The Iraqis knew that the British would send assistance to their embattled MSG, and that there was only one route those reinforcements could take. What this said about the enemy was interesting, but of only secondary importance at that moment. The situation was serious: twenty marines were spread out in whatever cover they could find, pinned down by enemy fire. The Iraqis had seized the initiative, and D Company had to get out of the mess but hold on to the junction. It was impossible to call down artillery or mortar fire on the Iraqis without knowing where the twenty marines of the combat team were. That was the first priority and, second, it was important to find out where the enemy was, what his shape was and, if possible, what his intentions were. In order to do this it was necessary to establish contact with the Iraqis – in other words, restart the firefight and shift the balance of forces to put the Iraqis on the back foot. The second patrol group moved forward, with the tactical headquarters, and established a position. Then, slowly, two sections pushed forward on foot, each group pouring covering fire at the enemy while the other four ran forward until they were taking the fight to the enemy. At the same time they were trying to rescue their comrades and provide a secure area to which they could retreat. The two damaged Pinzgauers, with their anti-tank missiles, ammunition, radios and other valuable equipment, had to be denied to the Iraqis, and the marines fired LAW missiles at them to destroy them, setting them ablaze.

It was a confusing fight, the Iraqis mounting an extremely mobile attack, running from cover to cover, firing assault rifles and RPGs, threatening to out-flank D Company's position. At the same time members of Combat Team 1 were retreating through the trees, and the chance of killing a comrade was high. In one incident Marine Thomas had sought shelter behind a wall, while another three members of his troop were trapped on the other side of an alley by an Iraqi machine-gun squad. Thomas moved down to the bank of the Shatt al-Arab, swam along the water-way towards a rowboat, which he unmoored and brought back along the bank close to where he had been sheltering. He climbed back up, and lobbed a grenade over the wall, killing the three Iraqis manning the machine-gun on the other side. His three comrades ran across the gap and all four got into the boat and made it back behind D Company's line.

The fight continued, using up a vast amount of ammunition. Corporals in the Royal Marines are trained to call down mortar fire, and as the conflict deepened it was possible for individual sections to direct light mortar shells on to Iraqi troops. Members of 8 Troop climbed on to roofs to pour down covering fire and spot any movement by Iraqi forces threatening to outflank D Company's positions.

The enemy was everywhere, and Major Pierson was staggered when his tactical headquarters were approached by a group of men carrying white flags in one hand, and AK-47s in the other. These 'men for all seasons' were quickly fired on and retreated.

After an hour of fighting all of the marines of the ambushed combat team had made it back safely. The mortar fire was brought down more heavily, and clearly the Iraqis had judged that their gambit had failed because they started to retreat. After a very nasty ninety minutes the fighting had lessened. Around thirty-five Iraqi soldiers had been killed, and many more injured. D Company had suffered no casualties, apart from one marine who had been rendered stone deaf by the blast of an RPG, but had otherwise escaped the near miss unharmed. They had, however, lost two Pinzgauers, four quad bikes, two heavy machine-guns, a number of LAW missiles and a pair of Milan launchers.

But their day was not over. The MSG, still under fire from a large force of Iraqi troops, was running out of ammunition, and a group of vehicles from Commando Headquarters was passing through D Company's area when it was ambushed. Now Matt Pierson was ordered to recover from his firefight and send forces to rescue the supply vehicles.

Gordon Messenger was becoming worried. With the MSG tied down and still heavily engaged, and D Company in a firefight, he was concerned that the first move to kicking down the door to Basra was becoming an opportunity for the Iraqis to ensure that it was slammed in the face of the British.

He talked to Brigadier Dutton, at Brigade Headquarters, who had been following the day's events with close attention. Dutton suggested to Colonel Messenger that he call in the brigade reserve, which was L Company of 42 Commando. Gordon Messenger agreed and L Company were taken by Chinook to a landing site in D Company's area of responsibility. By the time it arrived, the supply troop had managed to fight off its attackers, and D Company was no longer needed to rescue them. They could turn their attention back to the fate of the MSG. But evening was approaching and D Company was ordered to join up with L Company and go into a harbour formation for the night.

Operation James was now in the balance.

13

THE FIFTH AXIS – THE MANOEUVRE SUPPORT GROUP

On the morning of 30 March, the unit that was going to advance along the most western axis of the multi-pronged assault into Abu al-Khasib, which was Operation James, was 40 Commando's Manoeuvre Support Group (MSG) under Captain Paul Lynch. The rectangular area occupied by this suburb was about five kilometres deep and ran parallel to the Shatt al-Arab for around seven kilometres. The MSG would advance along the western flank, closest to the city of Basra.

This was a late development. At the orders-group meeting on 28 March, Lynch had been disappointed to learn that his unit was slated for a reserve role, in a secondary position to 42 Commando's Unit Manoeuvre Support Troop (UMST). But, as we have seen, the UMST was ordered later that day by Brigade to return to 42 Commando. B Company was tasked to take over their guard position, while Paul Lynch and his MSG were now ordered to take on their role in Operation James.

Paul Lynch rapidly went back to Commando Headquarters to back-brief Colonel Messenger on what was now his main task. There was some slight confusion, because Lynch had understood his orders were to clear along the whole of his line of advance, but Gordon Messenger indicated that his most important task was to secure two key areas, the first of which, following the James Bond theme, was called Galore, and the second, the most important, was Pussy, a crossroads that linked Abu al-Khasib to Basra and through which Iraqi reinforcements would pass from Basra to the area.

Controlling Pussy would not only prevent those reinforcements arriving from Basra it would also prevent Iraqi troops retreating, bottling them up either to be killed or to surrender to 40 Commando, who were sweeping through the suburb. As 40 Commando had rolled up the al-Faw peninsula, they appeared to be just one step behind Iraqi forces that had, for the most part, retreated before them. Successfully blocking the main route out of Abu al-Khasib meant that Operation James could inflict a major defeat on the local forces, prevent any strengthening of Basra's defences and send a powerful signal to the Iraqi commanders in the city.

Captain Lynch, like A Company, was going to be

reinforced by a section of Challengers from the Royal Scots Dragoon Guards. It was a small well-armed column that would go into action. The MSG was smaller than a full company, with around forty men, but it was mobile, and its vehicles were modified to carry heavy machine-guns and Milan anti-tank missiles. Originally the unit had had six Pinzgauers, three fitted with Milan anti-tank missiles and three mounting two general-purpose machine-guns in the sustained-fire role. One of these vehicles was lost right at the beginning of Operation James when, on the drive to the MSG assembly point, it rolled down an embankment and cracked its cylinder head. All the weapons, men and ammunition had to be reloaded on the remaining five vehicles. Even so, the MSG should have been able to give a good account of itself in any fight. With the addition of three Challengers very little should have been able to stand in its way. The unit also had two Land Rovers carrying the communications and forward-observer party, and a Humvee with the attached US marines' ANGLICO team in it.

As they formed up at their assembly area, the night sky was lit by lurid flames from a burning building, called Oddjob, that was blocking D Company's line of departure, thick black smoke rising into the sky, tinged red from the fire, the stink of burning rubber and oil hanging heavy in the air. It was a Wagnerian backdrop to the start of the operation, and not one they could get away from: the friendly-fire artillery barrage that had fallen on B Company had delayed their orders to move until daylight was breaking.

A night assault had turned into a daylight one, and Captain Lynch was unhappy about their vulnerability, but it quickly turned into a blessing: the Iraqis had planted hundreds of surface anti-personnel mines on the road, which would have been invisible at night. If their advance had started when it was intended to, the air would have been filled with lethal shrapnel slicing through the soft-bodied vehicles of the marines and their own flesh.

As it was, they still had the problem of dealing with them. It was impossible to bypass them because the ground on either side of the raised road was soft yielding mud, in which the tanks and Pinzgauers would quickly become bogged down. The mines might have been laid as part of an ambush, but there were no shots, and no RPGs were flying in, so it appeared that they were not part of a co-ordinated defence. But they needed to be got rid of quickly. Then one of the Challenger commanders had a brainwave. Their squadron, now in position at objective TAKU, included an armoured recovery vehicle, in effect a Challenger that mounted a crane and a bulldozer blade instead of a 120-mm gun. It could drive back to the MSG's position and bulldoze away the scattered anti-personnel mines.

After an hour the road had been cleared, and the

formation of vehicles continued its advance. In the lead was a tank, followed by two of the marines' Pinzgauers, then another tank, another two Pinzgauers and so on. The road was straight; on either side there was an expanse of low, boggy ground, still flooded from the storm a few days earlier, then dense palm groves and low vegetation. The sound of tank shells, mortars and heavy machine-gun fire from the other company's assault carried to the ears of the marines over the noise of the Challengers.

The lead tank approached the area of the crossroads and slowed. Its commander reported back to Captain Lynch that he could see movement in the palms: people were carrying what appeared to be RPG launchers and small arms. He requested advice about what to do. Captain Lynch, after his experiences in the monitoring and metering station, was abrupt: 'I thought, What's the problem? Kill them.' But the Challengers' commander was more circumspect. He was armed with a huge 120-mm cannon and a hull-mounted chain gun, both of which were fairly blunt instruments against foot soldiers. He was also concerned about the possible presence of civilians in the area, and felt, rightly, that his rule of engagement didn't justify blasting the palms wide open with high explosives.

Captain Paul Lynch moved forward, and a group of marines went up the road to investigate. Two went forward on foot, bold as brass, and a line of machine-gun bullets stitched a row of small explosions between them. Simultaneously they heard the rattle of a Soviet-built machine-gun hidden in a strongpoint among the palms. The two marines dived to the side, and rolled away. At the same time, RPGs started to come in, and the group realized they were being fired on from both sides of the road, and from directly ahead.

The marines' initial response was to advance, make contact with the enemy and assess who they were facing. A section moved forward to the nearest buildings, but they found families cowering inside, not fighters. The glimpses they caught of men running from shelter to shelter provided evidence that they were facing the black-clad insurgents they now recognized as the Fedayeen Saddam and Ba'ath Party Militia, who were more motivated and organized than the Iraqi Army. The MSG was having difficulty coming to grips with them.

The palms and the houses provided good cover, and the presence of civilians meant that the marines were forced to be more discriminating about whom and what they were shooting. The firefight was becoming increasingly intense. RPGs were finding their targets, and it was obvious that the marines' vehicles were vulnerable.

Paul Lynch realized that he was in the killing ground of a planned ambush and needed to get out. It wasn't easy. The vehicles were spread out along the road for three hundred metres; they couldn't venture on to the soft mud at either side so the drivers started to reverse. Then a Pinzgauer was hit by an RPG and stopped. The vehicle had to be stripped of its radios, weapons and maps, to stop them falling into the hands of the Fedayeen.

Paul Lynch radioed to Colonel Gordon Messenger, and asked for supporting artillery fire and heavy mortars while the MSG finished the job on the damaged Pinzgauer, and the other vehicles did three-point turns and got out of the area. The shells came in, air-bursting barely 150 metres from the forward marines, dangerously close, but they suppressed the Iraqis' onslaught.

They succeeded in moving back, and quickly went into a huddle, trying to assess, from the varied reports of contact, how many Iraqis there were and what sort of defensive position they occupied. The progress of the fighting had been relayed to Colonel Messenger, who was in almost constant communication with Brigadier Dutton at Brigade Headquarters.

Operation James contained an element of risk that Gordon Messenger readily acknowledged. Intelligence on the size and shape of the Iraqi forces in Abu al-Khasib was sparse. It was an advance to contact, rather than a conventional commando assault, and it carried with it the possibility of a battle with a significantly larger enemy force. Paul Lynch's MSG had originally been designated a reserve, but they were now committed, and Gordon Messenger had nothing left.

While the members of the MSG were working out what to do next, the three tanks reassembled, and advanced back up the road towards Pussy on a reconnaissance patrol. The lead tank fired a high-explosive round at the damaged Pinzgauer, which destroyed it and killed many Iraqis who were clambering on it, trying to restart it. The tank continued and swept the plantations using its thermal imaging system and radioed back an estimate that there were seventy-five to a hundred fighters, and asked Captain Lynch if he had the men to deal with them. He had to accept that his small force was outnumbered. They were blocked. Advancing up the open road towards the crossroads made them extremely vulnerable. The tanks could not leave the road, and could not penetrate the densely overgrown date palms.

It was now that Brigadier Dutton suggested to Colonel Messenger that it might be time to organize reinforcements before the situation became desperate. The battle for control of Abu al-Khasib was on a knife-edge, with every unit involved in a firefight. L Company landed on a cleared area to the rear of D Company's zone of responsibility and moved towards the MSG's location to set up a secure perimeter for the night. Captain Lynch began to brief

L Company's commanding officer about the events of the day and the current situation, and was asked, naturally, whether the area was sufficiently secure to establish a company headquarters. No sooner had Captain Lynch assured him that it was than an RPG narrowly missed them, flying past to explode harmlessly in the mud. The situation was now extremely fluid, and it was spinning out of their control.

The Fedayeen had moved past the tanks on the road, using the cover of the trees and shrubs on either side of it, and outflanked the MSG's position. The marines were now in a serious situation. They had lost sight of the enemy, were unaware of the Iraqis' strength and disposition and there was now a danger that TAKU, secured at the beginning of the day by the Challengers of C Squadron, Royal Scots Dragoon Guards, might itself be overrun, threatening the security of the gains made by the other companies in Abu al-Khasib.

This, however, was of secondary importance as the troops in the MSG and L Company realized they had a severe fight on their hands, as small arms and RPG rockets once again filled the air. Lance Corporal Justin Thomas of the Machine-gun Troop leaped on to a Pinzgauer and, in full view of the enemy, poured heavy machine-gun fire at their positions in the palm groves. While the bullets shredded palm fronds, gouging splinters out of the trunks, the rest of the MSG crouched behind the vehicles gathering their kit, filling magazines and reloading before they, too, started returning fire. Corporal Thomas stayed in his position for more than fifteen minutes, pounding the Fedayeen with a hail of bullets until it was safe for the marines to move.

Over the last few hours, the Iraqis had been able to reinforce their positions. The Royal Scots Dragoon Guards squadron commander at TAKU had observed Iraqis arriving from Basra at a disused factory a couple of kilometres forward of their position, then buses and other vehicles loaded with people heading down a side road to the western end of Abu al-Khasib, and the Pussy crossroads.

A tank round might have stopped them but the tank commander could not see any weapons. It was highly unlikely but the buses might have been carrying civilians home at the end of a day's work, and shelling a busload of civilians was definitely excluded by the rules of engagement.

L Company moved forward, passing through the MSG line and advancing to where the Challengers had taken up a position close to the crossroads. At this point, when the arrival of a full-sized company should have tilted the balance of forces in favour of the Royal Marines, the Iraqis showed that they were capable of raising their game. The forces confronting the MSG were much more skilled and determined than the conventional troops 40 Commando had confronted ten days earlier on the tip of the al-Faw peninsula. They knew they were defending Basra, and that if the marines were successful in this battle for Abu al-Khasib, the psychological effect on the civilian population, in the suburb and in the city itself, would threaten the regime's hold on the area. Whether they were Fedayeen, Iraqi special forces or a combination, a sophisticated group of combatants was waiting for the marines to advance up the only route open to them. At the same time, they were co-ordinating a defensive position further east that would spring the ambush on the reinforcements that were coming from D Company to join in the battle for these vital crossroads.

Still confident, especially now with the increased weight of firepower and more feet on the ground provided by L Company, the marines once more advanced towards the crossroads. The Challengers were in the lead, and the footborne marines moved slowly behind them. This was no armour-driven juggernaut that A Company had advanced behind earlier that day: instead, the forward movement was at walking pace, the marines watchful, firing at any movement in the palm groves, and laying down machine-gun fire as the lead sections went forward.

They got closer and closer to the line of palms and the inhabited banks of the Shatt al-Arab when suddenly the lead Challenger was hit by five RPGs, all exploding against the turret and hull, aimed deliberately, and accurately, by brave Iraqis who had crept close enough to pick out the key vulnerable points of the massively strong, powerful machine.

The warheads struck the gunner's sights, the driver's periscope, the hull-mounted chain gun, the commander's cupola, and one exploded against the turret. In an instant there was confusion inside the tank, no one in the crew fully aware of the extent of the damage, and the driver, temporarily disoriented, slewed the tank over the edge of the road. It tilted, and as he desperately engaged reverse to bring it back on to an even keel, both tracks were shed, the sprockets spinning uselessly as the metal links unravelled from the wheels. The driver, hoping against hope, revved the giant diesel engine in vain. The tank was immobile, and the route to the crossroads was blocked. The fire was coming thick and furious as the Iraqis scented victory. They had achieved a major coup. One of the best main battle tanks in the world, with almost impregnable armour, had been disabled and brought to a standstill by shoulder-launched rocket-propelled grenades, whose warhead was puny in comparison to the thick armour of the tank. The commander of the Challenger called urgently on his radio, 'I need infantry.'

Captain Lynch thought that the crew of the tank were safer in their vehicle than anybody would be outside it, but they couldn't leave the disabled Challenger at the mercy of the Fedayeen.

The machine-gun section of the MSG moved forward, with the other tanks. A call went out for the armoured recovery vehicle, which had cleared the roadway of mines at the beginning of the day, to venture out from its squadron at TAKU and make another journey into Abu al-Khasib.

When it arrived, a group of engineers dismounted and started work on the damaged Challenger. There was one saving grace in the increasingly precarious situation and that was the clear area of glutinous mud that stretched perhaps fifty metres on either side of the road before the palms and buildings started. The open ground prevented the Iraqis approaching and overwhelming the tank with its defenders. The machine-gunners were pouring fire into the trees and buildings to protect the Armoured Corps engineers, who were braving assault rifles and RPGs while they worked.

The day had been a long one, and not only was a tank under siege but D Company had had to fight its way out of a deadly ambush.

Colonel Gordon Messenger considered the situation, and thought about the coming night. It would be a serious mistake for sections of sixty or so marines to be scattered across the area, subject to attack and incapable of offering each other mutual support. He reached a hard decision. The MSG must stay in place to defend the tank while it was repaired, while L and D Companies must combine and retreat to a harbour area, where they could set up sentries, establish defensive arcs of fire and the men could take turns to rest. Tomorrow was another day. L Company retreated.

When D Company was ambushed that afternoon, they were able to destroy the two Pinzgauers they had abandoned to prevent them falling into the hands of the enemy. It's almost impossible to destroy a Challenger tank, but nobody wanted to do that. The work to repair it continued as night fell, and the marines used whatever weapons were necessary to hold the Iraqis at bay. An Iraqi sniper was on a rooftop, firing on the small force defending the tank. Bullets struck fountains of dust off the surface of the road, and ricocheted off the tank's armour. A marine climbed on to the top of a Pinzgauer and aimed a Milan anti-tank rocket at the building. With a roar and a streak of flame it flew from the tube, trailing its guiding wire behind it. Skilfully the marine directed the missile through a window, then dropped it inside the house where it exploded. Whether the sniper was killed or merely beat a retreat no one knew, but he didn't fire again from that position.

The thermal imager on the tank was picking up hotspots now, the infrared signature of the Iraqis surrounding the position. The tank commander estimated there were around two hundred enemy fighters circling the position. The marines were seriously outnumbered, but the concentrated fire from the machine-guns and assault rifles was keeping them away.

At last the Challenger was secured to the recovery vehicle, the attempt at repairing the tracks having been abandoned because of the heavy fire, and it was towed back two and a half kilometres to TAKU, the Pinzgauers following it, machine-guns pouring fire into the surrounding darkness as the little convoy journeyed slowly down the road. The machine-gun troop used up 30,000 rounds of 7.62 ammunition that night, plus any number of Milan and LAW missiles.

The crippled Challenger was hauled safely back to TAKU, where the tanks and the marines of the MSG deployed into a compact harbour area. It was now almost two in the morning on 31 March and daybreak was not far off. Nobody had slept since three o'clock on the afternoon of 29 March, and exhaustion was reducing them to zombies. Despite that, Captain Lynch was concerned that the Iraqis had tracked them back to TAKU and would still pose a threat. He ordered everybody to stay alert, but within ten minutes of sitting down he had fallen asleep, waking with a start a few minutes later. He gave in, and issued instructions for a fifty-fifty watch-keeping rota. Most people had the chance of at least an hour's sleep before the next day dawned.

* * *

The rays of the rising sun filtered through the column of black smoke that was still rising from Oddjob.

The day brought no peace. The Iraqis had indeed tracked them to TAKU, and rounds of RPG fire and mortars descended on the marines. The first mortar landed a few metres from Captain Lynch but buried itself in the soft sand and he was unhurt, although deafened and shaken to the core. No orders were needed. The marines sprang to their vehicles and weapons, and once more barrels grew hot as bullets cut swathes of suppressive fire into vegetation and palm groves.

Fortunately, a few kilometres north, D and L Companies were about to make a combined assault across country to the crossroads at Pussy, and it was the Iraqis who were now facing the danger of being outflanked. The two companies advanced in a deliberate rhythm, one laying down enormous quantities of covering fire while sections moved forward clearing buildings and targeting any Iraqis they saw. They went through the area quickly, with far less resistance than the MSG had encountered the day before. The Iraqis had realized their chance of inflicting a defeat on the British had disappeared. Two hundred marines of D and L Companies were advancing from the east, while the MSG had started to move north up the road again, their vehicle-mounted machine-guns firing at anything that moved. The Fedayeen were outgunned, and had lost control of the terrain.

The marines finally took the crossroads at Pussy, and D Company stayed there in a defensive position, close to a school building. That afternoon, as the Iraqi forces disappeared, sentries observed a group of civilians coming towards them with coffins. It was a funeral party, to bury those killed in the fighting yesterday, and they wanted to come through D Company's position. A sergeant major went forward with a white flag to say that they could not pass through the marines' lines. For Major Pierson it was a surreal moment that was typical of the marines' war in Iraq, where the most vicious fighting was taking place among a population that wanted to go about its daily affairs, where donkey-driven cartloads of tomatoes would creak through roadblocks, past bodies, piles of shell cases and burned-out tanks.

D Company, at Pussy, were in a forward position, on a main route just three or four kilometres from Basra and the presidential palace, in a huge complex on the southern border of Basra abutting the banks of the Shatt al-Arab, like a modern Tower of London on the river Thames. Major Matt Pierson expected a response from the Iraqis sooner or later. Every night RPGs and mortars were fired against their position. Although they were random, poorly aimed and ineffective, they were tiring.

Then a few days after they had taken the position, on the final day of Operation James, a signal was sent to D Company headquarters from Brigade. The radio watch-keeper called in Matt Pierson to read it: a Predator unmanned spy plane flying over Basra had spotted two thousand armed men advancing towards their position. As he recalled, 'It was a sobering thought. I asked for clarification, via the signals officer, and they said in reply, "Believe three hundred." Even so it was a problem.'

As he pondered what to do, the sniper section on the perimeter reported that an advance guard of thirty armed men was in sight and had taken up a position behind the school. 'We imagined that the larger group was forming up to their rear, out of our sight.'

The commander of 40 Commando's Mortar Troop, which was part of the Commando Headquarters Company, was visiting D Company's position. Pierson remembered, 'He said to me, "They have formed up behind the school." I said, "We know they're behind the school." I was quite irritated. It wasn't the time for idle chat, and he said, "Well, that's where we put the FPF!"' It was shorthand for final protective fire. In a defensive position the Commando Mortar Troop, who have the larger 81-mm mortars under their control, with a range of more than five kilometres, will calculate a number of different aiming points so that they can quickly fire on a potential enemy if a position is attacked. The significance of the mortar commander's remark now became apparent to Matt Pierson: 'The final protective fire position is the one that is closest to your position. It's the last one they aim for if you're in a fix.'

He called for a minute and a half of mortar fire on the company's final protective fire position and the mortar commander was quick to authorize it. The mortars were fired from a rear position and passed directly overhead before landing behind the school.

'It was like Armageddon. It was only a hundred and fifty metres away, danger close. It was deafening, flashes of yellow and white, and we all dived for cover. Everyone was deaf. We waited a long time, forty-five minutes, but no one approached us. Finally we went out. We found blood, bits of uniform, weapons, a few injured survivors. The rest must have seen what had happened to their vanguard and gone back. It would have been a horrific lesson for them.'

There were no more attacks on Pussy or any other positions that 40 Commando had taken in Operation James. They had accomplished all that they had planned, sailing through the Mediterranean in *Ocean*, and much that they had only thought a vague possibility. All that was left, just a few kilometres away, was the city of Basra.

14

BASRA

The lengthy and hard-fought occupation of Abu al-Khasib by 40 Commando had been the final and most important piece of the jigsaw in the capture of Basra.

While 3 Commando Brigade and General Brims in Divisional Headquarters had been considering Colonel Messenger's plan to seize Abu al-Khasib, other units of the 1st Armoured Division had taken up positions around Basra and were applying pressure on the defending forces. At the start of the invasion of Iraq, the division had moved north past Umm Qasr on the right flank of the US 1st Marine Division, along Highway 7, moving through the Rumailah oilfield and separating from the US Marines at Az Zubayr. The US Marines continued north to Baghdad, while the British 1st Armoured Division had headed for Basra. Once on the outskirts, they spread out.

The 16th Air Assault Brigade, with the Parachute Regiment, took up a position to the north of the city, straddling Highway 6 to Baghdad but not closing it off. The 7th Armoured Brigade took up position to the south-west, and Operation James brought 3 Commando Brigade close to the city limits in the south-east. 42 Commando had also moved forward.

It would have been possible at this stage to tighten the grip on the city, cut off food and water, making life difficult for the inhabitants and the Ba'ath Party leadership, potentially inciting a revolt against the latter.

A number of informers and agents had been infiltrated into the city before the invasion, and information had been passed to Divisional Head-quarters about signs of opposition and an apparent mutiny by some regular soldiers. The Ba'ath Party had responded brutally. Some military leaders who had wanted to get rid of Chemical Ali had been executed, artillery had been fired against the civilian population, and people who had tried to flee the city and reach British lines had been mortared and machine-gunned. There were also reports that the Ba'ath Party had taken the families of soldiers hostage to force them to remain in their positions.

If General Brims now raised the stakes and imposed an iron siege on the city there would be escalating civilian deaths, and Basra might collapse into anarchy. It would be harder for the British to seize it and the troops would be walking into a humanitarian crisis that would be difficult to deal with, and give the lie to the coalition's expressed aims of bringing peace and security to the population of Iraq.

General Brims adopted a much more subtle and effective tactic. He set up a series of roadblocks and checkpoints on the routes leading into the city. Vehicles were searched for arms, their goods given a cursory inspection, and then they were allowed on their way. Every day there were queues of vehicles, buses, cars and lorries loaded with tomatoes, watermelons and other produce, waiting to pass through the checkpoints. People would be spoken to, given leaflets; often they would give the interpreters information about the state of the Iraqi Army and conditions inside the city. No one attempted to prevent ordinary people going in and out of Basra. The British tactic was calculated to apply psychological and political pressure on the leadership without creating a humanitarian disaster.

The Ba'ath leadership in the city, who were trying to influence the population and fearful of another uprising from the predominantly Shia inhabitants, were unable to respond to this. They knew that information was leaking to the British. They also knew that people were being influenced by British propaganda, but short of closing down Basra, and cutting off supplies of food, there was little they could do.

The leadership was becoming isolated, a wedge being driven between them and the population.

Of course, the Iraqi Army and the Fedayeen could use this freedom of movement to gather intelligence about the disposition of British forces around the city and use it to counter-attack. Fedayeen raiding parties would occasionally come out to attack the British checkpoints, in taxis or buses, but they would be fired on by snipers or machine-gun teams before they could get close enough to do any damage. Militarily the regime had already lost. The time for a counter-attack had been at the very beginning, when 40 Commando were establishing a position on the al-Faw peninsula. It was now too late, and the Fedayeen's ineffectual raiding parties had more of a propaganda function than a military one.

The loose cordon had another advantage for the British. It was possible for covert groups of special forces and reconnaissance troops to infiltrate the city, and spy on the defenders.

By 30 March incursions were being made into the city from various points on the periphery. Small teams of Warrior tracked vehicles, each armed with a 30-mm cannon in a turret and seven troops in the hull, would drive into various areas of the city. They would attack previously identified army barracks or guardposts, then leave quickly.

These harassing raids were another form of pressure on the leadership. Snipers targeted Iraqi military figures and Fedayeen members, which was deeply unsettling for the regime's representatives, and made clear that there was nowhere to hide, that an attack was inevitable. They also wore down the defenders, who could never tell whether or not a raid was the start of a bigger incursion. Those mobile sweeps were also a way to insert sniper teams and forward-observation officers who could target the Ba'ath Party infrastructure, pinpointing their offices and leading figures in the city.

A Royal Marine amphibious unit, 539 Assault Squadron, had sailed with the task group to assist with the clearance of the beach near the pipelines on the al-Faw peninsula, and also to control the waterways at Umm Qasr. They had established a crossing point on the Khawr Az Zubayr river and patrolled it with landing craft and small, fast patrol boats. While conducting these operations, one of the landing craft had been hit by a Milan missile fired by a unit from 42 Commando, who were providing force protection for the Royal Engineers at the crossing point. Marine Christopher Maddison was killed, and several others injured in this friendly-fire incident. However, the next day the unit continued its operations and expanded to begin patrols on the Shatt al-Arab. They integrated their operations with 40 Commando, and patrolled the banks of Abu al-Khasib, monitoring the movement of Iraqi fishing-boats and preventing reinforcements entering Basra via the river. They also started providing assistance to some of the fishermen, and used those contacts to gather intelligence about the defences along the waterway in Basra. On 3 April they made an incursion up the Shatt al-Arab, alongside the compound housing the enormous presidential palace and further up into the old port, encountering almost no resistance.

On 5 April the covert intelligence-gathering operations inside Basra bore fruit, with information about the hiding-place of Chemical Ali, Saddam Hussein's representative in southern Iraq. A GPS-guided JDAM attack was authorized, based on targeting information given by a covert forward-observation officer. An F-16 aircraft carried out the mission, which destroyed the targeted building. Rumours of his supposed death spread rapidly throughout Basra and another JDAM attack was directed at a supposed Ba'ath Party meeting that was taking place at a hall in the city. Sadly, Chemical Ali escaped, and the air raid killed several innocent civilians, including ten members of the family of Dr Akram Hassan, the director of Basra's teaching hospital. His villa had been wrongly identified as Chemical Ali's refuge.

However, the belief that the raids had succeeded, and other information that resistance in the city seemed to be crumbling, prompted General Brims to mount a larger, more co-ordinated raid on the outskirts of Basra. On the morning of 6 April the Challengers accompanied Warrior armoured vehicles to the north of the city. The intention was that they would drive deep into Basra and establish a position, then retreat at nightfall. However, as they advanced they met no resistance. They drove on until they encountered Iraqi soldiers and Fedayeen at concrete pillboxes and fortified houses. These positions were quickly abandoned, and it became obvious that the Iraqi defence was falling apart.

General Brims was still under the command of General McKiernan of the US Marines: he phoned McKiernan and suggested that now was the time to go into Basra. McKiernan concurred, and at 1100 Brims gave the order for a full-scale assault on the city.

The first and most serious fighting was experienced by the Challengers and Warrior-mounted infantry, who had made the initial advance into the city. After their confrontation with the Iraqi Army they continued their advance and met serious opposition centred on the university, known as the College of Literature. This was defended by more than three hundred militia, and it took at least three hours to clear the buildings of opposition. The infantry had to fight their way through building after building, room after room, using grenades and assault rifles, but eventually it was in the hands of the British. 7th Armoured Brigade set up a forward operating base there. The back of Fedayeen resistance in Basra had been broken. General Brims had left open routes to the north for some time, and only now started to move the 16th Air Assault Brigade to close them, although the regular Iraqi Army and many of the Basra leadership had already taken this route out of the city.

3 Commando Brigade was ordered to move north from the front line at Abu al-Khasib and sweep along the Shatt al-Arab to seize the south-east of the city and the presidential palace.

Over the past few days Major May, commander of M Company, 42 Commando, had moved forward from Az Zubayr and was ready to pass through 40 Commando's lines at Blofeld, the polytechnic that Major Pierson and D Company had taken hours to clear at the start of Operation James. They went through 40 Commando's lines at night, then in the morning had a hurried orders group. Colonel May remembers he was given the execute order and told to be ready to advance from his line of departure within forty-five minutes.

Colonel Buster Howes called it 'a slight sort of creeping start off our line of departure'. It may have been rushed, compared with the 120 pages of orders that had been written for the original airborne assault on the al-Faw peninsula, and it was an *ad hoc* operation, but it was well organized and effective nonetheless. 42 Commando went forward with C Squadron of Challengers from the Royal Scots Dragoon Guards, who had previously combined with

40 Commando in Abu al-Khasib. Once again, their advance was an advance to contact, a move forward searching for enemy forces, with orders to secure bridges carrying roads leading into the city.

Howes, commanding 42 Commando, thought there were a considerable number of unknowns in the equation. 'We weren't at all sure what we were going to confront. I remember expecting some very heavy fighting and we had a squadron of tanks and I pushed the tanks. I peeled the tanks out because they were making really good progress, and as the opportunity unfolded I pushed more and more of them. I stripped them out of the combined-arms groupings and they ran a seam up the side of a river. I got them right into a screening position to guard my flank so I could punch my companies in at speed behind them. There was a risk that they were going to be isolated, but it was almost the classic liberation of Paris. In very short order it went from expecting a pretty serious urban fight to people waving palm leaves, applauding and all the rest of it.'

It was 'Daisy' May's job to put Buster Howes's scheme of manoeuvre into practice. He found that his route north was through the palm groves running along the side of the Shatt al-Arab, the same plantations that the Brigade Reconnaissance Force (BRF) had fought through as they cleared the way up the peninsula in Operation Leah. May was not happy with this: it would be slow and he wanted to advance up the main road that ran parallel to the plantations on a raised levee through the mudflats.

M Company had to secure five bridges, and charged up the road with the squadron of Challengers, leaving a tank at each bridge with a troop of marines. The speed of their advance took the Iraqis by surprise. According to May, 'We had unhinged their plan and they were just streaming over the bridges, which we closed after them.'

There was panic among the Iraqi forces as M Company and the tanks advanced. The marines could observe that cars and lorries were being commandeered by Fedayeen, who were using them to retreat into Basra. J Company followed up the road in their Pinzgauers. The BRF under Captain Chris Haw had been relieved from its post guarding the bridge at Sennen by D Company, and the BRF had been split. Chris Haw now found himself on the boats of the amphibious 539 Assault Squadron in the Shatt al-Arab working with another SEALs team. They had attempted a waterborne approach to Basra up the Shatt al-Arab via the sea. However, when they approached the mouth of the channel as it entered the Gulf, they had been intercepted by Iranian armed patrol craft. Not wanting to engage the Iranian Revolutionary Guards the SEALs withdrew and their boats were carried by truck and helicopter to 539 Assault Squadron's forward base on the al-Faw peninsula. On 6 April they had set out on the water, and Chris Haw revelled in the equipment the SEALs brought to everything they did.

'So, again, we were right at the front of everything, effectively to do a pincer movement on to the palace. I found myself with some American special forces [the SEALs] and they were pretty pumped up. They had all sorts of kit and these mini unmanned aerial vehicles [UAV], which were flying around. They were great and we had downlinks from the UAV on to the laptop to see what was in the palace. We had Iran on our right-hand side and there had been a few engagements from the Iranian side of the bank, but the lads were under precise instructions not to return fire.'

While the boats were moving up the waterway, M Company had stayed firm on the road junctions and bridges, blocking access to them, and J Company moved towards the palace. It was surrounded by a high wall with watchtowers, and a canal had been dug round it that connected with the Shatt al-Arab and acted like a moat. Three gates controlled access to the compound. It was easy to defend, with the watchtowers covering extensive killing areas and with overlapping arcs of fire covering the approach roads to the gates.

The surveillance pictures from the SEALs' Predator revealed a number of armed troops inside the compound. Buster Howes decided that a show of force was necessary and requested that a US Marine Corps Harrier carry out an attack on one of the buildings in the compound. A 1000-pound bomb penetrated the roof and exploded, the building disappearing in a cloud of smoke and dust from pulverized brick and plaster.

The Iraqi guards left the compound. J Company, closely followed by the Commando Tactical HQ, were now free to enter the building, a symbol of Saddam Hussein and the Ba'ath Party's domination of the city and its inhabitants for more than twenty years.

Captain Haw was still on the Shatt al-Arab, becoming increasingly worried about the possibility of another friendly-fire incident. He knew that there were guards in the palace, and that 42 Commando would attempt to clear it from the landward side. If the guards spotted them and opened fire, or the SEALs believed they were under attack and started firing at the palace, there was a distinct possibility that they would be firing on members of 42 Commando too. It was an extremely fast-moving situation, and nobody had complete situational awareness. 42 Commando's recce troop had moved far forward and were close to the rabbit warren of streets that was the old town of Basra, inaccessible to Challenger tanks and Warrior armoured vehicles. Part of the BRF had entered the city with members of the SEALs team and was heading directly for Chemical Ali's house – or, at least, the house that had been bombed the day before. They had an Assigned

Specialist Site Exploitation (ASSES) team with them, in a mission to find evidence of chemical weapons. They would spread across Iraq in the days to come, hoping to uncover what Saddam had so successfully, it was claimed, hidden from the UN inspection teams that had scoured the country in the weeks preceding the war.

Chris Haw recalls thinking, ' "I'm in charge of this, and if these American guys start firing in what they think is self-defence they're gonna mow down 42 Commando guys on the bank." We discussed this with the 42 hierarchy and it was a really tense situation. It was tempting to land and go into the palace, but that would have been tempting fate, and also we'd been told by Colonel Howes that that was not to happen because they had to clear it through from the land side. And we effectively cleared the water flank of the palace.'

J Company, the rest of the BRF and the Commando Headquarters Company entered the palace to find that it was grossly ornate, with huge chandeliers, giant murals, silk curtains and rugs, the obligatory gold-plated door handles and gold-plated taps in the bathrooms. They went through room after room and it seemed to stretch on endlessly. It was a sharp contrast with the poor shanty town on the edge of the industrial area, which had seen the first fighting between the Challengers and the Ba'ath Party militia that morning.

However, Buster Howes and the men of 42 Commando were determined to make it their home for a while.

The next day the Parachute Regiment moved into the old town and met very little resistance. Basra, the administrative and commercial centre of southern Iraq and the Rumailah oilfields, had fallen, and was under British control. 42 Commando started putting patrols in place the next day. M Company stayed on their blocking positions on the bridges and junctions for two days, then moved into the city, setting up sniper positions on roofs and starting patrols.

Captain Haw felt entry to the palace was a significant and fitting end to the Royal Marines' operation in the al-Faw peninsula, an exceptional conclusion to the débâcle of their aborted landing. 'Thank God for that. We've done it, we're in the palace, we've salvaged ourselves.'

In retrospect he was proud, too, of the way that the Royal Marines were able to adopt a peacekeeping role after the occupation of Basra. 'We switched from high-intensity war fighting, which is effectively what we had been doing, to peace-support operations literally overnight. Guys had been driving around, waiting for an engagement, then opening up on an enemy or an insurgent. Now they were driving around with seatbelts on in the Land Rovers, getting out, rifles by their sides, chatting to the locals. And the lads were extremely professional and adapted very well to it. But there was a definite challenge in changing the mindset from being in high-intensity war fighting to being in a peace-support operation.'

The problems they were about to confront became obvious in the next few days. In al-Faw, Umm Qasr, and Abu al-Khasib, despite the retreat of the Iraqi forces and militia, residual conflict continued, manifesting itself in an RPG being fired, or an assault rifle being loosed off at a distance. Now, in Basra, the removal of authority unleashed a wave of pent-up anger and resentment against the privations and shortages of the old regime.

Colonel Howes said, 'Mayhem occurred. A bit like a cork coming out of a champagne bottle, they all went berserk and started looting and burning, and an area that had been appallingly undercapitalized for years under the Ba'ath regime was completely trashed. There was much subsequent criticism – why didn't we stop it? There were hundreds of thousands of people just going berserk, and short of shooting them in large numbers there was no way of deterring them, none at all. If we'd done that, we would have been involved in some hideous wide-scale urban fight against the populace, which would have been totally counter-productive.'

There was mass looting of shops, offices, clinics and hospitals, and people carted anything they could carry out of every government building they could enter. There were also attacks on Ba'athists and local representatives of the regime who had not escaped out of the city. They were lynched or beaten to death.

The British armed forces were now responsible for a city of over 1.5 million people, and an area of Iraq with towns and villages containing another million at least. In those areas that 40 Commando had occupied in the al-Faw peninsula, the marines were now attempting to take over as the interim authority. It was a far cry from orders groups and schemes of manoeuvre. As company commanders searched for offices and permanent company headquarters in Abu al-Khasib and al-Faw town, Colonel Gordon Messenger had little advice to offer beyond the injunction 'Don't act like God.'

15

DON'T PLAY GOD

After Operation James the majority of 40 Commando remained in their area of responsibility in Abu al-Khasib, now policing the districts through which they had just fought. Foot patrols were sent out to dominate the ground, and vehicle patrols went to control key junctions and make mobile patrols through more rural areas. Operation James had been a victory, but the war was not yet over.

Companies searched out buildings where they could establish headquarters and living quarters, and Major Holt of A Company elected to occupy the barracks from which Iraqi troops had fled, leaving cups of coffee on the table. He set up Company Headquarters in the former commander's office, although it was in a squalid state.

A Company had been sent a field human-intelligence team, a group of Arabic-speaking intelligence officers from Divisional Headquarters, so they could start to process the information the patrols brought back. Barely twenty-four hours after the end of the fighting, a delegation of leading citizens came up to the main gate of the barracks, asking to discuss with their occupiers what would happen in the town. Justin Holt thought it was a helpful proposal, and agreed to a meeting the next day.

Major Matt Jackson, whose B Company had fought through to the Shatt al-Arab on the right flank of A Company, set up his headquarters in a school. His area included part of the old port and some military docks along the waterway; foot patrols found that the area was being looted by the local population. In fact, anything that couldn't be protected was 'liberated' and one of B Company's patrols saw someone driving away a bus.

Matt Jackson went to visit Justin Holt about a signal he'd received concerning the local Ba'ath Party headquarters in Abu al-Khasib, which were located in B Company's area of responsibility. He noticed the marked difference between Holt's palatial quarters and the wrecked building B Company was occupying. They talked about how to deal with the presence of Ba'ath Party members in the area and how to co-ordinate their patrols. They both knew that there were still Ba'ath militia and Fedayeen in the area, and that the Party headquarters and other government buildings would be a focus of resistance. In fact, a B Company patrol had found an enormous cache of arms and ammunition in the docks that included thirty RPG rounds, 8000 rounds of small-arms ammunition and twenty 82-mm mortar shells.

Colonel Messenger had paid a visit to the various company areas during the day with the news that each would have the opportunity to go for a day's rest and refurbishment in a rear area. This sounded like good news to everybody, but the downside for B Company was that they would be, according to Matt Jackson, 'the rent-a-company that moves in to take over everyone's area while they go. B Company would be the last, reinforcing our company motto of "First in last out".' There was also some indication that B Company would be sent back to the al-Faw peninsula to guard the pipelines, which, again, they did not look forward to.

Jackson visited Commando Main Headquarters to make enquiries about the members of his forward-observation team, which had been the accidental target of the preliminary artillery fire at the start of Operation James. The most seriously injured had been sent to Cyprus for treatment, but most were recovering from shrapnel wounds. A marine who had escaped with minor bruises and a lot of shrapnel through his respirator container had been allowed back to the company, and told Matt that all of the forward-observation party had already taken cover because they thought the Scimitar covering their line of departure was about to open fire. It was for this reason, he believed, that nobody had been killed.

When Matt Jackson returned to his company headquarters, a local resident had come to see him with the information that two houses close to the bridge where B Company had been ambushed were now occupied by ten or twelve soldiers with RPGs. He had more information: armed men were hiding near the fire station in A Company's area. He was escorted to the intelligence team at Justin Holt's headquarters to give them the details.

Both Justin Holt and Matt Jackson organized patrols to keep a discreet watch on the buildings. The next morning the human intelligence team and a patrol went out to raid the suspect locations but found nothing. The buildings were empty, although apparently had been occupied until very recently.

Intelligence was being received at Commando Main Headquarters, and passed down to Holt, that the threat from militias was increasing. Although Operation James had been a major defeat for the Fedayeen and Iraqi forces, Justin Holt suspected that Ba'ath Party hardliners and militia were moving freely about the town. They were unarmed and in civilian clothes, watching what the marines were up to and intimidating anyone who was prepared to speak to the British forces. If the patrols couldn't find where they were operating from and take them out of circulation, they would remain as a threat to security and do long-term damage to the marines' credibility.

The next morning a delegation of local dignitaries arrived at the gate of the barracks to talk to Justin Holt, as they had arranged on their visit the day before. They sat down in the open under a shade tree and discussed what the town needed and what the marines could do to help. There was a lunch invitation, which Justin accepted: he enjoyed a lavish meal, a welcome change from the marines' rations. His assessment was that his host, the leader of the Iraqi delegation, was a shrewd businessman who was prepared to recognize British authority and hoped to benefit as the first to establish a working relationship with them.

The next day Major Jackson and B Company were given orders to move up to the forward area and replace L Company around Pussy and Galore. A Company was going to expand its area and take over part of B Company's patrols. The handover was completed successfully, but several incidents reminded the marines that their occupation of Abu al-Khasib was not very secure. A section guarding Sennen, the bridge that the Brigade Reconnaissance Force (BRF) had captured on the morning of 30 March, came under mortar attack. Holt sent a quick-reaction force to the area. The mortars were erratic, and the Iraqis were probably firing blind because the enemy fire didn't follow the section as they deployed to a defensive position. The quick-reaction force arrived after twenty minutes but it wasn't possible to locate where the mortars had been fired from. It had alarmed the residents though: they rushed out of their houses and demanded to know what was happening, prepared to flee if fighting was about to start.

Later that evening the compound of the barracks in which A Company was based came under fire from machine-guns and rocket-propelled grenades. There were shouts of 'Stand to', and at the sounds of gunfire and the explosions of the RPG, Holt raced to the roof to try to spot the firing points, but it was a fruitless effort in the dark. He went to the operations room and talked a patrol into position by radio, hoping they might be able to block the Iraqis' escape, but this also came to nothing.

Earlier that day, some walk-in informers had come with information about two buildings close to the barracks, which were supposed to be sheltering Ba'ath Party activists. They overlooked the compound and could be used to spy on the marines' movements. It seemed likely that this was where the firing had come from.

The next day at first light, around 0530, the marines conducted two simultaneous house raids. One of the suspect locations was empty, but the other was occupied by a woman, her daughter and son. They were terrified by the armed marines who were storming around her house. The informer had said that she was a Ba'ath Party spy. Her husband was a colonel in the Iraqi Air Force, still in Baghdad, still fighting the war, although the air force had been absent so far from the fighting. Only a few days earlier Justin had followed his company as they advanced, firing, through the suburb, the accompanying Challengers blasting 120-mm shells into houses and other targets from which resistance was coming. Now he found the distress of this woman deeply upsetting. She was so frightened that she could barely speak. The marines left her. Justin Holt knew that the searches were not what was needed: 'The men had been professional, but it was violent, aggressive and aimed at civilians, who couldn't be anything but terrified.'

Five houses were searched that morning, and eleven people brought in for questioning; they provided little information. In the evening Holt sent large patrols into the streets when people were out of their houses. There was some small-arms fire at a troop, and information was received about another attack on the barracks but nothing happened that night.

The next day it was A Company's turn to go back to Brigade Headquarters, where there were facilities for the men to wash, put on clean clothes, attend to their kit and have proper meals for the first time since they had landed more than a fortnight ago.

B Company had an interesting time in L Company area. On 5 April two Iraqi T-55 tanks were observed rumbling down the road that led to the crossroads, TAKU; they were immediately destroyed by the Challengers stationed there. There was also a half-hearted attack on the recce troops' area, which resulted in one Iraqi soldier being killed and six others taken prisoner. Major Matt Jackson was told that after his day of rest and refurbishment in the rear-echelon facility at Az Zubayr, B Company would return to where it had landed in Iraq, this time to guard the monitoring and metering station (MMS), the pipelines, and maintain security in al-Faw town. His heart plummeted. He had had an opportunity to talk to the commander of C Company, which had been left on the al-Faw peninsula while the rest of 40 Commando had fought its way up to the outskirts of Basra. This officer had felt abject at being sidelined, and missing the fighting, and complained to Jackson that he had been driven almost insane with boredom, having nothing to do but look out at the river.

Matt Jackson was worried that the same might happen to him and his men, particularly if there was any fighting in Basra.

When he reached Az Zubayr he spoke to Colonel Gordon Messenger, who could offer him nothing except the advice that he had to remain positive when discussing the issue with his men.

B Company drove to the metering station, reaching

it on the day before the assault on Basra. Jackson sent the company out into the compound; half were to occupy the pipelines and the perimeter that had been set up around them. When he heard that the British had entered Basra, with little fighting, and that there had been no repeat of an assault like Operation James, his despair at being given a 'made-up job' abated, and he reflected that there were some benefits to the peace and quiet of the al-Faw peninsula. His accommodation was the most comfortable he had enjoyed for weeks.

Al-Faw town was quiet. The marines returning from their first patrols reported that the residents were friendly and that the children were giving them bullets as though they were sweets. There was, however, a problem with looting and lawlessness after dark.

The next day Matt Jackson toured the town, observing that the most damaged part was the Ba'ath Party headquarters, which A Company had blown its way into and left burning on the first night after the invasion. It was completely trashed, and had been further damaged by subsequent looting. Inside, he walked over shattered glass, collapsed ceilings and piles of singed files from overturned cabinets.

He visited the hospital, and found a developing crisis because of the lack of drinking water. Gastro-enteritis was common and there were fears it would become an epidemic. The two doctors in charge were also concerned that, now Basra had fallen, their supply of drugs would dry up. The next day Jackson called a meeting at the hospital, hoping to get not only the two doctors but a water engineer, an electrical engineer and the police chief to attend, as well as the imams from the Sunni and Shia mosques. He was concerned about the water situation, but in any event he had to get some form of local authority working.

The response was good. It was clear from the discussions that water was a priority, and the town needed two tankers-full daily. In addition the power lines had been destroyed in the first days of the war, cleared to make helicopter landing sites, and needed urgent repair. Matt Jackson was dubious about how long this would take. But there were two generators at the metering station that the hospital could take if they worked. In the meantime, the leading town representative requested a delivery of a tanker of diesel each day to fuel individual generators.

Jackson wanted the schools back in business, and the police to get back on the streets. The police chief wasn't prepared to send his men back to work without more security, so Jackson agreed to set up joint patrols in the town. As the meeting closed, a doctor pointed out that the police chief was a Ba'ath Party member. It didn't matter, said the leader of the meeting; he was necessary for the administration. Jackson had to agree.

B Company did not stay long in al-Faw town, however. Matt Jackson oversaw the arrival of the water tankers, and assisted with the removal of the two generators from the MMS to the hospital, but then he received fresh orders to move to a guard position for the forward operating base of the Royal Marine Assault Squadron, Neptune, on the Shatt al-Arab. Before the Company left, with their quad bikes and other equipment loaded on to the backs of two tank transporters, Jackson saw the first delivery of humanitarian aid to the town. The two thousand boxes caused an enormous crowd of people to descend on the metering station, which the Iraqi police were barely able to control. Jackson was amazed to see the contents: washing powder, soap, buckets, brooms and sanitary towels.

B Company spent a peaceful time at Neptune, then returned to Kuwait, via Az Zubayr, and boarded HMS *Ocean* for a long period of decompression. They were looking forward to a lengthy trip home, but Matt Jackson was told that some senior army officers at the Ministry of Defence believed that the Royal Marines had been receiving too much publicity, and didn't want a triumphant return, with HMS *Ocean* sailing into Portsmouth harbour, the marines of 40 Commando lining its flight deck. After a few days on board, with the marines doing a great deal of drinking and sleeping, they finally flew home on 11 May.

A Company returned to Abu al-Khasib after its day of rest and relaxation. Basra had fallen, and although they were on notice for rapid deployment, they were not needed. The routine in the suburbs of searches and arrests continued. Although inform-ation came in, the searches never turned up any of the suspects the patrols were looking for, and the inform-ers still seemed frightened of reprisals. A night foot patrol had one success when it stopped a taxi, and found that the two occupants had a cargo of ten AK-47s. The marines had fired shots to extinguish some street-lights and the residents thought that the two men had been killed. Throughout the next day, people approached the barracks to find out what had happened to the men and recover their bodies for burial.

Major Holt wanted to make progress, and thought he needed to establish more of a presence in the town. A permanent patrol in the centre of Abu al-Khasib would be possible if it had a permanent patrol base, and he identified a building that would be perfect as such. It was new, had been built as offices just before the invasion, and never used by any of the regime's organizations. It had two storeys and the plan was that a troop of marines could stay on the first floor on a forty-eight-hour duty, providing security and running regular patrols, while the ground floor could be used as offices where local Iraqis could talk to the marines. It was located prominently, next to one of the town's big mosques, and would take a lot of security pressure off the barracks. A Troop went in and secured the building, which started operating the next day. Justin hoped it would encourage the residents to take some initiatives in getting the town going again. In Commando Headquarters it was already being referred to as A Company's 'drop-in centre'.

One local dignitary did come forward to offer his services, and Holt recruited him to help in making a shortlist of people who were senior figures in the old Ba'ath regime from the hundred-plus names he had been given. Whittling it down, they selected those whose names were most mentioned by the informers, and were left with around ten. The BRF had now been attached to A Company and Holt preferred its members to carry out the 'snatch' operations. Planning to arrest the two men at the top of the most-wanted list, the BRF went into the area close to their houses and started to distribute leaflets about the current situation with the war. A crowd gathered and the marines took two men who had come out of one of the houses to see what the fuss was about; they turned out to be the brother and nephew of one of the wanted men. They were taken back to the drop-in centre where they were questioned. Although they were very frightened, they insisted that the target, a leading Ba'ath Party enforcer, had left town some time ago. Justin Holt let the brother of the wanted man, who was weak with fear, return home, but detained the nephew overnight as a hostage for the appearance of the Ba'athist who, Justin was convinced, was still active in Abu al-Khasib.

It was a schizophrenic policy, and Justin Holt was the first to acknowledge it as such. During the day the marines would attempt to win over the hearts and minds of the local residents, and encourage them to use the offices as a meeting place, but at night houses were raided and people dragged off for questioning. Justin didn't know what to do: the presence of the Ba'ath Party and its agents hung over the town, and the marines only realized how potent the threat was when they attempted to take two of their chief informant's associates with them to identify five houses belonging to members of the Ba'ath Party security organization. As the patrol vehicles got closer to the location of the first house, the two Iraqis became more and more agitated, until they begged the marines to stop, got out of the Land Rover and ran for it as fast as they could. The mission was aborted.

While the search for senior members of the regime continued, without any success, the marines were sometimes asked to assist in local disputes. One day the offices were disturbed by crashing and shouting as four men dragged another up to the door. He was under arrest and they wanted to hand him over to the British. Under questioning it turned out that he was a member of the Security Services Organization, one of the most feared units of secret police, and had been responsible for abducting and torturing many people. However, the four men, who were brothers, had arrested him because he had stolen a dowry paid to him to marry their young sister. She had eloped with him, become pregnant, yet they had not married. They wanted their dowry money back and also help with locating their sister so they could kill her for dishonouring the family. Justin Holt was grateful to them for bringing in the prisoner, but declined to interfere in the other matter.

Some local incidents had to be addressed, however, and one was the murder of a fourteen-year-old boy who had been shot while fishing with his uncle. Two armed men had tried to murder the uncle, in an on-going family feud, and the boy had been killed. Holt sent a squad to arrest the men, and arranged for a Royal Military Police squad to start a murder investigation.

By 14 April Iraqis were visiting the offices, but Holt was suspicious of the motives of many who were informing on others who had committed crimes under the Ba'ath regime. He had an ever-growing list of people's names given by walk-in informers, and believed most of them were the result of old scores being settled between clans or families. It seemed to him that half the male population between the ages of sixteen and sixty had been accused by someone of deserving arrest and questioning. He reduced the list to thirty names. The process got him no further: that afternoon they went to arrest three people but they were long gone.

Gradually, other things started to improve, giving the impression that some progress was being made in restoring a semblance of a functioning administration to Abu al-Khasib. The members of the local fire brigade returned now that the war was over, asked for their salary and would often drive around in their fire engine. Most of its hoses and pumps had been looted, so it was largely ineffectual, but the men were followed back to work by the police chief, who in Justin's judgement was fairly popular, and members of the police force. Shortly after, the marines and some local policemen were making joint local foot patrols at night. How effective the local police would be in fighting the wave of robberies and looting was hard to judge. Vehicle checkpoints were set up on the road to Basra, manned jointly by police and marines, looking for arms and explosives being brought into the town. The police met old friends, and started long conversations, catching up with everything that had happened in the past three weeks. They moved off for a coffee and a sit down with their old acquaintances, and very quickly the checkpoint was manned solely by British marines.

Justin Holt invited representatives of the clans and heads of outlying villages, as well as dignitaries from the town, to a meeting to elect a council. Twenty-two people arrived at the drop-in centre, most of whom had brought their eldest sons to observe the meeting. Holt wanted them to select seven representatives, who would take responsibility for security, education and the administration of justice. He left the room while they got on with it. After twenty minutes they had chosen seven people. The man selected to take care of education was an Iraqi Army colonel. His unit had been wiped out in the war; those soldiers surviving the first attack had either surrendered or run away. He had two young children and, according to Justin, seemed more interested in running the local schools than in returning to the army.

Justin had told the chairman of the council that he would only provide enough security for them to function. His instructions had been vague. Beyond Gordon Messenger's injunction not to behave like God, he had been flying blind. He had no authority to do so, but Justin informed the chairman of the council that he would now take advice from them.

He had one other success. A few nights previously, one of the informers who had run away when taken to a suspect house had agreed to work with the marines, but only at night and in disguise. Justin Holt detailed A Company's Mortar Troop as the snatch squad, and they rehearsed the operation during the day. At night they went to two suspects' houses, under the guidance of their informer, where they charged and arrested two men. Both were members of the Iraqi special forces and responsible for the attacks on the bridge.

On 20 April the centre of Abu al-Khasib was crowded and noisy. Residents were gathering for a Shia religious festival that had not been celebrated publicly for more than twenty years.

The town council had been established, but there were few resources for it to administer. The overall governance of the country was still in the hands of US forces. There was a feeling that humanitarian aid would soon flow over the border with Kuwait, once the fighting had ended but, as Justin Holt remarked, 'That myth was beginning to turn sour because we did not see a single organization other than a man from the Red Cross, who decided that our hospital, although secure, was insufficiently needy.' However, there were still enormous problems with inadequate supplies of clean water, electricity and fuel. The only petrol was being brought into the town by the army, and was being distributed on the basis of need. First on the list were buses and taxis, then agricultural tractors, and then individuals for their electricity generators. The petrol was free, but the first supplies were quickly offered for sale by the local petrol station at an extortionate price, and a huge crowd of protesters gathered at the pumps. Justin told the owner that he would let the crowd lynch him if he didn't stop profiteering.

On 24 April A Company left the barracks at Abu al-Khasib and the town with all its problems. Some order had been achieved, and Holt felt that, compared to the situation in Basra, the town and its residents had made enormous progress in the transition to peace. A Company were driven to Brigade Headquarters ready to return home. On 27 April they embarked on RFA *Sir Percivale* for four days' decompression, then flew back to the UK, by chartered 747, on 9 May. Their return was low key.

The Commandos never went back to Iraq. They had carried out their mission, had suffered few casualties, and were proud of what they had done. Saddam Hussein's government had been overthrown, although he was not captured for some months. No trace of chemical or biological weapons was ever found in Iraq.

Iraq and its population remained, however, a country and a people that had been destroyed by a ruthless dictatorship and twenty-three years of war. It was an opportunity to return to normal, but the politicians of the US and Britain had forgotten that in its history Iraq had never experienced democracy or a free market. There was no normal.

CONCLUSION: AFTER THE FALL

On 9 April 2003, a large statue of Saddam Hussein, in Firdos Square, Baghdad, was pulled from its pedestal by Iraqi civilians, with the assistance of a US Marines tank. The dramatic scene was televised live around the world, and the collapse of the statue, toppled to the ground by a rope and chain round its neck, became an instant symbol of the downfall of the Iraqi dictator. The image became as iconic as the photograph of the raising of the Stars and Stripes over Iwo Jima, or the Russian red flag being hoisted above Berlin's Brandenburg Gate in 1945.

Reality is sometimes less clear cut than visual symbols suggest. Overt military resistance to the invasion from conventional Iraqi forces had practically ceased. Basra had been liberated, and Allied aircraft were already landing at Baghdad international airport without opposition. In the absence of Saddam Hussein and representatives of Iraq's rulers to admit defeat, the statue was the next best thing, serving as a convenient full stop. In the general rejoicing it obscured the important question it raised: what did victory look like?

As the cities of Basra and Baghdad were occupied by the Allies, the totalitarian regime collapsed, and with it went any semblance of law and order. A power vacuum ensued, which the troops on the ground were unable to fill. They had been given no clear instructions on what to do; neither were they numerous enough to maintain order on the streets.

Although Iraq is a major oil-producing country, the ravages of the Iran–Iraq war and the sanctions that followed Saddam Hussein's invasion of Kuwait had impoverished it and the majority of its population. Consumer goods were in short supply, and basic foodstuffs rationed. As soon as the old authority was overthrown, looting started on a truly gigantic scale. At first British troops were amused by this, seeing it as a blow against the old regime by a newly liberated people, but it soon became extremely damaging. The first response, to seek out furniture or electrical goods from government and Ba'ath Party offices, soon took on criminal dimensions.

The shortages and rationing of the previous fifteen years had created a thriving black market, and a network of criminal gangs in Iraq that had been tolerated by the regime. The gangs now came into their own. Hospitals and clinics were ransacked, as were government offices and schools. Everything was fair game.

The impact of their activities was profound. A doctor, visiting shortly after the end of the fighting, wrote, 'There are no drugs, hospitals have run out of oxygen and have been looted of beds and equipment. Laboratories are stripped. There is intermittent power. There is a public-health crisis. Water is contaminated with sewage, there is not enough fuel, food is scarce and expensive. There are cases of cholera, typhoid and whooping cough.'

With the troops' inability to run an effective police operation, the gangs' activities exacerbated the problems the coalition was faced with. Power stations were run down and poorly maintained, as part of the legacy of sanctions, and fuel supplies were disrupted as a result of the war, but now gangs were cutting down electricity-transmission cables and pylons for the metals they contained, the copper and aluminium being melted down and shipped to Syria, Jordan or Iran. As they tried to increase their influence, they threatened and killed those who attempted to stand up to them, including hospital doctors and university professors. The decision to disband the Iraqi Army and remove even low-level Ba'ath Party members from their jobs created unemployment and fuelled the growth of lawlessness.

This facet of Iraqi life took the coalition by surprise, but almost nothing had been planned for post-war Iraq. The Office of Reconstruction and Humanitarian Assistance, established under the retired US General Jay Garner who had led the humanitarian assistance to the Kurds after the Kuwait war, was nominally charged with assuming control of the reconstruction of Iraq, but had almost no funds, few staff, and certainly did not command the manpower, in the form of police or military forces, to quell the looting. Ironically Garner and his staff remained in Kuwait because Baghdad was considered too dangerous for them to take up residence there. The representative councils that had been set up by 40 and 42 Commandos in Abu al-Khasib and Az Zubayr were inevitably dependent on support from Basra and Baghdad. Without a central organization to take responsibility for channelling aid and assistance, it was impossible for the Commandos to supply sufficient equipment to bring the schools and clinics up to scratch, improve the local power supply and deliver fresh water. Failure meant that the representative councils lost credibility in the eyes of the population.

Although in the first instance British forces had responsibility for Basra and southern Iraq, Britain had no independent mechanism or funds for administering these areas separately from those of the US. The Coalition Provisional Authority was run by a

US appointee, Paul Bremer, who prepared to focus on Baghdad in the belief that the city was the key to stability in Iraq. This left British civilian representatives and military forces responsible for security in Basra and the surrounding provinces of Al Muthanna, Dhi Qar and Maysan, but with almost no power or resources to effect change.

The focus on Baghdad was partly justified by the belief that Basra and the south, being dominated by Shiites and long oppressed by Saddam Hussein, would not throw up significant resistance to the occupation by Allied forces. Initially there was some truth in this, but there had never been a complete end to the fighting. Even after the conclusion of Operation James, and the fall of Basra, British troops would occasionally come under small-arms fire. At night, the marines' bases were attacked by RPGs or mortars. They were not serious enough to worry the marines unduly, but they were a reminder that opposition to the occupation was by no means dead.

In June 2003, a few weeks after the statue of Saddam Hussein was pulled down, it was dawning on many that the structure of Ba'ath Party power was broader, with far deeper roots in the Sunni clans and their tribal allegiances, than anyone had anticipated.

On 25 June General John Abizaid, who had taken over from General Franks as head of US Central Command, said to a Senate Committee, 'We shouldn't kid ourselves about the fact that we can be the subject of terrorist attacks in Iraq. We are certainly in for some difficult days ahead.'

The occupation of Iraq and the destruction of the Ba'ath Party exacerbated the sectarian difference in Iraq. The Shias largely welcomed the occupation while the Sunni did not. The five million strong Sunni community supported resistance to the occupation and were alarmed when it became clear that the Shias and Kurds would not give up their bid for power after centuries of marginalization. Sunni organizations and the remnants of the anti-occupation Fedayeen united in attacks not only against coalition forces but also against collaborators, the Shia community and its political leaders.

This sectarian warfare fuelled the growth of the militias, as communities sought to defend themselves, and the power of the state decreased even further. Again, this fragmentation was aided by the troops' lack of knowledge of local conditions, and by the policy of root-and-branch 'de-Ba'athification'. When fighting broke out in Basra or another area it was impossible for the patrols to know what the causes were. Tribal and local militias took the law into their own hands and community leaders established vigilante gangs to thwart attacks on their turf.

Across Iraq the community-based allegiances of former Iraqi soldiers and police were sapping the power of the state. In Sunni areas the only people well enough armed to defend the communities were the resistance fighters.

In the south, the coalition made serious efforts to train a new police force. The Danish government established a training centre in Umm Qasr, staffed by Danish military and police instructors. British Royal Military Police were also co-opted into training programmes, but on 24 June six members of the force were killed by a mob in Maysan province, and the policy was rapidly changed. In the two months since the end of the fighting the security situation had deteriorated so far that the protection of the armed forces and civilian members of the Coalition Provisional Authority became a priority.

The first real sign that the resistance had regrouped was seen in August 2003. A car bomb exploded in Baghdad outside the Jordanian embassy killing eleven people. Two weeks later, in a more serious and far more politically damaging attack, a bomb exploded outside the UN headquarters, killing seventeen UN officials and Sergio Viera de Mello, the UN secretary-general's personal envoy to Iraq. Kofi Annan had sent him to Iraq partly in the hope that the UN would be able to assist in the rebuilding of the country, and to negotiate a way forward with a new government. The car bomb destroyed that ambition, and the UN withdrew from the country. Other attacks on international organizations followed. In October the Red Cross headquarters was hit by a car bomb, and simultaneously three police stations were targeted. Thirty-five people were killed.

At 1015 on the morning of 12 November a truck bomb was driven into a building in Nasiriyah housing an Italian base. Nineteen members of the Italian *carabinieri* and twelve Iraqi civilians were killed. It was the most serious attack on coalition forces in the south since the end of the war.

The security situation was clearly unravelling and the British base in Basra was sealed off under a security alert. In the weeks that followed, it became much more dangerous to travel by road to other parts of the region administered from Basra, and serious precautions had to be taken before a member of the Coalition Provisional Authority in Basra could journey the few kilometres to Basra airport.

In January 2004, mortars were fired at the Provisional Authority base in Basra, which was moved back to the military headquarters in the presidential palace. Ordinary Iraqis working with the occupation forces also became targets. Two women who ran a laundry for the British base in Basra were killed.

Moves on the part of the US to create a new Iraqi government ironically exacerbated the violence. Any progress towards some form of democracy would inevitably reduce the Sunnis' power, and attacks against representatives of the occupation forces were directed against the Shia community as well. It led to sectarian killing on a grand scale, the cleansing of whole areas of Baghdad and the displacement of some two and a half million people.

In an attempt to suppress the resistance, US forces mounted a major assault on the town of Fallujah in the centre of Iraq in April 2004, but it had no effect on the situation in the country. The attacks soared and the violence spread south. Basra was hit in the same month, on 21 April, when five car bombs were directed at police stations in and around the city, including Abu al-Khasib, and at least sixty-eight people were killed, eighteen of them schoolchildren. Many of the Sunni inhabitants were driven out by death threats from a variety of Shia militias. A car bomb exploded in the town in January 2005; the most recent incident took place in September 2007, when a bomb went off outside the mosque close to the drop-in centre that Justin Holt had set up. A new local police chief had been appointed after Holt had left, but was assassinated in 2006.

In August 2004, the holy Shia shrine of Iman Ali in Najaf was destroyed by a bomb, killing Ayatollah Mohammad Bakir Hakim, and ninety of his followers. The Grand Ayatollah Ali al-Sistani called on his Shia followers not to retaliate against this outrage, but restraint did not last long, and Iraq was convulsed by a series of increasingly bloody tit-for-tat killings. Thousands died and the militias split the country apart. Car bombs exploded in crowded markets, in busy streets during rush-hour, and people became afraid to leave their neighbourhood, sometimes even their houses, for fear of being kidnapped and killed at a militia checkpoint. Just two examples of the violence are enough to show its magnitude.

In February 2006, a holy Shia shrine in Samarra was attacked by bombs. In Baghdad, a few days later, the bodies of 1300 people, mostly Sunnis, were found in and around Baghdad. In early March, car bombs exploded in the markets of the Shia slum area of Baghdad, Sadr City, killing scores of people. A few days later a pit was uncovered that contained the bodies of twenty-seven Sunnis who had all been stripped, tortured and shot in the head.

Basra was also affected by sectarian violence but the situation never reflected the major splits occurring in the rest of Iraq. It was between three Shia groups in a bid to seize political power and control the revenues of organized crime and oil smuggling.

The major political organization that sprang up in Basra was the Supreme Council for the Islamic Revolution (SCIRI), which had had its leadership in Iran since 1991 and the abortive Shia revolt in the south. Since the overthrow of Saddam Hussein, its military wing, the Badr Army, had started to develop independently from SCIRI. These organizations were initially in support of the Coalition Provisional Authority, believing that they would achieve political power in a new Iraq. There were also two rejectionist movements: the Fadhila, under the direction of a cleric called Abu Salam, and the Sadrists, under the leadership of Moqtada al-Sadr, both of which were under the influence of another cleric from the holy city of Najaf, Muhammad al-Ya'qoubi; they support significant well-armed militias.

Much of their funding comes from corruption and smuggling. The city of Basra was once called the Venice of the Middle East but has now become its Naples. Business in Basra can only be conducted with the approval of one or other of these political organizations. Any contract with the Basra council requires payments to the parties, and a percentage of the total price must be paid to their associated militia for the sake of security. The process of reconstruction helps fuel the growth of armed gangs, all of whom have a vested interest in removing British troops from the area.

The largest source of funding, however, and the biggest obstacle to regeneration of the country is oil smuggling. During the UN-imposed sanctions, oil was regularly diverted illegally from the southern oilfields to makeshift facilities along the Shatt al-Arab. With the collapse of the regime, they have been taken over by the political organizations and gangs, often clan-based. Convoys of tankers transport oil from the southern oilfields to unofficial holding tanks along the waterway, and from there it is loaded on to small barges for transport down the river to waiting tankers. It is then delivered to refineries as far away as India. Sometimes the oil crosses sectarian boundaries, but so lucrative is the trade that payments can be made to militias, Customs officials and government surveyors. The biggest beneficiaries are the militias who cream off as much as 30 per cent of the profit. It has been estimated that as much as $200 million worth of oil is smuggled out of Basra each year.

It was impossible for British forces in Basra and the surrounding area to make any impact on a society so dominated by Mafia-style organizations. Their presence was a lightning rod for attacks and roadside ambushes for any organization that needed to prove its rejectionist credentials, or defend its black-market trade.

By the time that the British government announced that its troops would withdraw from the city to Basra airport, 149 British servicemen had been killed, and more than 350 wounded.

British forces finally handed over control of Basra on 16 December 2007. The invasion had achieved the overthrow of Saddam Hussein, but five years later there was still a major US troops presence in Iraq, very little security and a divided nation. There were still serious deficiencies in health services; unemployment and homelessness affected large numbers of Iraqis, and many areas of the country still had no supplies of clean water or power.

Not only did the occupation fail to deliver a free and revitalized Iraq, it has been responsible for serious atrocities and breaches of international law. The members of 40 and 42 Commando believe that, even in the heat of battle, they observed the rules of engagement that had been issued to them, and that after the fighting had stopped they did what they could to effect change in the areas for which they became responsible. They are paid and trained to fight wars, not to act as policemen or run local authorities. That, they believe, is the responsibility of politicians who send them to fight. Most have now moved on to different positions in the Royal Navy, or in the Ministry of Defence hierarchy. At the time of writing, some are expecting to start work in the other theatre of British intervention: Afghanistan.

APPENDIX

Members of 40 and 42 Commando received several honours as a result of their actions during the invasion of Iraq.

They are as follows:

Order of the British Empire
Colonel F. R. Howes, 42 Commando

Member of the British Empire
Major J. S. Holt, 40 Commando
Major D. P. May, 42 Commando

Distinguished Service Order
Colonel G. K. Messenger, OBE, 40 Commando

APPENDIX

Conspicuous Gallantry Cross
Lance Corporal J. R. Thomas, 40 Commando

Military Cross
Corporal D. J. Beresford, 42 Commando
Captain C. E. Haw, BRF
Captain P. P. Lynch, 40 Commando
Marine G. Thomas, 40 Commando
Corporal P. R. Watts, 40 Commando

Mentioned in Dispatches
Corporal J. E. Broughton, 40 Commando
Marine A. T. Cullen, 40 Commando
Corporal R. J. Storey, 40 Commando
Medical Assistant 1st Class M. A. Sumner, 40
  Commando
Marine J. T. Thompson, 40 Commando
Corporal J. Twycross, 40 Commando

Queen's Commendation for Valuable Service
Captain O. A. Lee, 42 Commando
Captain T. N. Leyden, 42 Commando
Corporal A. I. W. Phillimore, 42 Commando
Marine M. Qarajouli, 40 Commando
Marine P. M. Tucker, 40 Commando
Lance Corporal N. J. Young, 42 Commando

BIBLIOGRAPHY

Blix, Hans, *Disarming Iraq*, Bloomsbury, 2004

Campbell, Alastair, *The Blair Years*, Hutchinson, 2007

Danner, Mark, *The Secret Way to War*, New York Review of Books, 2006

Donnelly, Thomas, *Operation Iraqi Freedom,* American Enterprise Institute, 2004

Eppel, Michael, *Iraq: From Monarchy to Tyranny*, University Press of Florida, 2004

Friedman, Norman, *Desert Victory*, Naval Institute Press, 1991

Gordon, Michael, and Trainor, Bernard, *Cobra II*, Atlantic Books, 2006

Hiro, Dilip, *Iran Under the Ayatollahs*, Routledge & Kegan Paul, 1987

HMSO, *Paiforce*, 1948

Murray, Williamson, and Scales, Major General

Robert, *The Iraq War*, Belknap Press of Harvard University, 2005

Simons, Geoff, *Targeting Iraq*, Saqi Books, 2002

Sluglett, Peter, *Britain In Iraq 1914–1932*, Ithaca Press, 1976

Synnott, Hilary, *Bad Days In Basra*, I. B. Tauris, 2008

Timmerman, Kenneth, *The Death Lobby: How the West Armed Iraq*, Fourth Estate, 1992

Woods, Kevin M., *The Iraqi Perspectives Report*, Naval Institute Press, 2006

Woodward, Bob, *Plan of Attack*, Simon & Schuster, 2004

PICTURE
ACKNOWLEDGEMENTS

First section
George W. Bush and Tony Blair, Crawford, Texas, 6
April 2002: Reuters/Win McNamee; US Secretary of
State Colin Powell speaks before the United Nations
General Assembly, 16 September 2002: Reuters/Chip
East

Exercise Akrotiri Bay, Cyprus, 29 January 2003:
photograph by Angie Pearce/© Crown Copyright/
MOD, image from www.photos.mod.uk.
Reproduced with the permission of the Controller
of Her Majesty's Stationery Office; Royal Marines
boarding a Chinook, 6 February 2003: photograph
by Angie Pearce/© Crown Copyright/MOD, image
from www.photos.mod.uk. Reproduced with the

permission of the Controller of Her Majesty's
Stationery Office; Sea King supplying *Ark Royal*, 19
February 2003: photograph by Jim Gibson/© Crown
Copyright/MOD, image from www.photos.mod.uk.
Reproduced with the permission of the Controller
of Her Majesty's Stationery Office; Sea King in the
northern Arabian Gulf, 1 March 2003: photograph
by Nathan Dua/© Crown Copyright/MOD, image
from www.photos.mod.uk. Reproduced with the
permission of the Controller of Her Majesty's
Stationery Office; 3 Cdo Brigade on the range in
Kuwait, 21 February 2003: photograph by PO Tam
McDonald/© Crown Copyright/MOD, image from
www.photos.mod.uk. Reproduced with the permission of the Controller of Her Majesty's Stationery
Office; Col Gordon Messenger: Reuters/Stephen
Hird; Matt Jackson in Kuwait and 40 Cdo under
tarpaulin: courtesy Matt Jackson; Challenger tank
fires live ammunition in the desert: PA Archive/PA
Photos

3 Cdo Brigade HQ, 21 March 2003: ©
Reuters/Corbis; 40 Cdo disembark from HMS *Ark
Royal*, 20 March 2003: photograph by LA Sean
Clee/© Crown Copyright/MOD, image from
www.photos.mod.uk. Reproduced with the
permission of the Controller of Her Majesty's
Stationery Office; 40 Cdo being airlifted by US

CH53s: Jon Mills/DPL; Royal Marines attend to an unidentified Iraqi, 21 March 2003 (two photos): both Reuters/Terry Richards; Justin Holt: courtesy Justin Holt; Royal Marine fires a Milan wire-guided missile, 21 March, 2003: Reuters/Jon Mills; MMS pipelines: courtesy Matt Jackson

Raising US flag over Umm Qasr, 21 March 2003: Reuters/Desmond Boylan; US 15th Marine expeditionary unit (MEU) commanding officer Thomas Waldhauser and Jim Dutton: Reuters/Desmond Boylan; Royal Marine stands in front of Saddam mural, 24 March 2003: Reuters/Jon Mills; Royal Marine stands guard at new port, Umm Qasr, 25 March 2003: Getty Images; Royal Marines secure area around the port: Reuters/MOD-LA Angie Pearce; Iraqis watch as Royal Marines patrol in Umm Qasr, 29 March 2003: Reuters/Andrew Parsons

US Special Forces with dolphin, 26 March 2003: Reuters/Alan Evans; *Sir Galahad* enters Umm Qasr, 28 March 2003: US Navy photo by Photographer's Mate 1st Class Brien Aho

Second section
Marines Baird, Anderson, Lewis, McDonald, Williams and Lt Cpl Thomas, 23 March 2003; Paul

PICTURE ACKNOWLEDGEMENTS

Lynch; Paul Lynch's MSG at the MMS: all courtesy
Paul Lynch

Challenger tank, Abu al-Khasib, 30 March 2003: PA
Archive/PA Photos; Royal Marine from 40 Cdo fires
his GMPG, 30 March 2003: PA Archive/PA Photos;
Royal Marine from 40 Cdo runs for cover, 30 March
2003: PA Archive/PA Photos; Royal Marine from 40
Cdo fires at Iraqi positions, 30 March 2003: PA
Archive/PA Photos; Russian tank smoulders, 30
March 2003: PA Archive/PA Photos; Iraqi militia
surrender, 30 March 2003: PA Archive/PA Photos;
Matt Pierson and Objective Blofeld sequence:
courtesy Matt Pierson

Iraqi man and boy flee Basra, 28 March 2003: PA
Archive/PA Photos; road block on the road to
Basra, 24 March 2003: Reuters/Jerry Lampen; Royal
Marine from 40 Cdo puts up a poster, 6 April 2003:
© Reuters/Corbis; young Iraqis welcome British
troops, 27 March 2003: Reuters/Jon Mills; Royal
Marine from 42 Cdo hands out food and water,
March 2002: Reuters/Dave Husbands

Royal Marines from 42 Cdo move into Basra, 7
April 2003: photograph by PO(Phot) Tam
McDonald/© Crown Copyright/MOD, image
from www.photos.mod.uk. Reproduced with the

permission of the Controller of Her Majesty's
Stationery Office; Royal Marine from 42 Cdo looks
out over Basra, 7 April 2003: photograph by
PO(Phot) Tam McDonald/© Crown
Copyright/MOD, image from www.photos.mod.uk.
Reproduced with the
permission of the Controller of Her Majesty's
Stationery Office; Royal Marines from 42 Cdo
occupy palace grounds, 7 April 2003: photograph by
LA(Phot) Husbands/© Crown Copyright/MOD,
image from www.photos.mod.uk. Reproduced with
the permission of the Controller of Her Majesty's
Stationery Office; Royal Marines from 3 Cdo
Brigade enter grounds of presidential palace, 7 April
2003: © Reuters/Corbis; Royal Marines from 3 Cdo
patrol Basra, 7 April 2003: ©Reuters/Corbis; Royal
Marine from 3 Cdo patrols outside presidential
palace of Basra, 7 April 2003: © Reuters/Corbis;
Royal Marines from 42 Cdo enter palace: photograph
by LA(Phot) Husbands/© Crown Copyright/MOD,
image from www.photos.mod.uk. Reproduced with
the permission of the Controller of Her Majesty's
Stationery Office; Royal Marine Rigid Inflatable
Boats outside presidential palace, 8 April 2003:
photograph by PO(Phot) Tam McDonald/© Crown
Copyright/MOD, image from www.photos.mod.uk.
Reproduced with the permission of the Controller
of Her Majesty's Stationery Office; looting at the

PICTURE ACKNOWLEDGEMENTS

Sheraton Hotel, 8 April 2003: PA Archive/PA
Photos

Stills from a video sequence of the destruction of a
statue of Saddam, Basra, 5 April 2003: Associated
Press

Index